N37/2

THE CHURCH

Its Changing Image Through

Twenty Centuries

JAY   78/166

The Church
Vol.1.

D1419812

THE CHURCH
Its Changing Image Through Twenty Centuries

VOLUME ONE

The First Seventeen Centuries

ERIC G. JAY

LONDON

S P C K

First published 1977
SPCK
Holy Trinity Church
Marylebone Road
London NW1 4DU

Text set in 11/12 pt Photon Times, printed and bound in Great Britain at The Pitman Press, Bath

ISBN 0 281 02990 3

Contents

Acknowledgements

Thanks are due to the following for permission to quote from copyright sources:

A. & C. Black: *Early Christian Doctrines* by J. N. D. Kelly.

Cambridge University Press: *The Doctrine of the Church in the New Testament* by G. Johnston (by permission also of the Reverend Professor G. Johnston); and *The Protestant Tradition* by J. S. Whale (by permission also of Dr J. S. Whale).

Les Editions du Cerf: *L'Ecclésiologie du haut Moyen-Age*, and *L'Eglise de saint Augustin à l'époque moderne*, both by Yves Congar.

Fortress Press: *Luther's Works*, vols. 39, 41, and 44.

Institut Français d'Etudes Byzantines: 'Conférence sur la Primauté du Pape à Constantinople en 1357' by J. Darrouzès, *Revue des Etudes Byzantines* 19, 1961 (Mélanges Raymond Janin).

Professor Nikos A. Nissiotis: Background Paper on the Lectures for the Seminar on Orthodox Worship and Theology, 5–18 April 1971, at the Ecumenical Institute, World Council of Churches.

Oxford University Press: *The New Temple* by R. J. McKelvey.

Paulist Press: *Ancient Christian Writers*, vol. 26, edited by R. P. Lawson.

Penguin Books Ltd: *Western Society and the Church in the Middle Ages* by R. W. Southern, 2 (1970), pp. 92–3, 100, © R. W. Southern 1970; and *The Orthodox Church* by Timothy Ware (1963), p. 35, © Timothy Ware 1963.

SCM Press Ltd and The Westminster Press: *Calvin: Institutes of the Christian Religion*, vols. xx and xxi, The Library of Christian Classics, edited by John T. McNeill and translated by Ford Lewis Battles. Published in the USA by The Westminster Press. Copyright © MCMLX, by W. L. Jenkins.

Biblical quotations from the Revised Standard Version of the Bible, copyrighted 1946 and 1952 by the Division of Christian Education of the National Council of the Churches of Christ in the USA, are used by permission.

Preface

Since 1958 I have regularly taught a course on 'The Nature of the Church' to theological students representing various churches, and most of whom have been preparing for ordination. Bibliographies have been provided; students have been directed to certain authorities, ancient and modern, required to read selected passages from them, and encouraged to gain the good habits of wide reading and study in depth. But undergraduates have other courses to take, and there is a limit to the number of books they can be expected to read in a single term. There is need, it has seemed to me, for a single textbook which, in the hands of a student, would give him a review of this subject and help him to gain more from the lectures, and contribute more to the tutorials, during the term in which the course is offered.

This, then, is an attempt to provide for what I feel to be a need. I have chosen to do so by way of tracing the history of the idea of the Church, following the example of others who, some decades ago, produced historical studies of such doctrines as the Person of Christ and the Atonement (Sydney Cave), the Eucharist (Darwell Stone), and Penance (O. D. Watkins) which have proved of great help to students. While I recognize ruefully that it is impossible to overcome subjectivity in any historical survey, objectivity has been sought in allowing theologians to speak for themselves by an extensive use of quotation or by providing summaries of their thought as fairly as I can.

The book has been written with the theological student in mind, but also in the hope that it may find other readers in days when many are asking the questions 'What is the Church?' and 'What is the Church for?'

I owe a particular debt of gratitude to Mrs Kenneth Naylor of Montreal for typing the manuscript, and for many useful suggestions (including the wording of the title).

McGill University, Montreal   ERIC G. JAY

Abbreviations

Adv. Haer.	Irenaeus, *Adversus Haereses*
ANCL	Ante-Nicene Christian Library (Edinburgh 1864 ff)
A.V.	Authorized Version of the Bible
Church	Hans Küng, *The Church*
Ep.	*Epistle*
E.T.	English Translation
L'Eglise	Yves Congar, *L'Eglise de saint Augustin à l'époque moderne*
LEP	Richard Hooker, *The Laws of Ecclesiastical Polity*
LW	*Luther's Works* (St Louis and Philadelphia 1955 ff)
LXX	The Septuagint Version (Greek) of the Old Testament
NPNF	The Nicene and Post-Nicene Fathers (New York 1886 ff)
N.T.	New Testament
O.T.	Old Testament
PG	*Patrologia Graeca*, ed. J. P. Migne (Paris 1857 ff)
PL	*Patrologia Latina*, ed. J. P. Migne (Paris 1844 ff)
R. S. V.	Revised Standard Version of the Bible
Structures	Hans Küng, *Structures of the Church*

Part 1

THE CHURCH IN
THE NEW TESTAMENT

1

The Word 'Church'
in the New Testament

The word 'church' is the usual translation of the Greek word *ekklesia*. Its first occurrence as applied to a group of Christians is in the first verse of St Paul's First Epistle to the Thessalonians: 'Paul, Silvanus, and Timothy, to the church [*ekklesia*] of the Thessalonians in God the Father and the Lord Jesus Christ: Grace to you and peace.' First Thessalonians is the earliest extant Christian document, being written about A.D. 50,[1] some fifteen years before the earliest date which scholars are prepared to allot to St Mark's Gospel.

What is this church which Paul addresses in this letter? What can be learned about it from this document? If the Christian movement had been a short-lived phenomenon, and if 1 Thessalonians were the only documentary evidence for it, what could we know about the church? Relying on the internal evidence alone, we can make several assertions:

1   The church includes a group of people in Thessalonica, a town in Macedonia which Paul had visited some months before (2.1).
2   On this visit he had communicated to them 'the gospel of God' (2.2,9). This gospel was also the gospel of Christ (3.2). It declared that one named Jesus, whom Paul calls 'Christ' and 'Lord', is the Son whom God the Father has sent into the world to bring salvation to it (5.9). Jesus had suffered and died (2.15), but he rose again (1.10; 4.14) and will come again to 'establish' them before God (3.13) so that they may always be with their Lord (4.17).
3   This group in Thessalonica had accepted this gospel and had become believers (2.13). As a consequence they had received power and inspiration from the Holy Spirit (1.5–6; 5.19), and had become imitators of Jesus, of Paul and other apostles, and of other churches in Judaea, especially in the courageous enduring of suffering (1.6; 2.14). In their turn they had proclaimed and spread the same gospel to

others (1.8; 4.10). An outgoing love had become characteristic of their lives day by day (3.6,12; 4.9–10), motivated by the desire to please God (4.1), and they lived in the expectation of the coming of Jesus, their Lord, who would bring them to their final salvation (1.10; 5.1–11).

4   The group of people whom Paul addresses is a local church. It is the church of the Thessalonians. But it is not a self-contained group isolated from other Christian groups. It is actively in contact with 'all the believers in Macedonia and in Achaia' (1.7; 4.10). Paul conceives of them also as having an intimate relationship with 'the churches of God in Christ Jesus which are in Judaea', despite the difference in race (2.14). Paul himself and Timothy, who had recently paid them a second visit (3.2), provided their main links with the churches in the more distant places.

5   The group met together regularly. This is implied by the references to prayer (5.17), prophesying (5.20), and mutual encouragement (5.11), and by Paul's assumption that there would be opportunities for his greetings to be conveyed and his letter read to the brethren.

6   The church of the Thessalonians evidently regarded Paul as a person of authority. He himself, though he addressed them as 'brethren' (1.4), thought of himself as a father over them who not only had the duty of exhorting, encouraging, and charging them while he was with them (2.11), but also claimed the right to do so by letter when he was absent (5.12 ff). That this claim was recognized is shown by the content of the report which Timothy, after his second visit, had brought back to Paul (3.6–8). Nevertheless the community had its local leaders, 'those who labor among you and are over you [*proistamenoi humōn*, literally 'those who stand before you'] in the Lord and admonish you', whom Paul charges the Thessalonians to respect and esteem (5.12–13).

These six paragraphs summarize what we could learn about the Church if 1 Thessalonians were the only document at our disposal. The letter has much to tell us about what the members of this church believed and how they acted, but little about its nature and constitution. The argument from silence may not legitimately be used here. For example, because 1 Thessalonians contains no reference to an initiatory rite or a communal meal, it does not follow that Paul at the time of writing considered baptism and the Lord's supper unimportant or that they had no place in the life of the Thessalonian Christians. We do not pack into the letters we address to friends references to matters which are taken for granted among us. We should not expect Paul to do so.

But the Christian movement was not short-lived, and 1 Thessalonians is not our only documentary evidence for it. Within a few years the Church had been planted in many places, from Palestine and Syria westward to Italy. Within the next few decades a lively literature grew up to which Paul himself contributed several more letters. The most significant of these writings were collected together in what we now call the New Testament. Before turning to inquire what the New Testament as a whole has to tell us of the nature of the Church, it will be useful to examine the word *ekklesia*. The study of the root meaning of a word and its general usage often provides information about the nature of that to which it refers.

EKKLESIA

This word had a long history before Paul employed it. In Athens, the city from which Paul probably wrote 1 Thessalonians, it had for several centuries been used of the assembly of the whole body of citizens, met together to elect magistrates, to confirm political decisions, and to hear appeals arising from judicial decisions. Other Greek cities also had their *ekklesiai*, varying in the powers they enjoyed. After the subjugation of Macedonia and Greece by the Romans, completed about 150 B.C., Greek cities still had their *ekklesiai*, although they retained little political power.

In classical Greek literature, therefore, the word was used of an assembly of citizens, officially constituted to do such business as the laws of the city appointed for it. *Ekklesia* is closely connected with the Greek verb *kaleo*, 'call', in its compound form *ekkaleo*, 'call out'. This signifies that an *ekklesia* is a gathering of people who have been duly summoned, or called out. The Greeks had another word, *sullogos* (connected with the verb *sullego*, 'collect together'), for unofficial or chance gatherings. The two words were sometimes used interchangeably, but strictly *ekklesia* means an officially summoned body, and *sullogos* an unofficial gathering of the people.

The use of the word *ekklesia* in another body of literature, the Septuagint (LXX), is more significant for an understanding of the Christian use of it. This was the Greek version of the Hebrew Scriptures, produced in Alexandria during the second century B.C. Its name, the Greek word for 'seventy', derives from the tradition that seventy scholars were simultaneously engaged in the translation. The LXX was familiar to Hellenistic Jews, from among whom came many of the earliest converts to Christianity. The New Testament takes its Old Testament citations much more frequently from the LXX than from the Hebrew.

In the Hebrew Scriptures the two most common words for a gathering of people are *ĕdhah* and *qāhāl*.[2] The root of *ĕdhah*[3] means 'appoint', and that of *qāhāl* means 'call'. Although both words are used of gatherings of all kinds, they also appear very frequently in the phrases '*ĕdhah* (*qāhāl*) of Israel' and '*ĕdhah* (*qāhāl*) of Yahweh' (the congregation, or assembly, of Israel, or of Yahweh). The root meaning of the two words would indicate that Israel is here regarded as a people appointed or called by God. Thus used the words have a technical and theological meaning and designate a people, called into being by God, who from time to time are gathered together for such solemn religious occasions as the receiving of the Law (Deut. 5.22), the dedication of Solomon's Temple (1 Kings 18.14 ff), and the reading of the book of the Law by Ezra (Neh. 8.2).[4]

In the LXX *ĕdhah* is uniformly translated by *sunagōgē*, literally 'a gathering together' (connected with the Greek verb *sunago*, 'bring together'). *Qāhāl*, however, is translated by *sunagoge* in Genesis, Exodus, Leviticus, Numbers, and in the Prophets; but by *ekklesia* in Deuteronomy (with a single exception), the historical books from Judges to Nehemiah, and in the Psalter (with the exception of Ps. 40.10).[5]

It is probably an unprofitable task to seek for some special significance in the way in which the LXX translation of *qāhāl* is distributed between *sunagōgē* and *ekklesia*. It might be worth attempting if the LXX came from one hand or a single team of translators. But 'the Alexandrine Bible is not a single version, but a series of versions produced at various times and by translators whose ideals were not altogether alike'.[6] Moreover, texts were subject to the errors of scribes, their well-meant efforts to correct, and all the other hazards involved in textual transmission before the invention of printing. And, as K. L. Schmidt says,[7] *ekklesia* and *sunagōgē* in the LXX, like the Hebrew words behind them, have much the same meaning: 'Both words are used both technically and non-technically, as underlined by the fact that translation varies between "assembly", "company" and "congregation".'

It is more to our purpose to inquire why Paul, writing about A.D.

50, chose *ekklesia* rather than *sunagōgē* to designate the community of those who accepted Jesus as Lord. Schmidt says[8] that the Hellenistic Christians found *ekklesia* preferable, because this word was falling into disuse among Greek-speaking Jews, who at the same time were tending to give *sunagōgē* a purely local meaning. It is perhaps not so certain as Schmidt implies that the word *ekklesia* was falling into disuse by the Jews, but there does seem to have been a tendency to employ *sunagōgē* for the local Jewish community and for the building in which they met for worship.[9] It is probable that more than one reason determined the Christian choice of the word *ekklesia*: (a) founders of early Christian groups, like Paul, must have known that in the LXX *ekklesia* was more frequently used than *sunagōgē* to translate *qāhāl*, and that *qāhāl* and not *ʻedhah* was the word used to designate official gatherings of the people on certain especially significant occasions (see p. 6 above); (b) *qāhāl* and *ekklesia* both have the consonantal sounds k and l,[10] and both have the root meaning of 'call'; (c) *ekklesia*, with its continuing secular usage in the Hellenistic world to denote a gathering of citizens 'was not so distinctively Jewish as to be unsuitable for a society which quickly accepted Gentiles to membership on the profession of their faith in Christ as Lord';[11] (d) the frequent use of *sunagōgē* for the building in the town or village where Christians were increasingly unwelcome.

THE USE OF *EKKLESIA* IN THE NEW TESTAMENT

St Paul frequently uses *ekklesia* of gatherings of Christians in a particular place, such as a house. He speaks of 'the church in your house' (Philem. 2); he sends greetings 'to Nympha and the church in her house' (Col. 4.15).[12] He employs the word also of a group of Christians assembled for worship (1 Cor. 11.18; 14.19). Appeal is made to such texts as these by those who maintain that the Church is essentially the gathering together of believers in a local congregation for worship.

But Paul also uses *ekklesia* of all the Christians in a city. In Thessalonica, for instance, there were no doubt a number of house churches. He speaks of these together as 'the church of the Thessalonians' (1 Thess. 1.1; 2 Thes. 1.1). Consequently it is natural for him to use *ekklesia* in the plural when he wishes to refer to all the Christian communities in an area: 'the churches of God in Christ Jesus which are in Judaea' (1 Thess. 2.14); 'the churches of Galatia'

(Gal. 1.2); he assures Christians in Rome that 'all the churches of Christ greet you' (Rom. 16.16).

This language is not to be taken to imply that Paul thinks of Christ's faithful simply as a number of smaller or larger local groups. When he confesses, 'I persecuted the church of God' (Gal. 1.13), he means something more than that he harried a number of Christian congregations in Jerusalem and Judaea. He was conscious that his offence was against the whole body of believers, wherever they might be (and, indeed, against their Head), even though it was but a few local gatherings which seemed to be affected. These local gatherings were the Church, the new people of God, embodied in those localities. Some have seen, probably correctly, the same significance in Paul's wording of the address in his letters to the Corinthians: 'to the church of God which is at Corinth' (1 Cor. 1.2; 2 Cor. 1.1). The *ekklesia* in Corinth, itself consisting of a number of *ekklesiai* (house churches), was the whole Church expressed and concretized in that city. It is not that the *ekklesia* is divided into *ekklesiai*. It is not that the *ekklesiai* are added up to make the *ekklesia*. Rather, the *ekklesia* is to be found in the places named.[13]

In the Acts of the Apostles *ekklesia* is also used both of believers in a single locality and of believers everywhere. The usage in the course of the narrative describing the growth of the Christian movement is instructive. The *ekklesia* in Jerusalem was the local church in the city, but originally it was also the 'whole church' (Acts 5.11). As the gospel advances beyond Jerusalem and Judaea we find *ekklesia* used in two ways, of the whole brotherhood and of a local community. Acts 9.31 records that 'the church throughout all Judea and Galilee and Samaria had peace and was built up; and . . . was multiplied'. Here 'church'[14] is most naturally taken of the Church as a whole, even though particular areas are mentioned. It was *the* Church which was growing. In Acts 20.28 Paul is recorded as exhorting the elders of Ephesus 'to feed the church of the Lord which he obtained with his own blood'. It is the church in Ephesus in which these elders have pastoral responsibilities, but it is the Church as a whole which Christ 'obtained'. On the other hand, in 14.27 and 15.3, *ekklesia* is used of the local Christian community of Antioch, in 15.4 of Jerusalem (which was now no longer the whole Church), and in 18.22 of Caesarea.

In the four Gospels there are only two occurrences of the word *ekklesia*, both in Matthew. This is not surprising, since the evangelists were concerned with the significance of the person, words, and work of the one who called into being the new community of the people of God, the one without whose suffering, death, and resurrection it would never have been. Writing after several decades of Christian expansion, they were certainly aware that the word *ekklesia* had gained wide usage.[15] Their failure to use the word may simply be because they were also aware that in the lifetime of Jesus it, or an Aramaic equivalent, was not yet used of believers.

Little need be said here of the two occurrences in Matthew. Matthew 16.18, 'You are Peter, and on this rock I will build my church', is a text which later became crucial because of the claim that the primacy which it appears to give to Peter among the apostles devolves upon the bishop of Rome as the successor of Peter. If it is an authentic saying of Jesus, which many scholars have doubted, it was probably spoken in Aramaic, and Schmidt gives reasons[16] for holding that the word used was *kᵉnishta* which could be the equivalent either of *qāhāl* or of *édhah*. Matthew 18.17, which prescribes the role of the *ekklesia* in cases of dispute among the faithful, seems to use the word of the kind of local group of Christians which came into being after Pentecost. The saying has the stamp of a very early piece of ecclesiastical legislation, placed anachronistically by the evangelist within the teaching of Jesus.[17] The whole thrust of the New Testament is that the *ekklesia* is the fellowship *of the risen Christ*. This is neither to deny that its foundations were being laid upon the apostles in the lifetime of Jesus nor to assert that it had no continuity with ancient Israel.[18]

'CHURCH' IN OTHER LANGUAGES

Ecclesia, the Latin transliteration of the Greek *ekklesia*, became the technical term for the Church in the Latin-speaking West, rather than such possible translations as *convocatio, contio,* or *comitia.* From the Latin it has passed into the French *église* and the Spanish *iglesia.*

The English word 'church' is almost certainly derived from the Greek adjective *kuriakos*, 'the Lord's', 'belonging to the Lord'.[19] This adjective is found in the New Testament in the phrases 'the Lord's supper' (1 Cor. 11.20) and 'the Lord's day' (Rev. 1.10), but is not applied to the Christian community. Other forms of the word are the German *Kirche*, Swedish *kerke*, Gaelic *kirk*, Russian *cerkovi*. In all of these it will be observed that the same consonantal sounds are used, k, r, and k, the k sound being sometimes aspirated. It is not known certainly where the word first gained currency as a synonym for *ekklesia*, or when precisely it came into the languages of northern and western Europe.

2

The Doctrine of the Church
in the New Testament

Turning from our consideration of the word 'church' (*ekklesia*), we now inquire what the New Testament has to say about the *nature* of the Church. We find nothing in the way of a formal definition. The N.T. is not a textbook of dogmatic theology. Rather we find that certain broad themes like 'people of God' and 'fellowship of the Spirit' are employed in speaking of the relation of the believers to Christ and to one another, and that the various writers seek to sharpen the reader's understanding of the relationship by using striking images (some would prefer to say 'metaphors') such as body, bride, sheepfold, vine, house, temple. These themes and the more frequent images we must now examine.[1]

THE CHURCH AS THE PEOPLE OF GOD

In a discussion of the words which might have been adopted as the name for the Christian community, Professor George Johnston mentions *laos* (the Greek word for 'people'): 'It particularly denotes the people of Israel, God's chosen. But it was not generally adopted: national limitations probably caused its rejection.'[2] Hebrews 4.9 and 1 Peter 2.9–10 are the only N.T. instances of its application to the Christian community. Yet many N.T. writers use language which suggests that they thought of Christians as the continuance, renewal, and enlargement of God's chosen people, Israel. Paul, who has come to realize that 'neither circumcision counts for anything, nor uncircumcision, but a new creation', prays that 'peace and mercy be upon all who walk by this rule, upon the Israel of God' (Gal. 6.15–16). Those who belong to Christ are 'Abraham's offspring, heirs according to promise' (Gal. 3.29).[3] The Epistle of James is addressed to 'the twelve tribes in the dispersion', and 1 Peter to 'the exiles of the dispersion in Pontus, Galatia, Cappadocia, Asia and Bithynia'. In 1 Peter

2.9–10 we find several designations of the Church which are used in the O.T. of ancient Israel. With Peter's 'chosen race' compare Deuteronomy 7.6 and 10.15; with 'royal priesthood' and 'holy nation', Exodus 19.6; with 'God's own people' (A.V. 'peculiar people'), Deuteronomy 4.20, 7.6, and 14.2.

Paul's image of the olive tree from which some branches are broken off and into which others are grafted from a wild olive (Rom. 11.17–24) recalls Jeremiah 11.16. The discourse in John 15 in which Jesus speaks of himself as the vine, of the vine-dresser as the Father and of those who abide in him as the branches recalls the imagery of Israel as God's vine in Isaiah 5.1–7 and in Psalm 80.8 ff. Some of the other N.T. images of the Church which will be discussed below also have clear O.T. parallels. Moreover, themes like the new covenant (e.g. in Mark 14.24, 1 Cor. 11.25 and elsewhere in Paul, and frequently in Hebrews) and the messiahship of Jesus give strong support to the suggestion that N.T. writers conceived of the Christian community as the ancient people of God reconstituted, Israel renewed and revivified.

Many scholars have agreed with T. W. Manson[4] in his argument that the N.T. doctrine of the Church rests upon the O.T. theme that Israel is the elect people of God, bound by a covenant sealed with blood to remain faithful and to keep God's law. The O.T. frankly faces the fact of the apostasy of the majority in Israel, and the idea of the remnant emerges, the righteous few who survive the catastrophe which overtakes the nation because of its apostasy. In the thought of several O.T. writers the remnant idea seems to attach itself closely to Israel's expectation of the Messiah (e.g. Isa. 11.1, 10–11; Jer. 23.3–6; Mic. 5.2–9). There is much in the N.T. which suggests acceptance and further development of this interpretation of biblical history. The remnant is seen as narrowed down to Jesus alone, the one true representative of Israel, utterly faithful and obedient. The priests of the temple and the guardians of the law reject him; the multitudes who at first heard him gladly, melted away; in the end his most intimate disciples 'forsook him and fled' (Mark 14.50). Hoskyns and Davey[5] believe that the considerable use made by all four evangelists in their Passion narratives of Psalm 22, 'treating of the afflictions of the "afflicted"; his rejection by men, and apparent forsaking by God' is significant. It points to the climax of the history of Israel as God's people. Jesus in his own person is the remnant. He accepts for himself the catastrophe of death which must overtake the apostasy of the many. He accepts it actually at the hands of those many who have taken offence at his own firm obedience to God's will, and it is for these many that he accepts it as the one true representative of God's people. But the temporal finality of death was cancelled by the act of God in raising him from death. 'Strictly speaking,' writes G. Henton Davies,[6]

> the Resurrection of our Lord is the end of the remnant idea. Here he who is truly the righteous remnant 'survived' the ultimate catastrophe, 'death', by resurrection. In that 'survival' life was maintained and indeed made available by the act of God, and thereafter the Presence and Kingship of God are manifested in and bound up with the resurrected Lord.

Christians believed that, through repentance and faith, they shared in this life of the risen Christ, were conscious of this presence, and thought of themselves as the continuing people of God. Paul could speak of them still as 'a remnant chosen by grace' (Rom. 11.5). But in fact the shrinking process was now reversed: 'Henceforth it is the destiny of the Christian remnant not to dwindle but to expand',[7] and Luke, the earliest Church historian, marks the advance stage by stage.[8]

This *Heilsgeschichte*[9] of the diminishing and expanding remnant has been challenged as an arbitrary and unverifiable interpretation of certain events in Jewish history and of Christian origins. But it is undeniable that early Christian writers did view the events in this way. There is so much reference either directly or by allusion to the remnant idea, and to the Church as Israel which has emerged into new life through the gift of God in Jesus the Messiah, that it cannot be ignored as evidence of what these writers conceived the nature of the Church to be.

THE BODY OF CHRIST

The idea of the Church as the people of God is closer than may at first appear to what is usually thought to be the most prominent N.T. image of the Church, that of the body of Christ. What brings them together is the concept of Christ as the remnant implicit in the former, and the concept of Christ as a corporate personality implicit in the latter.

Paul has several very frequent phrases which describe the relationship of the believer to Christ.[10] These are 'in Christ', which first appears in 1 Thessalonians 1.1; 'with Christ', which is frequent in passages which speak of the Christian suffering and dying, rising and

living with Christ (e.g. Rom. 6.1–11); 'into Christ', in passages which
deal with the significance of baptism (e.g. Rom 6.3; Gal. 3.27).
Christians thus brought 'into Christ' become 'members of Christ' (1
Cor. 6.15), a phrase which brings us close to the idea of the body of
Christ.

Ernest Best writes:[11] 'Behind all these descriptions (i.e. of the Christian community as a body, a bride, etc.) and behind the descriptions of
the Church as "in Christ" or "with Christ" there is a conception of
Christ as a corporate or inclusive personality and of believers as solid
with him'. The idea of Christ as corporate personality appears clearly
in 1 Corinthians 15: 'For as in Adam all die, so also in Christ shall all
be made alive' (v. 22), and 'The first man Adam became a living being;
the last Adam became a life-giving spirit' (v. 45), and the following
versus continue the argument. Romans 5.12–21 presents the same
idea, which may be summed up in the words of verse 18: 'Then as one
man's trespass led to condemnation for all men, so one man's act of
righteousness leads to acquittal and life for all men'. As men are
physically in racial solidarity with Adam, so the believer is in spiritual
solidarity with Christ, and this is proleptically true of all mankind. In
these Pauline passages the universalism is very marked.[12]

The solidarity of mankind is not a concept which is readily grasped
by those who have not freed themselves from the 'rugged individualism' which was perhaps the nineteenth century's main legacy
to the western world. But modern genetics in its doctrine of
transmitted characteristics, and the modern psychology which
emphasizes the significance of racial memory, have each made it clear
that the concept cannot be dismissed as merely primitive mythology
not to be taken seriously by twentieth-century scientific man.
'Solidarity', says J. A. T. Robinson, 'is the divinely ordained structure
in which personal life is to be lived.'[13] St Paul's claim is that in Jesus
Christ who died on the cross and overcame death by his resurrection
an analogous solidarity is being created: 'If any one is in Christ, he is
a new creation . . . the new has come' (2 Cor. 5.17).

First Corinthians 12.12–27 is the earliest passage in which Paul
treats at length the idea of the Church as a body. On the surface it
seems that he presents us with a simile—the Church is *like* a body.
Comparison with the human body is worked out vividly, even
humorously. The human body would be limited indeed if it were
nothing but a seeing instrument: 'If the whole body were an eye, where
would be the hearing?' Stress is equally laid on the necessary co-

operation between the diverse members: 'The eye cannot say to the hand, "I have no need of you".' Even what appear to be less important members are indispensable (v. 23). Paul then goes on to speak of the varied ministries appointed by God in the Church.

But there are several indications here that Paul is doing more than suggest a simile. 'You are the body of Christ and individually members of it' (v. 27) says more than 'you are like a body' or 'you may usefully think of yourselves as a kind of body'. The language of verse 12 which opens the passage is instructive:

> For just as the body is one and has many members, and all the members of the body, though many, are one body, so it is with Christ.

Had Paul been employing simile, we should have expected the last phrase to be 'so it is with the Church'. But what Paul is saying is that *Christ* possesses many members, those who have been baptized into him and have received the Holy Spirit (v. 13). Christ is this body. The members, too, are the body of Christ, but only in him; without integration by faith, baptism, and the gift of the Spirit of God they could not be this kind of body, the body of Christ.

There have been many scholarly discussions about whether Paul was using the phrase 'body of Christ' in a simile, metaphorically or analogically, literally or ontologically. E. Best, who interprets the phrase as a metaphor, provides an example.[14] I am of the opinion that, whatever difficulties it presents to the modern mind, Paul is asserting that, in *reality*, Christ, now risen and glorified is, to use Best's own words, 'a corporate or inclusive personality',[15] into solidarity with whom God has already brought believers and wills to bring all men. What is 'a corporate or inclusive personality' but a body? Not, indeed, a body which corresponds to any body, animal, human, or societal, which can be empirically studied, for it is the body which God has willed before the foundation of the world, the body of the redeemed by and in his eternal Son.[16]

The Epistles to the Colossians and Ephesians develop the body of Christ theme further. That these came from the hand of Paul has been seriously disputed, but scholars who reject Pauline authorship are generally inclined to admit that the thought is Pauline.[17]

Colossians declares that God's purpose in the incarnation of his Son, 'the image of the invisible God' in whom and for whom all things were created (1.15–16), was the reconciliation with himself of all that is estranged (1.20). Jesus Christ has done the work of reconciliation in 'his body of flesh' (1.22). In his risen body 'he is the head of the body, the church; he is the beginning, the firstborn from the dead, that in everything he might be pre-eminent' (1.18). From this 'beginning', which is Christ, the body develops, but only as believers hold fast 'to the Head, from whom the whole body, nourished and knit together through its joints and ligaments, grows with a growth that is from God' (2.19).

Ephesians at greater length works out the theme of the 'mystery' of God's purpose now revealed in Christ and his Church. God's mighty act has brought it about that Christ, raised from the dead, has become 'the head over all things for the church, which is his body, the fulness of him who fills all in all' (1.22–3). This body is the body of those who are reconciled to God (2.16), of which Gentiles are now fellow members (3.6). It is a body which is to grow to maturity, the maturity of Christ the head, aided by gifts of the Holy Spirit which he has made available, by the work of the apostles, prophets, evangelists, pastors, and teachers whom he has called (4.11–12), living in unity and love (4.2–3, 15; 5.2). The thought of Colossians 2.19 is repeated:

> We are to grow up in every way into him who is the head, into Christ, from whom the whole body, joined and knit together by every joint with which it is supplied, when each part is working properly, makes bodily growth and upbuilds itself in love (4.15–16).

It has seemed to some that Ephesians 1.23 which speaks of the Church as the fulness of Christ, suggests that Christ is not complete without the Church. It is unlikely that the writer who speaks of Christ in 4.13 as already possessing the fulness to which the Church must attain can have meant this. The Christ is complete. There is fulness in him which Colossians 2.9 speaks of as 'the whole fulness of deity'. We cannot enter here into a full discussion of this admittedly difficult verse which is capable of various translations.[18] But three facts are to be borne in mind: (a) the Pauline epistles everywhere affirm the perfection, completeness, and sovereignty of Christ; (b) they express the conviction that within the body of Christ all will attain the measure of the stature of the fulness of Christ (Eph. 4.13; cf. 1 Cor. 15.27–8); (c) they recognize realistically that the Church is still far from attaining this fulness.

The whole passage, Ephesians 1.15–23, expresses the consciousness of Christians that in Christ victory has been accomplished (v. 20), but that its fruits are yet to be claimed (vv. 17–19). The

Church experiences a perplexing tension in its recognition that salvation and fulfilment belong to it *now* by the grace of God, but also are *not yet* fully manifested in its life. This tension appears at several points in Paul's thought, and we refer to it again below (p. 20). We shall therefore not be far wrong if we interpret Ephesians 1.22–3 as intended to convey the sense that the fulness of Christ, which is his even though the Church be small and sinful, is to be claimed by the Church, is in fact being continually imparted to it, and will be wholly experienced in the age to come.

THE EUCHARISTIC BODY OF CHRIST

Paul speaks also of the body of Christ in connection with the Lord's supper. His account of the institution of the eucharist in 1 Corinthians 11.24 records the words of Jesus in breaking the bread: 'This is my body which is for you.' In an earlier passage, where he exhorts the Corinthians to have nothing to do with pagan sacrifices, he writes:

> The cup of blessing which we bless, is it not a participation in the blood of Christ? The bread which we break, is it not a participation in the body of Christ? (1 Cor. 10.16).

The next verse makes clear the connection in his mind between the supper and the community:

> Because there is one loaf, we who are many are one body, for we all partake of the same loaf.

It perhaps goes further than the evidence warrants to say with A. E. J. Rawlinson[19] that the occurrence of the word 'body' in the words of institution and his grasp of the significance of the eucharist suggested to Paul the application of the term 'body of Christ' to the Church. What is clear, however, is that Paul sees the supper, instituted, according to the tradition which he had received, by Christ himself, as integral to the life of the Christian community. Paul's understanding of this is well elucidated by G. Johnston in the book which has already been cited several times:

> The Lord's Supper has a similar place (i.e. to baptism) in the life of the Church as the growing Body of Christ. It is distinctive from other fellowship meals (e.g. those of the mystery religions) because it is associated with the living Christ who has died to save the world. It must be the *Lord's* Supper or nothing (1 Cor. 11·20). Here the dying Christ is

recalled and the death proclaimed 'till he come', by the eating of the loaf and drinking the cup (1 Cor. 11.26). In the blood shed a new Covenant had been ratified; hence to drink this cup is to share the promise. Surely all who do so must be one in Christ! As the loaf was broken, so the mortal body of Christ had been slain. But in Him, the triumphant Saviour, all the redeemed became one spiritual body. It is in this capacity that they meet to celebrate the Supper. As they eat they all participate in Christ's death. Surely that should cement their unity! The Lord himself is in their midst, judging their attitude as they come to his table. That is why division here is so heinous.[20] Christ suffers in the suffering of His people. This mutual sharing in the dying Jesus is the very highest point of the Church's unity. Christ's spirit of sacrificial love is to be the ideal and inspiration of its corporate life. Only so can it really be the Body of Christ.[21]

The intimate connection of the eucharist with the very life of the Church has been stressed throughout the history of Christian thought. We shall find this in Ignatius of Antioch (p. 35 below) and St Augustine (pp. 84–5 below). It is implied in excommunication which was early introduced as a disciplinary measure against those whose lives were judged to belie their Christian membership. In the Confessions of the Churches of the Reformation the definition of the Church which is proffered invariably includes among its marks the administration of the sacraments of baptism and the supper according to Christ's ordinance. Both in the teaching and the practice of the Orthodox Churches of the East, which generally refrain from dogmatic definitions, the Church is regarded as essentially a eucharistic community.

Paul, as we have seen, can use the image of the body in a very practical way to assure each Christian, however humble, of the importance of his place and function within the whole membership. But for him this image primarily concerns the inward relationship of the faithful with Christ and with one another. 'Body of Christ' speaks of a fellowship more closely knit and deeply rooted than any other known to men, a fellowship in which the faithful enter into the experience of the Redeemer himself, dying with him, and living with him, feeding upon the nourishment and abounding in the energy which he gives. Each who truly enters into this Christ-centred experience is in unity and love with every other who shares it.

THE BRIDE OF CHRIST

In the Pauline writings the image of the Church as a bride appears in 2

Corinthians 11.2 and Ephesians 5.22–33.[22] Precedent for this exists in O.T. passages in which the relationship between God and Israel is likened to that between husband and wife (Hos. 1–3; Isa. 54.1–8). Certain elements in the tradition of the teaching of Jesus may also have suggested the Pauline use of the image, namely, Jesus' reference to himself as the bridegroom (Mark 2.18–20) and the parables of the marriage feast in Matthew 22 and the ten virgins in Matthew 25.

In 2 Cor. 11.2 Paul is referring to the local church in Corinth when he writes: 'I betrothed you to Christ to present you as a pure bride to her one husband.' But in Ephesians 5.22–33 the bridge is the whole Church. The context is one in which the mutual love and duties of husband and wife are discussed. The relationship between Christ and the Church is suggested as the perfect model:

> The husband is the head of the wife as Christ is the head of the church, his body, and is himself its Savior. As the church is subject to Christ, so let wives also be subject in everything to their husbands. Husbands, love your wives, as Christ loved the church and gave himself up for her, that he might sanctify her, having cleansed her by the washing of water with the word (Eph. 5.23–6).

The passage itself seems to recognize the inadequacy of the parallel. Christ is the Saviour of his Church, and that cannot be said in any ultimate sense of a husband in relation to his wife. A man, loving his wife, and knowing that she is utterly worthy of his love, may be ready to die for her. But Christ in his love for the Church dies for it, and *then* makes it worthy (vv. 25–6). His will is

> that the church might be presented before him in splendor, without spot or wrinkle or any such thing, that she might be holy and without blemish (v. 27).

It will be noted that in this passage the image of the head and body is interwoven with that of the husband and bride. This is an appropriate place to note that in each of these images an ambiguity is implicit.

The body and head may be thought of as two separate parts of an organism. The head has its own special function within the organism, and the body, considered as the trunk in distinction from the head, is a collection of members each having its own function. But while head and body can be thought of in this compartmental way, in reality they are an integrated unity within the living organism. Without the head, which is the governing member, the body, considered as trunk, is lifeless.

Similarly, husband and wife may be thought of as two individuals, each with obligations to the other which may or may not be fulfilled. But the will of God is that 'the two shall become one' (Eph. 5.31; cf. Gen. 2.24, 'one flesh') in a mutuality of love and responsibility. There is a sense, then, in which a man's love of his wife is a nourishing and cherishing of his own flesh (Eph. 5.28–9), that one flesh which he has become with his wife.

The ambiguity inherent in the relationship of head to body and of husband to wife remains when they are taken as images of the relationship between Christ and the Church. The two in principle have become an integrated unity, yet it is still possible, and even necessary, to think of them in distinction. Body and head are not identical; the bride is not the bridegroom; the Church is not the Christ. There is a tension of thought here: integrated unity, yet not identity. In its unity with Christ the Church shares in his glory and perfection. But thought of as one partner in a marriage, or as a body distinguishable from its head, the Church owes obedience to Christ which is nowhere and never completely rendered. It is far from glory and perfection. In the history of doctrine this tension of thought comes to the fore whenever the sense in which the word 'holy' may be attributed to the Church is discussed.[23] The same tension is experienced in the life of the individual believer, whose status Luther was to sum up in the phrase *simul justus et peccator*, 'justified, yet at the same time a sinner'. It is the tension between the 'now' of appropriating in faith the redemption that Christ has once for all won for man, and the 'not yet' of conscious unworthiness and the realization that life with its temptations lies ahead. The Church is holy; the Church is to become holy.

Paul, whose realism has already been mentioned, was well aware of this tension. He can turn immediately from the most exalted language about the Church to warnings against divisive and uncharitable behaviour. He had no illusions about the perfection of the members of the church in Corinth.

THE CHURCH AS GOD'S BUILDING

In the four Gospels, the Acts, the Pauline Epistles, 1 Peter, the Epistle to the Hebrews, and Revelation allusions to the people of God as a building, a house, a sanctuary, or temple abound.[24] The building image has roots in the O.T. The prophets frequently speak of God's people as 'the house of Israel' or of Jacob. Isaiah 28.16 and Psalm 118.22–3 introduce the idea of God's building containing a 'cornerstone'. The stone of Psalm 118 which is rejected by the builders as unsuitable but is reinstated by God as the chief cornerstone is most naturally taken to refer to some person in the community. The application of this to the person of Jesus Christ by the early Church (Matt. 21.42; Acts 4.11; 1 Peter 2.7) doubtless helped to suggest the image of the Church as a building whose principal stone is the rejected and crucified, but now risen, Lord.

Paul frequently speaks of 'building up' the Church in his letters to the Corinthians.[25] This is the work not only of apostles, but of every member. In Ephesians the idea of building up the Church is combined with the idea of the Church as a body: 'building up the body of Christ' (4.12); 'the whole body . . . makes bodily growth and upbuilds itself in love' (4.16).

This language describes the *process* of building. Elsewhere the Church is spoken of as *a building*. Paul tells the Corinthians that they are God's building. He himself has laid a foundation, and that foundation is Jesus Christ (1 Cor. 3.9–15). The other main Pauline passage which speaks of the Church as a building is Ephesians 2.19–22:

> You are . . . members of the household of God, built upon the foundations of the apostles and prophets, Christ Jesus himself being the chief cornerstone, in whom the whole structure is joined together and grows into a holy temple in the Lord; in whom you also are built into it for a dwelling place of God in the Spirit.

There is a division of opinion about the Greek word *akrogōniaios*, translated 'cornerstone'. Some[26] take it to be a stone connected with the foundations of a building; others[27] to be the important locking stone at the crown of the archway above the main entrance of a building. The first interpretation presents the picture of a number of foundation stones, the most important of which is Christ, the others being the apostles and prophets. The second identifies the apostles and prophets as the foundation, and likens Christ to a stone which is the last to be put into position, and which secures the whole building.

In either case the imagery is deficient. If the 'cornerstone' which is Christ is the last to be built in, it is suggested that the building of the Church originated in human enterprise. If the 'cornerstone' which is Christ is a foundation, the image fails to do justice to the concept of the continuing activity of the risen Christ in the life of the Church. But the basic defect of the image is that stones are lifeless things. The author of the Epistle is evidently aware of this, for by the use of the phrase 'grows into a holy temple' in verse 21 he alludes to the body image which he expounds elsewhere. 1 Peter, which also employs this imagery, attempts to overcome its inadequacy by speaking of Christ as the 'living stone' (2.4) and of Christians as 'living stones' (2.5).

We noted above that the images of the Church as the body of Christ and the bride of Christ both contain an ambiguity which reflects the tension in which the Church of Christ always exists. We spoke of it as the tension between the 'now' and the 'not yet'. The same ambiguity is found in the image of the Church as God's building. From one point of view the building is complete and perfect in Christ. From another it is incomplete: stones are continually being added, and the building will not be complete and perfect until the full number is built in. R. J. McKelvey's comment[28] on this ambiguity is helpful:

> The conception of the church as a building under construction, with no suggestion of when the work will be completed, and at the same time as a temple in which God is actually dwelling and worship is being offered, looks like a contradiction. What we have here, however, is a paradox which is basic to much New Testament thinking, the paradox of present possession and future hope. Like each of its members, the Church is called to become what it is, the dwelling-place of God in the Spirit. Recognition of this fact preserves the church from the twin evils of complacency and despair.

THE FELLOWSHIP OF THE SPIRIT

I have left to the end of this very selective treatment of the N.T. doctrine of the Church consideration of the theme which many believe to be the most significant, that of the Church as the fellowship of the Holy Spirit. The idea of the constitutive role of the Holy Spirit is, however, often present in the themes which I have already discussed: 'Do you not know', writes Paul to the Corinthians, 'that you are God's temple and that God's Spirit dwells in you?' (1 Cor. 3.16). The Church as the Lord's holy temple is 'a dwelling place of God in the Spirit' (Eph. 2.22). Listing the bonds of Christian unity and peace, Ephesians 4.3–7 places the 'one body' and the 'one Spirit' together. Christians are baptized into the one body by the one Spirit (1 Cor. 12.13), whose enabling gifts Paul discusses at length immediately following his first major treatment of the body image in 1 Cor. 12.12–27.

The idea of the Holy Spirit as the creator of the Church is already implicit here. A discussion of the relationship between Christ and the Spirit would lead us beyond our present task into the field of Trinitarian theology. But G. Johnston is clearly correct in affirming that in the thought of Paul 'God is the Father of the Lord Jesus Christ; God's Spirit therefore is Christ's Spirit'.[29] For Paul the Spirit of God and of Christ is active throughout and from the very beginning of the saving process. The Christian's confession that Jesus is Lord (1 Cor. 12.3) is prompted by the Spirit, and 'the graces of the Christian life are the fruit of the Spirit, since those who belong to Christ possess His Spirit and are temples of the Spirit of the living God. ... To be in Christ is also to be in the Spirit.'[30] The Christian man is 'led by the Spirit of God' and by the same Spirit becomes aware of membership in the community of the sons of God (Rom. 8.14–17).

Consider the word 'fellowship'. Familiarity tends to obscure for us the extraordinary phenomenon of a body of ancient literature in which the idea of and the words for fellowship and sharing abound as they do in the N.T. Of frequent occurrence are the adjective *koinos*, 'shared in', 'held in common', and its cognates, the nouns *koinōnia*, 'sharing', 'fellowship', and *koinōnos*, 'sharer', 'partner', and the verb *koinōneo*, 'to have (or give) a share in'. Frequent synonyms for *koinōneo* are *metecho* and *metalambano*. The prefix *sun*, 'together with', is used with nouns far more frequently than in any other ancient writings, and we read of 'fellow-workers', 'fellow-prisoners', 'fellow-soldiers', 'fellow-servants', 'fellow-heirs', 'fellow-citizens'.

The N.T. speaks of Christians as sharing in the benefits which Christ has made available. They are partakers of grace (Phil. 1.7), of God's promise (Eph. 3.6), of glory to be revealed (1 Pet. 5.1), even of the divine nature (2 Pet. 1.4). They also share *with* Christ in his experience. Baptism signifies being united with Christ 'in a death like his' and 'united with him in a resurrection like his' (Rom. 6.5). This theme often recurs: 'You were buried with him in baptism, in which you were also raised with him through faith' (Col. 2.12; cf. 2 Cor. 4.10). The Christian can therefore recognize that personal adversity is to 'share his sufferings, becoming like him in his death' (Phil. 3.10).

There is also a fellowship and sharing of Christians with each other. Passages which teach the privilege and duty of brotherly love, sympathy, and forgiveness are numerous and to be found in almost every book.[31] Practical expressions of it are the experiment in the sharing of goods by Christians in Jerusalem (Acts 2.44; 4.32) and a collection which Paul organized among his Gentile converts for poor Christians in Jerusalem (Rom. 15.26; 2 Cor. 8.1 ff and 9.1 ff). The word which Paul uses for this collection is *koinōnia*, which in this context might be translated 'an expression of fellowship'.

All this describes the content which the New Testament Church gave to the word *koinōnia*, what Christians understood it to mean in their daily lives. The inspiration and motive power for it they ascribed to the Spirit of God and Christ. They believed themselves to be living in 'the fellowship (*koinōnia*) of the Spirit'.

What does the word 'of' mean in this phrase? The English 'of' can be as ambiguous as the Greek genitive case which it here represents. Does '*koinōnia* of the Spirit' mean 'participation in the Spirit' as in the R.S.V. translation of Philippians 2.1? Or does it mean 'fellowship which the Spirit bestows'? This would seem the better interpretation in 2 Corinthians 13.14 where Paul obviously has the divine prevenience in mind. It is not necessary to decide between these interpretations, for both are valid.[32] They complement each other. It is because the Holy Spirit bestows fellowship that participation in the Spirit and the gifts of the Spirit is made possible.

Again and again the N.T. insists on the prevenience of the Spirit in the life both of the individual believer and of the whole Church. The life of the believer originates with the Holy Spirit: 'God's love has been poured into our hearts through the Holy Spirit which has been given to us' (Rom. 5.5). In the baptism which opens the believer's heart to receive his continuing influence the Holy Spirit is already at work (1 Cor. 12.13). Of those who are truly in Christ it must be said that they are 'in the Spirit' (Rom 8.9–11), are 'led by the Spirit' (Rom 8.14; Gal. 5.18), and 'walk by the Spirit' (Gal. 5.16, 25) so that the 'fruit of the Spirit' is seen in their lives, 'love, joy, peace, patience, kindness, goodness, faithfulness, gentleness, self-control' (Gal. 5.22–3). The Holy Spirit is the creator and sustainer of the Christian's life.

The Holy Spirit is also the creator and sustainer of the Church's life. The account of Pentecost in Acts 2.1 ff, which is presented as the fulfilment of Christ's promise to clothe his disciples with power from on high (Luke 24.49; Acts 1.8)[33] testifies to the conviction that the Church's historical existence was empowered by the Holy Spirit. 'The Church is a creation through the act of God in Christ'; but it is 'at the same time a fellowship created by the Holy Spirit'.[34] The creator Spirit is also the Church's guide and sustainer. To his guidance are attributed decisions taken at certain crucial points in the Church's early history: the baptism of the first Gentile (Acts 14.44 ff); the first overseas mission (13.2); the admission of Gentiles without requiring their circumcision (15.28); the bringing of the gospel to Europe (16.6–10). It is the Spirit of God, too, who distributes the varieties of gifts and ministries which nourish the Church's life.

This self-understanding as 'the fellowship of the Spirit' is another indication that the early Church thought of itself as the people of God, renewed and living in the day of the Messiah. According to the prophets the messianic age was to see a renewed activity of the Spirit (Isa. 11.1–2; Ezek. 36.26–7, 37.1–14; Joel 2.28 ff). So the N.T. portrays it. The coming of Jesus the Messiah is by the power of the Spirit who is present at his conception (Luke 1.35), at his baptism (Mark 1.10), as he faces the implications of his vocation (Matt. 4.1; Mark 1.12; Luke 4.1) and as he opens his ministry (Luke 4.14, 18). The messianic kingdom is inaugurated. Joel's prophecy begins to be fulfilled (Acts 2.16) with the outpouring of the Spirit on the Messiah's first followers at Pentecost. To those who by faith and repentance subsequently enter the messianic community the Spirit comes and brings his gifts and graces of which the greatest (1 Cor. 13.13) is that love 'which binds everything together in perfect harmony' (Col. 3.14), the unity of the Spirit.

The Kingdom is *inaugurated*; it is yet to come to fulfilment. Consequently the Church in history is not identical with the Kingdom. The Kingdom, says G. Johnston,[35] 'is a realm in which God, Christ, and the Ecclesia are united in the Spirit. . . . The Church is the sphere on earth of the incarnating of this Holy Spirit, a visible society with an invisible life, a divine-human phenomenon.' He prefers to speak of the *incarnating* rather than the *incarnation* of the Spirit. It is more true to the Church's experience of tension between the 'now' and the 'not yet' and to its consciousness of imperfection while it lives in hope of the gift of maturity in the body of Christ and in the unity of the Spirit.[36]

THE CHURCH AND THE INDIVIDUAL

The N.T. throughout lays great stress on the corporate nature of the Church. It is apparent in all the Church themes and images which we have studied: people of God, body, marriage relationship, fellowship of the Spirit; it is true even of the seemingly inanimate image of the building, for God's building is at once 'the household of God' (Eph. 2.19) and the temple of a worshipping community (Eph. 2.21). Whatever may be the validity of the concept of a private Christian withdrawn from membership of the community, the N.T. knows no such person. 'Church' does not mean the sum of individuals who have a private relationship with Christ and a private inspiration of the Holy Spirit. It is a community of believers incorporated into Christ's filial relationship with God by the adopting initiative of God himself who 'has sent the Spirit of his Son into our hearts' (Gal. 4.6). This is not to say that the individual is submerged. In the body all members have their necessary place (1 Cor. 12.14 ff); in the household and temple all have their priestly work (1 Pet. 2.5, 9; Rev. 1.6). 'Let every one lead the life which the Lord has assigned to him, and in which God has called him,' writes Paul (1 Cor. 7.17). And he is confident that in the consummation God will raise man's physical body into a spiritual body (1 Cor. 15.42–50). This resurrection body is 'none other than the Body of Christ in which we have a share'.[37] Man's destiny is the completion of his incorporation into the body of Christ which began at baptism, the fulfilment of solidarity with Christ's risen and glorious body. But this does not mean the loss of individuality. The teaching of Jesus contains a strong emphasis on the worth of the individual. Paul and other N.T. writers were doubtless too well aware of this, and of Jesus' own concern for persons, to suggest any eschatology of absorption.

Part 2

THE PATRISTIC PERIOD

3

From Clement of Rome
to Irenaeus

A quarter of a millennium elapsed from the birth of Jesus Christ before the first work dealing specifically with the nature of the Church was written. This was *On the Unity of the Church* by Cyprian, Bishop of Carthage, 248–58.[1] The first theological concern of the early Church was the doctrine of the Person of Christ in relation to the doctrine of God. But the articles of Christian faith, later to be drawn together in the creeds, are all integrally related. The doctrine of Christ's Person has direct implications for a doctrine of man and man's relationship to God. We find indications, therefore, in the earliest Christian Fathers, of how they thought about the Church, even though they do not address themselves to the nature of the Church as a particular theological problem.

Empirically the Church existed as a number of congregations scattered over the Mediterranean countries. In view of the distance which separated them they might easily have become self-contained groups, developing in idiosyncrasy and showing great variety in teaching, modes of worship, and customs. Variations there were, but in general we have a picture of remarkable unanimity in doctrine, worship, and, certainly by the end of the second century, in forms of ministry and general structure. This unanimity witnesses both to the faithfulness of the Church's early missionaries and their converts to the tradition they had received, and to the excellence of the means of communication and travel in the Roman Empire which made it possible. Congregations were reminded that the Church which expresses itself wholly in the worship and work of the local Christian community nevertheless transcends it. 'Wherever Jesus Christ is, there is the Catholic Church,' writes Ignatius of Antioch.[2] Polycarp, Bishop of Smyrna, is reported, in the account of his martyrdom written soon after the event (c. 155), to have prayed for 'the whole Catholic Church throughout the world'.[3] The word 'catholic' is used here in its literal sense of 'universal' or 'in its totality' (from the Greek *kath'holon*) in distinction from a local church. It is somewhat later that the word is used to distinguish the Church which adheres to accepted doctrine from groups judged to be heretical or schismatic.

From the beginning Christian writers used the N.T. themes and imagery of the Church. The following is a list of the most notable instances in the earliest Fathers:

THE CHURCH AS THE NEW ISRAEL

Clement of Rome (*c.* 94), *To the Corinthians* XXIX, 1–3, where the argument is that whereas in time past Israel was 'the portion of the Lord', God has now 'made us [Christians] the portion of his choice for himself'; The *Epistle of Barnabas* (*c.* 70–100) III, 6 and V, 7: the Church is 'the new people'; Justin Martyr (*c.* 150), *Dialogue with Trypho* XI, 5 and CXXIII; Irenaeus (*c.* 180), *Adversus Haereses* V, 32.2: 'Abraham's seed is the Church', and V, 34.1.

THE CHURCH AS THE BODY OF CHRIST

1 Clement XXXVII; Ignatius, *Smyrnaeans* I: the crucified body of Jesus is seen as a standard which rallies the faithful in 'the one body of his Church'; the preacher of the sermon which is erroneously called the Second Epistle of Clement (*c.* 140) says: 'I imagine that you are not ignorant that the living Church is the body of Christ' (2 Clem. XIV); Irenaeus, *Adversus Haereses* IV, 33.7: the Church is 'the great and glorious body of Christ'.

THE CHURCH AS THE BRIDE OF CHRIST

2 Clement XIV: 'The Scripture says "God made man male and female"; the male is Christ, the female is the Church'. In the context in which this passage occurs the preacher ties together, somewhat confusedly, the three biblical images of the Church as the body of Christ, the bride of Christ and the dwelling-place of the Spirit.

THE CHURCH AS GOD'S BUILDING

Ignatius, *Ephesians* IX, 1; *The Shepherd* of Hermas (*c.* 140–50), Vision III and Similitude IX, where this image of the Church is worked out in great detail.

THE CHURCH AS THE TEMPLE OF THE HOLY SPIRIT

Irenaeus, *Adv. Haer.* III, 24.1:

> Where the Church is, there is the Spirit of God; and where the Spirit of
> God is, there is the Church and all grace; and the Spirit is the truth.
> Those, therefore, who do not participate in the Spirit neither feed at their
> mother's breasts nor drink the bright fountain issuing from Christ's body.[4]

Several of these writers, however, introduce new ideas, or attempt a
greater precision on matters concerning the nature of the Church of
which there are only hints in the N.T.

1 CLEMENT OF ROME (*c.* 94)

Clement's letter to the church in Corinth[5] was prompted by a quarrel
in that church which threatened its unity. Certain properly appointed
and blameless presbyters had been deposed (XLIV). Clement exhorts
the Corinthian Christians to restore them to their office and the
church in Corinth to good order and amity. He draws instances from
the O.T. to commend the virtues of brotherly love and patience and to
demonstrate the dangers of the vices of hatred and envy. He cites the
orderly movements of the heavenly bodies and the tranquil succession
of the seasons and of night and day to inculcate the lessons of
peacefulness and orderliness. Brotherliness and good order are essential to the Church.

APOSTOLIC SUCCESSION

Integral to his argument is what later came to be known as the doctrine of apostolic succession. This doctrine affirms that it is essential
that the ministers of the Church be appointed in a succession from the
apostles. Clement states (XLII and XLIV) that the apostles foresaw the
possibility of discord about the exercise of rule (the Greek word is
episkope) in the Church. They were therefore careful to appoint men
to continue the work of the ministry in the places to which they had
brought the gospel in their missionary journeys, and to make provision for a continuing succession of ministers. The Corinthians,
therefore, have acted unjustly in deposing men who were appointed by
apostles or by others whom the apostles had authorized to do so, and
who had done nothing to deserve such treatment. This is a sin against
the good order of the Church.

We have here, then, the first mention in Christian literature of the idea of apostolic succession. It is a passage which has been submitted to a good deal of scholarly scrutiny, but there are different opinions about its interpretation. It is clear, however, that in Clement the words 'bishop' (*episkopos*) and 'presbyter' (*presbuteros*) refer to the same order of ministry. The two words are synonymous, as they undoubtedly are in Acts and the Pastoral Epistles.[6] The term presbyter-bishop is usually employed to denote this identification. Some twenty years later in Ignatius of Antioch (see below, pp. 35–6) we find the word 'bishop' used of a single individual, distinct from the presbyters, in whom is invested the oversight (*episkope*) of the local church. For the bishop in this sense (which became universal towards the end of the second century) the term 'monarchical bishop'[7] is used.

The dispute about the interpretation of 1 Clement XLII and XLIV centres on the question of the ministerial *agent* of the succession. Does Clement mean that the succession is passed on by the presbyter-bishops in each community? Or does he mean that the apostles appointed men to a special ministry, comparable to that of the monarchical bishop, with the exclusive right to ordain? In other words, does he conceive of a presbyteral or an episcopal succession? To follow the arguments on either side, Clement's words must be studied:

> The Apostles . . . preached from district to district, and from city to city, and they appointed their first converts, testing them by the Spirit, to be bishops and deacons of the future believers . . . (XLII).

> Our Apostles also knew through our Lord Jesus Christ that there would be strife for the title of bishop. For this cause, therefore, since they had received perfect foreknowledge, they appointed those who have already been mentioned, and afterwards added the codicil that if they should fall asleep, other approved men should succeed to their ministry. We consider therefore that it is not just to remove from their ministry those who were appointed by them, or later on by other eminent men, with the consent of the whole Church, and have ministered to the flock of Christ without blame . . . (XLIV).

Much depends upon whether 'other approved men' and 'other eminent men' refer to the same people. Those who would see here a doctrine of apostolic succession of the monarchical bishop hold that the 'other eminent men' are *not* to be identified with the 'other approved men'. They interpret Clement as saying that the apostles appointed presbyter-bishops to continue the work of the ministry in the places which they had evangelized, and that they also appointed other men to a distinct office, an important element in which was the ordaining of a continuing supply of presbyter-bishops.

Others take the 'other eminent men' to refer back to the 'other approved men'. Clement, they hold, means that the apostles appointed reliable Christians as presbyter-bishops, and arranged that, when it became necessary, these should appoint their own successors. This is to say that the passage envisages a succession of presbyter-bishops, the oversight of the local community together with authority to ordain being lodged in the presbyteral body as a whole.

While there is nothing in the passage, grammatically or in its general flow, to forbid the first of these interpretations, I, episcopalian though I am, incline to the second. Had the monarchical bishop existed in Rome or Corinth when the letter was written it is odd that it provides no clearer indication of it than the ambiguous wording of this passage. We should also have expected it to have been addressed to the bishop under whose authority the Corinthian Christians lived, bidding him exercise a firmer pastoral control.[8] Clement himself, moreover, nowhere claims to write as *the* bishop of Rome. It is true that some eighty years later in the list of bishops of Rome given by Irenaeus (*Adv. Haer.* III, iii.2) his name appears as the third after Peter and Paul. But all that can be certainly affirmed of this letter is that it is written in the name of the church of Rome. It is reasonable to suppose that Clement enjoyed a position of leadership among the Roman presbyter-bishops, and was their spokesman. This may well be a clue to the way in which the monarchical episcopate emerged during the second century.

THE CHURCH AS AN ARMY

As we have seen, Clement uses N.T. language about the Church as the New Israel and the body of Christ. But there is one short passage where the idea of the Church as Christ's army is employed. This is not a N.T. image, although Ephesians 6.10–7 and 2 Timothy 2.3–4 apply the military metaphor to the Christian individual. In XXXVII, however, Clement is probably simply using the example of the organization and discipline of the Roman army to bring home once more to his readers the advantages of good order:

> Let us then serve in our army, brethren, with all earnestness, following his faultless commands. Let us consider those who serve our generals, with

what good order, habitual readiness, and submissiveness they perform their commands. Not all are prefects, nor centurions, nor in charge of fifty men, or the like, but each carries out in his own rank the commands of the emperor and of the generals. The great cannot exist without the small, nor the small without the great.

Comparison of the Church with an army appears frequently in Christian thought: for example, in the directions for his monks of Pachomius (*c*. 363–424) who himself had been a Roman soldier; in the organization of the Society of Jesus (established in 1540) founded by Ignatius Loyola who had also been a soldier; and in the widely used phrase 'the Church militant'. The establishment of the Salvation Army (1865), which was a model for similar organizations within several denominational churches, and the popularity of S. Baring-Gould's hymn 'Onward, Christian soldiers', testify to the appeal of this concept of the Church, slight though its N.T. foundations may be.

THE LAITY OF THE CHURCH

It is noteworthy that as early as Clement a distinction is drawn between clergy and laity. In XL, impressing on his readers the importance of orderliness, Clement cites the regulations in Leviticus by which special responsibilities are assigned to the high priest, priests, and Levites,[9] adding that 'the layman (*laikos*) is bound by the ordinances for the laity'. Clement does not draw the distinction so sharply as to reduce the layman to the passive nonentity which he tended to become in the Middle Ages. Note the concluding words of the quotation from XXXVII above. Clement also says (XLI) that each member of the Church has his ministry with its own appointed rules. The early Fathers are as insistent as the N.T. that the baptized Christian is to be no mere nominal member. Even though he holds no office he has an active part in the worship and mission of the Church.

The word 'layman' (*laikos*) is the adjective of the Greek *laos* (people), the biblical word in the phrase 'people of God', by which is meant the whole people, those who hold office and those who do not. Strictly, therefore, the individual 'layman' in Clement's and the modern sense of the word represents the whole Church and bears responsibility for its total life (worship, order, mission), a truth which the idea of the priesthood of the laity preserves. And on the other hand, since office-bearers bear their responsibilities on behalf of and as representatives of the whole Church, the early Fathers carefully note that the whole Church, which includes the *laikos*, has a voice in their appointment.[10]

2   IGNATIUS OF ANTIOCH (died *c.* 115)

During a journey under guard to Rome from Antioch where he had been condemned to death by the Roman magistrates, Ignatius wrote seven letters, two to churches where he had stopped en route (Philadelphia and Smyrna), three to churches which had sent representatives to greet him when he stayed in Smyrna, one to the church in Rome, and one to Polycarp, Bishop of Smyrna, who had shown him much kindness. It is probable that Ignatius suffered martyrdom in Rome *c.* 115.

His letters have doctrinal importance in several ways, but especially for the early trends in Christology and for the doctrine of the Church. As we have seen, Ignatius uses the N.T. images of the Church, and shares Paul's understanding of the catholicity of the Church (*Smyrn.* VIII, 2). But his main concern, like Clement's, is for the Church's unity and good order, and for a similar reason: the occurrence of schism in the church in Philadelphia (*Phil.* III and VII) and its threat elsewhere (*Eph.* VII, *Magn.* VIII, *Trall.* VII).

A THREEFOLD MINISTRY

It is clear that in the churches in Syria and Asia Minor which Ignatius knew, a threefold ministry of bishop, priest, and deacon had emerged. A detailed study of the doctrine of the ministry is not the intention of this book, but the first appearance of the pattern of ministry which was to prevail in the Church from the second to the sixteenth century demands a brief discussion here. Moreover, Ignatius obviously sees the bishop's role as essential to the Church.

THE BISHOP

The bishop presides over the council of the local church[11] (*Magn.* VI). He presides also at the eucharist and at baptisms, though apparently he may depute these functions, and the holding of a love-feast (*agapē*), to others, presumably the presbyters:

> Let that be considered a valid eucharist which is celebrated by the bishop, or by one whom he appoints. Wherever the bishop appears let the congregation be present, just as wherever Jesus Christ is, there is the Catholic

Church. It is not lawful either to baptize or to hold an 'agape' without the bishop; but whatever he approve, this also is pleasing to God, that everything which you do may be secure and valid (*Smyrn.* VIII).

The bishop is also seen by Ignatius as the focus of the unity of the local church. Again and again he insists on the duty of obedient submission to the bishop.[12]

THE PRESBYTERS

Ignatius does not say how many presbyters there were in these churches. Since he frequently likens them to the apostles it is tempting to think that in each church there were twelve. If this number seems too large for what must have been quite small communities, it is to be remembered that they were not full-time salaried officers. At all events Ignatius' use of the collective noun *presbuterion* (presbytery) (*Magn.* XIII) and his description of them as a council (*Magn.* VI) suggest that there were more than one or two. The phrase 'aptly woven spiritual crown' (*Magn.* XIII) may imply that they sat in council with the bishop in a circle. In the council they would no doubt collaborate with the bishop in matters of church policy and discipline, and exercise the function which Ignatius says (*Trall.* XIII) is particularly fitting for presbyters, namely 'to cheer the soul of the bishop'.[13]

THE DEACONS

Ignatius frequently mentions deacons, but says little about their functions. From other early Christian writings[14] we learn that deacons were closely associated with the bishop, under whose authority they administered the alms of the congregation to provide for the physical needs of widows, orphans, sick, and poor. That they had these duties in the churches Ignatius knew is implied in *Trall.* II:

> And they also who are deacons of the mysteries of Jesus Christ must be in every way pleasing to all men. For they are not the ministers of food and drink, but servants of the Church of God; they must therefore guard against blame as against fire.

Ignatius is anxious to show that, although the deacons deal in mundane things like food and drink, their ministry is a spiritual one. They are, he says (*Magn.* VI), 'entrusted with the service (*diakonia*) of Jesus Christ'. In their office they represent the ministry of Christ and the whole Church to the needs and sufferings of men.

Ignatius sees this threefold ministry as patterned on the relationship between God the Father, Jesus Christ, and the apostles. Although he is not always consistent, he usually correlates the bishop with the Father, the presbyters with the apostles, and the deacons with Jesus Christ, as in *Magn.* VI:

> Be zealous to do all things in harmony with God, with the bishop presiding in the place[15] of God and the presbyters in the place of the Council of the Apostles, and the deacons, who are most dear to me, entrusted with the service of Jesus Christ.

And in *Trall.* III:

> Likewise let all respect the deacons as Jesus Christ, even as the bishop is also a type of the Father, and the presbyters as the Council of God and the college of Apostles. Without these the name of 'Church' is not given.

Ignatius is silent on several matters about which we should like to know what he could have told us. How, for instance, were the bishop and presbyters chosen and commissioned? It is probable that all were chosen by the local church, but we should like to know whether the bishop was ordained by the presbytery (presbyteral consecration), or by other bishops from neighbouring places (episcopal consecration). And was the ordination of a presbyter at the hands of the presbyterate, or was ordination the prerogative of the bishop alone?

Ignatius does not invoke the principle of apostolic succession. On the other hand he strongly repudiates the suggestion that the pattern of ministry which he advocates is no more than a human invention to counteract schism:

> I cried out while I was with you, I spoke with a great voice—with God's own voice—'Give heed to the bishop, and to the presbytery and deacons.' But some suspected me of saying this because I had previous knowledge of the division of some persons: but he in whom I am bound is my witness that I had no knowledge of this from any human being, but the Spirit was preaching, and saying this, 'Do nothing without the bishop' . . . (*Phil.* VII).

And in *Eph.* III he declares that 'the bishops, who have been appointed throughout the world,[16] are by the will of Jesus Christ'.

B. H. Streeter[17] interprets Ignatius' constant insistence on obedient submission to the bishop as evidence that monepiscopacy[18] was a recent development which he was over-anxious to bolster up. Streeter speaks of him as a neurotic with a 'will to power'. It is most probable that monepiscopacy was of recent development, but it may be doubted whether Streeter's estimate of Ignatius' character is consonant with the picture of him which emerges from these letters written on the way to martyrdom. It is important to note, too, that the bishop of whom Ignatius speaks is by no means an autocratic prelate. With him in the government of the local church is associated the council of presbyters. In most of the passages where the recipients are exhorted to be obedient to the bishop they are also called on to render obedience and respect to the presbyters and deacons. One who could write, 'Let not office exalt anyone, for faith and love is everything, and nothing has been preferred to them' (*Smyrn.* VI), can hardly have seen the bishop as a 'prelate'.

THE CHURCH OF ROME

The letter which Ignatius sent ahead to the church in Rome, imploring that no steps be taken to save him from death, presents a puzzle. In this letter alone there is no mention of the bishop. Is this because he assumed that the church which he describes in most congratulatory terms in the opening sentence must have had a paragon of a bishop and that the Roman Christians would surely be living in loving obedience to him, so that there was no need to insist on loyalty to the bishop as in the other six letters? But if so, why no greetings to the Bishop of Rome, no mention of him? Or is it because Ignatius knew that Rome had no bishop in the sense that he understood the term? We do not know. But we have noted that Clement's letter, written from Rome some twenty years before, provides no evidence that Rome had a monarchical bishop.

3 THE SHEPHERD OF HERMAS (*c.* 150)

This second-century 'Pilgrim's Progress' was written in Italy, probably in Rome. The Muratorian Fragment[19] informs us that Hermas was the brother of Pius who was the occupant of the *kathedra* (bishop's seat or throne) of the city of Rome, and implies that he wrote *The Shepherd* while his brother was bishop, *c.* 140–50.

The book recounts a series of visions, lays down a number of moral commandments (Mandates), and presents ten long and involved parables (Similitudes). Hermas is concerned throughout with the Church's holiness, and the moral purity of its members, and he advocates a rigorous exercise of discipline. He provides an early example of the ecclesiology[20] which in stressing holiness as an essential mark of the Church tends to neglect other important aspects of its nature.

THE CHURCH AS A PRIMAL CREATION OF GOD

We have already noted[21] that Hermas gives considerable elaboration to the N.T. image of the Church as God's building. In the 'Visions' he also introduces the idea of the Church as a primal creation of God which is not to be found in the N.T. unless Ephesians 1.4[22] be taken to imply it. Hermas records several visions of an old woman (Vis. I, ii; II, i, iv) who had encouraged and instructed him. A young man, appearing in a dream, asked Hermas who he thought the old woman was:

> I said, 'the Sybil'. 'You are wrong,' he said, 'she is not.' 'Who is she then?' I said. 'The Church,' he said. I said to him, 'Why then is she old?' 'Because', he said, 'she was created the first of all things. For this reason she is old; and for her sake was the world established' (Vis. II, iv).

In subsequent visions the old woman becomes progressively younger, until she is radiant with beauty (Vis. III, x-xiii).

The N.T. view of the Church as the renewal of the people of God provides a scriptural basis for the idea that it pre-dates the birth of Christ, but, apart from the possibility that Ephesians 1.4 implies it, the idea that it is the first of God's creations is new. It is one, however, which appears at much the same time in the sermon already mentioned on p. 30:

> Thus, brethren, if we do the will of our Father, God, we shall belong to the first Church, the spiritual one which was created before the sun and moon (2 Clem. XIV).

A tendency to allegorize the Scriptures in 2 Clement suggests that it emanates from Alexandria, where this hermeneutical method was prevalent. It is there that Clement of Alexandria towards the end of the second century, and Origen early in the third, were to expound a similar doctrine of the Church.[23]

THE MINISTRY

Most of Hermas's references to the ministry are vague. He speaks of 'elders [*presbuteroi*] who are in charge of the church' (Vis. II, iv). In two passages he mentions *episkopoi*, but as he does so in the plural it is impossible to say whether the word is a synonym for *presbuteroi* or not. In his vision of the Church as a building he tells us that the square stones which are firmly set are the apostles and *episkopoi* and teachers and deacons (Vis. III, v); and in Similitude IX, xxvii *episkopoi* are referred to as 'hospitable men who at all times received the servants of God into their houses gladly and . . . sheltered the destitute and the widows'.

But there is one passage which strongly suggests the existence in Rome at this time of the monepiscopate in a form which in one respect at least recalls the Ignatian bishop. In Mandate XI, 1 Hermas describes a vision of a group of men seated on a bench, and another man who is sitting on a *kathedra* (throne).[24] The application of this to the monarchical bishop on his throne with his 'aptly woven spiritual crown' (Ignatius, Magn. XIII) sitting around him is tempting. Can Hermas here be referring to Pius whom Irenaeus lists as the ninth bishop of Rome and the Muratorian Fragment identifies as Hermas's brother? Whoever he was, Hermas did not approve of him. He goes on to denounce him as a false prophet who corrupts the minds of the servants of God.

It is appropriate here to cite the evidence of Justin Martyr (died *c.* 165) whose *Apology* must have been written soon after *The Shepherd*. Justin nowhere mentions the *episkopos*. In the well-known passages which describe the Paschal eucharist and the Sunday eucharist (*Apol.* LXV–LXVII) the celebrant is spoken of as the president (*prohestōs*).[25] The evidence of Hermas and Justin Martyr taken together strongly suggests that in the middle of the second century Rome had an ecclesiastic who occupied the *kathedra* and normally presided at the eucharist, but that he was not yet commonly known as *the* bishop (*episkopos*). That he was so designated later in the second century is well attested by the Muratorian Fragment, Irenaeus,[26] and *The Apostolic Tradition* of Hippolytus.[27]

4 THE EPISTLE TO DIOGNETUS

Although written in the form of a letter this work is really an apology, the intention of which is to commend the Christian way of life to a pagan inquirer. Of its authorship, date, place of origin, and the identity of Diognetus nothing is known with certainty. That scholars tend to date it in the middle of the second century[28] justifies our treating of it at this point. It presents a different concept of the Church from anything we have so far met. The writer does not use the word 'church', but speaks simply about 'Christians'. The Epistle presents a strong Christology of incarnation (VII–VIII) and a doctrine of Atonement which sees Christ's death as a ransom and his righteousness as that which justifies the believer (IX), but does not develop this into a doctrine of the Church as the body of Christ. Rather, on the analogy of the Platonic view of the relation of soul to body, the writer thinks of Christians as the soul of the world:

> What the soul is in the body, that the Christians are in the world. The soul is spread through all members of the body, and Christians throughout the cities of the world. The soul dwells in the body but is not of the body, and Christians dwell in the world, but are not of the world. The soul is invisible, and is guarded in a visible body, and Christians are recognized when they are in the world, but their religion remains invisible. . . . The soul has been shut up in the body but itself sustains the body; and Christians are confined in the world as in a prison, but themselves sustain the world (Diogn. VI).

The Epistle develops the Pauline idea that the Christian's true citizenship is in heaven (Phil. 3.20), and at the same time explains the meaning of the Church's universality. His designation of Christians as 'this new race' (Diogn. I) is elaborated in the following words:

> The distinction between Christians and other men, is neither in country nor language nor customs. . . . While living in Greek and barbarian cities, according as each obtained his lot, and following the local customs, both in clothing and food and in the rest of life, they show forth the wonderful and confessedly strange character of the constitution of their own citizenship. They dwell in their own fatherlands, but as if sojourners in them; they share all things as citizens, and suffer all things as strangers. Every foreign country is their fatherland, and every fatherland is a foreign country. . . . They pass their time upon the earth, but they have their citizenship in heaven. They obey the appointed laws, and they surpass the laws in their own lives. They love all men and are persecuted by all men . . . (Diogn. v).

It is an attractive account of the significance of Christian life in the world. Its limitation is that it does not free itself from the Platonic idea of the body as the prison of the soul, and consequently regards Christians as imprisoned by the world. While the writer, nevertheless, conceives of the world as invisibly sustained by the Church, he gives no more than a hint that it is the field of the Christian's service and the Church's mission. His ecclesiology is, however, more true to the

nature of the gospel than those which, with a more thoroughgoing
Platonism, view matter, and consequently the body, as inherently evil,
and see the true Christian as one who restricts the demands of the
body to the utmost possible degree, and the Church as a 'holiness
group' separated from the world and its concerns.

5   IRENAEUS (*c.* 130–200)

Irenaeus became Bishop of Lyons in Gaul in 177 in succession to
Pothinus, who was martyred in a persecution during the reign of the
Emperor Marcus Aurelius. His most important book, *The Refutation
of False Knowledge*, is usually known as *Adversus Haereses*.[29] It is
mainly a refutation of the teachings and claims of Gnostic teachers.

THE GNOSTIC THREAT

Gnosticism was a mode of thought which was being actively
promoted in the Graeco-Roman world of the second century. The
Gnostic teachers differed greatly in the details of their systems, but
each claimed to possess a secret knowledge (Greek, *gnosis*) about God
and the world which a man must acquire if he wished to be assured of
salvation. Gnosticism was a mixture of philosophy and religion which
drew elements from most of the philosophies and religions of the ancient Near East, including Judaism and Christianity. The main tenets,
common to most of the Gnostic teachers, are that the Supreme Being is
spiritual, transcendent, and unknowable; he cannot possibly have any
contact with matter; the world of matter therefore originates from
some other being or beings. Gnostic mythology predicates a series or
hierarchy of beings, sometimes called 'aeons', proceeding by emana-
tion from the Supreme Being, less spiritual, more foolish or mischievous the lower their place in the hierarchy.

At this point Gnostic imaginative fancy is brought into full play.
The numbers, names, and characters of the aeons differ in the various
systems. Saturninus spoke of seven (*Adv. Haer.* I, xxiv.1), Valentinus
of thirty (I, i.1–2).[30] The origin of matter, and therefore of the world,
is attributed either to an unfortunate accident caused by the
foolishness of the aeons, or to the deliberately mischievous action of
one of them, often called the Demiurge, and by some identified with
the God of the O.T. Matter and the human body are uniformly
regarded as inherently evil. But in some human beings there has been

implanted an element of spirit. For these, and only these, salvation is possible, but the spiritual element must be freed from its imprisoning matter.

Gnostics like Valentinus who incorporated Christian ideas to any large extent, spoke of Jesus as a saviour.[31] Salvation, however, is not won by his sacrificial life and death and appropriated through faith in him. It is a matter of having correct knowledge about the world, the aeons and their relation to the Supreme God, knowledge which will enable the spiritual man to overcome the dangers which will face him after death, and to pass safely to his destiny with the Supreme Absolute Spirit. Jesus imparted this knowledge to his apostles. Gnostic teachers claimed to have received it from them by a secret tradition, and thus to be able to make it available to their adherents.

This was the kind of teaching which was gaining a grip on intellectuals and unlearned alike. Clothed in a Christian dress though it often was, for example by Valentinus, Basilides, and Marcion, it denied fundamentals of Christian faith. It was dualistic, it had no place for the doctrine of the incarnation, and its view of the body as intrinsically evil was incompatible with the Christian estimate of man's dignity as God's creation.

THE CANON OF TRUTH

Irenaeus' refutation of Gnostic teaching brings him into the realm of ecclesiology at the point at which he deals with the Gnostic claim to possess a secret tradition derived from the apostles. It is the Church, he insists, which possesses the true apostolic tradition. It is not secret; it is enshrined in the Scriptures, and is contained also in what he calls the canon (or rule) of truth, taught openly to all who will in sincerity and humility learn from the Church's authoritative teachers. He summarizes this canon of truth as follows:

> The Church, though dispersed throughout the whole world, even to the ends of the earth, has received from the apostles and their disciples this faith: (She believes) in one God, the Father Almighty, Maker of heaven, and earth, and the sea, and all things that are in them; and in one Christ Jesus, the Son of God, who became incarnate for our salvation; and in the Holy Spirit, who proclaimed through the prophets the dispensations of God, and the advents, and the birth from a virgin, and the passion and the resurrection from the dead, and the ascension into heaven in the flesh of the beloved Christ Jesus, our Lord, and His (future) manifestation from heaven in the glory of the Father 'to gather all things in one' (Eph. 1.10)

and to raise up anew all flesh of the whole human race, in order that . . .
He should execute just judgement towards all; that He may send . . . the
angels who transgressed . . . together with the ungodly . . . among men,
into everlasting fire; but may, in the exercise of his grace, confer immortality on the righteous and holy . . . and may surround them with
everlasting glory (*Adv. Haer.* I, x.1).[32]

Irenaeus' argument may now be presented under four headings:

a   The universality of the canon of truth

He claims that these doctrines, summarized in the canon of truth, are
taught everywhere in the Church:

> The Church, having received this preaching and this faith, although
> scattered throughout the whole world, yet, as if occupying but one house,
> carefully preserves it. . . . Although the languages of the world are
> different, yet the import of the tradition is one and the same . . . in Ger-
> many . . . in Spain . . . in Gaul . . . in the East . . . in Egypt . . . in Libya
> (ibid.).

The claim can be verified by comparing Irenaeus' canon of truth
with the passage in which his younger contemporary, Tertullian of
Carthage, summarizes what he calls 'the canon of faith',[33] and the
passage in which Origen of Alexandria, writing about 220, presents at
rather greater length what he calls 'the teaching of the Church'.[34] The
similarity in content is striking. Each might be a preliminary draft for
the later and more succinct 'Apostles' Creed'. Here is evidence, within
a period of about forty years, from places as far apart as Gaul, the
Roman province of North Africa, and Alexandria, to support
Irenaeus' contention that the Church 'believes these points just as if
she had but one soul, and one and the same heart, and she proclaims
them, and teaches them, and hands them down, with perfect harmony,
as if she possessed only one mouth' (ibid.). This is in strong contrast
with the widely differing systems of the Gnostic teachers. Irenaeus'
point is the simple and compelling one that the unanimity of Christian
teaching in so many different places is evidence that it is derived from
one source and genuinely represents the original teaching.

b   The succession of bishops

Irenaeus claims that the substantial identity of the Church's canon of
truth with the teaching of the apostles is further guaranteed by the unbroken succession in the various local churches of those who are the
official guardians and teachers of this canon, the bishops:

It is within the power of all ... who may wish to see the truth, to con-
template clearly the tradition of the apostles manifested throughout the
whole world; and we are in a position to reckon up those who were by the
apostles instituted bishops in the churches, and (to demonstrate) the
successions of these men to our own times (*Adv. Haer.* III, iii.1).

He says that if the apostles had known of 'hidden mysteries', such as
the Gnostics claimed to be able to impart, they would surely have
transmitted them to the men to whom they were entrusting the
churches. It would be tedious, he goes on, to give the succession lists
of all the churches. He takes Rome as an example:

... the very great, the very ancient, and universally known church
founded and organized at Rome by the two most glorious apostles, Peter
and Paul.... For it is a matter of necessity that every church should agree
with this church, on account of its pre-eminent authority (*Adv. Haer.* III,
iii.2).[35]

Irenaeus goes on to give a list of the bishops of Rome, a list which, according to the early fourth-century historian, Eusebius of Caesarea,
Hegesippus had begun to compile some twenty-five years before (*c.*
155). The list is Linus, Anacletus, Clement (whom he identifies as the
writer of the letter to the Corinthian church), Euarestus, Alexander,
Sixtus, Telesphorus, Hyginus, Pius (mentioned in the Muratorian
Fragment: see p. 38 above), Anicetus, Soter, and Eleutherus who
'does now, in twelfth place from the apostles, hold the inheritance of
the episcopate' (*Adv. Haer.* III, iii.3).

Irenaeus then mentions Smyrna and Ephesus which similarly
provide witness to the true apostolic line, but without listing their
bishops. In both cases, however, the lists would have been shorter. At
Smyrna, Polycarp lived until *c.* 165, and Irenaeus accepts the tradition
that the apostle John presided over the church in Ephesus 'until the
times of Trajan', who was emperor between 98 and 117.

c Succession to a see

It is important to notice that Irenaeus traces the apostolic succession
through the previous holders of a see (*kathedra*), and not through
bishops who lay on hands in consecrating. He conceives of each of the
important Christian centres as having a *kathedra*, a teaching chair,
which must be occupied by one who will faithfully and responsibly
guard the canon of truth. When, through death or for other reasons,
the chair falls vacant, the Church must choose a suitable successor.
There can be no doubt that Irenaeus believed that a bishop must be

properly elected and consecrated, but he says nothing of these things. Nor does he speak of the bishop's pastoral and governing functions, or of the bishop as presiding at the eucharist. In his argument against the Gnostics he concentrates on the bishop's role as the official teacher of the local church, the guardian of the purity of the canon of truth, who has succeeded to this office in a particular church in direct line from the apostles.

d The Scriptures

Irenaeus believed that the true doctrine of Christ was not only transmitted by oral teaching, but was also committed to written documents. But it was not possible for him to use the Scriptures as a sole court of appeal. The Gnostics were adept in criticizing the Scriptures (III, ii.1) and in twisting their meaning to suit their own theories (I, xix.1–2). They were also zealous in producing 'Gospels' and 'Acts', strongly tinged with Gnostic ideas, and purporting to be the work of apostles (I, xx.1). Moreover, in Irenaeus' day the canon of the New Testament Scriptures had not yet been settled. There was uncertainty, for instance, about whether works like the Epistle of Clement to the Corinthians, and *The Shepherd* of Hermas should be included. In these circumstances Irenaeus was on stronger ground in his controversy with the Gnostics in putting the stress on the canon of truth as it was handed down by the succession of the Church's official teachers, the bishops. It is not that he undervalued those writings which he was fully assured were the work of apostles or apostolic men. For him the written tradition and the unwritten tradition protect and interpret each other. A passage in *Adv. Haer.* IV, xxxiii.8 makes clear his position on this matter. Here he lists the various elements which contribute to a knowledge of the truth. They include the tradition taught by the bishops, which he says is 'safeguarded without any written documents'. It is, in other words, self-authenticating. He obviously does not mean that there were no documents to which, if necessary, appeal could be made, for in the same sentence he includes the reading of the Scriptures and their regular and careful exposition.

In the same passage Irenaeus speaks also of the distinctive life of the Church as the body of Christ, and the 'special gift' of love, more precious than knowledge, more glorious than prophecy (an allusion to 1 Cor. 13). For all his insistence on the importance of the apostolic succession for the preservation of true doctrine, he well understood that there are other important elements in the idea of succession. The tradition of true doctrine would be barren if there were not with it a tradition of the love which the apostles had met in Jesus Christ and learned from him.

EPISCOPAL OR PRESBYTERAL SUCCESSION?

Before leaving Irenaeus' doctrine of apostolic succession, two points must be noted. First, although there is no doubt that Irenaeus uses the word bishop in the sense of the monarchical bishop, here and there he speaks of a succession of presbyters: '... that tradition which originates from the apostles, which is preserved by means of the successions of presbyters in the churches' (III, ii.2); 'it is incumbent to obey the presbyters who are in the church—those who, as I have shown, possess the succession of the episcopate, have received the certain gift of truth' (IV, xxvi.2). What are we to make of this?

We saw reason to believe that Clement of Rome was concerned with the apostolic succession of presbyters.[36] The above quotations strongly suggest that Irenaeus also thinks of the succession as basically presbyteral. In his time, in the face of dangers posed by erroneous teaching, in particular that of the Gnostics, the practice of appointing one of the presbyters to occupy the *kathedra* as the official teacher and guardian of the faith in the local Christian community had been adopted. The title of *episkopos*, originally an alternative for 'presbyter', is now applied to him exclusively. But he is still a presbyter, and Irenaeus can therefore speak both of a succession of bishops and of a succession of presbyters.

An ecclesiastical problem is raised here. How in the second century did the bishop enter upon his office? Doubtless he was believed to be called by God, and his commissioning was thought of as an act of God through the Church. But by whose hands was he set apart for his particular ministry, those of the presbytery or those of other bishops from neighbouring places? The former would imply that the episcopate was not a distinct order of ministry, but that presbyters appointed one of their number to perform the functions of the *episkopos* as their representative, while remaining a member of their order. On the basis of evidence up to the time of Irenaeus it is impossible to give a confident answer to the question. Our authors are silent on the matter. However, Hippolytus in his *Apostolic Tradition*, written early in the third century but purporting to describe liturgical procedures in Rome at an earlier date, insists that in the consecration of a bishop bishops alone lay on hands.[37] This suggests strongly that bishops are regarded as a distinct order of ministry. Yet, 200 years after Irenaeus, Jerome (*c.* 342–420) recalls that originally it was not so, that churches were governed by a presbytery, and that later, as a protection against schism, one of the presbyters was chosen to preside.[38] But Irenaeus' argument that the apostolicity of Christian teaching had been protected by authorized teachers in a line of succession back to the apostles is not weakened whether the *episkopos* was consecrated by presbyters or by another bishop or other bishops. Whether Clement, for example, whom Irenaeus placed third in his list of bishops of Rome, was ordained to his office of leadership by the presbyters of Rome or by somebody who already held the same office does not affect the strength of the argument that the teaching of the Church was in fact handed down by persons duly chosen, accredited, and ordained by others who were everywhere in the churches acknowledged to possess the authority to do so.

THE GRACE OF ORDINATION

The second point arises in the sentence from *Adv. Haer.* IV, xxvi.2: 'the presbyters who are in the church . . . who, together with the succession of the episcopate, have received the certain gift of truth [Latin, *charisma veritatis certum*]'. This is sometimes seen as an early appearance of the idea of the transmission of grace through the apostolic succession. In later centuries the notion was conceived that Christ gave to his apostles a deposit of grace, a portion of which was transmitted by the laying on of hands in the consecration of those who followed the apostles in the episcopal succession. This doctrine (it is usually known as the pipeline theory) is open to grave theological objections: it conceives of grace as a material or quasi-material commodity, and it confines God to one method, and an indirect and almost mechanical method, of imparting what is by definition his own free gift. Such an idea, however, is not to be squeezed out of Irenaeus' words in this sentence. Nothing he says is inconsistent with the thought that grace for ministry is given directly by God to the man who, having been duly elected and tested, is consecrated to the office of bishop.

What Irenaeus does evidently hold is that the grace which the bishop receives includes a 'certain' (the word means nothing less than 'infallible') grasp of theological truth. Unhappily the history of the

Church does not justify such confidence. There have been heretical bishops, an awkward fact which was to provide the Church with difficult problems.

THE MINISTRY AND THE NATURE OF THE CHURCH

As we have investigated the idea of the Church in these early Christian writers, questions relating to the ministry have constantly arisen. The Church, being a community of persons, must have its servants or ministers; it needs leadership. In the earliest book of the N.T. we read of those who worked among the communities and were leaders (1 Thess. 5.12), and elsewhere apostles, prophets, teachers, *episkopoi* or presbyters, deacons, and other ministers are mentioned. The authors we have studied in this chapter make it clear that the early Church quickly came to realize that its well-being, its unity and effectiveness had much to do not only with the quality of its ministers, but also with their recognition, by the Church as a whole, as being properly invested with authority. There cannot long be a healthy life in any community if there are no leaders and servants who are recognized as such by the community. Consequently, the possession of an ordered and recognized ministry is integral to the nature of the Church.

It is not the purpose of this book to present a theology of Christian ministry or a detailed history of its development. As we trace the development of the idea of the Church, however, we shall realize that convictions about the structure of the ministry frequently affect a writer's views on what the Church is. We shall see that some wish to go beyond the fundamental concept that an ordered and recognized ministry belongs to the nature of the Church, and insist that a *particular* detailed structure of ministry is essential. The seeds of such a claim are doubtless to be found in the writings of Ignatius of Antioch. We shall shortly find Cyprian of Carthage pressing this point of view; and it was largely taken for granted throughout the medieval period. In the twentieth century this is still perhaps the most formidable obstacle to the success of ecumenical endeavours to bring separated churches together.

4

The Early Third Century

In this chapter we discuss the ecclesiologies of two western theologians, Tertullian of Carthage and Hippolytus of Rome, who have much in common, and of the two earliest representatives of the theology, strongly influenced by Platonism, which was characteristic of Egypt, namely Clement of Alexandria and Origen.

1 TERTULLIAN (*c*. 160–*c*. 220)

Tertullian of Carthage, trained as a lawyer, the first theologian we know of who wrote in Latin, laid down guidelines and provided a terminology for western theology in several areas, especially in Trinitarian doctrine, Christology, atonement, and penitential theology. He was converted to Christianity about 193, but by 213 he had associated himself with the Montanists, a Christian sectarian movement of a pentecostal and rigoristic type. His later ecclesiology presents a strong contrast in many respects to that of his pre-Montanist days.

SCRIPTURAL CONCEPTS

We find Tertullian in his *Apologeticus* using the N.T. body imagery in a simple way in order to present to non-Christian readers an impression of the corporate life of the Church. It is a body united by a common profession, discipline, and hope. Christians meet together in a congregation that they may present their unanimous prayers to God. These include prayers for emperors and those in authority. Their corporate life is expressed both in their own discipline, and more outwardly in their charitable ministrations to the poor, orphans, aged, and prisoners.[1] He uses also the scriptural image of the bride of Christ[2] with the closely connected idea of the Church as the mother of the faithful. He speaks of 'our lady mother the Church'.[3]

THE APOSTOLIC TRADITION AND SUCCESSION

He follows Irenaeus in claiming that the Church's unity, indeed its very essence, consists in its possession of a tradition of doctrine, which he usually refers to as 'the canon of faith', everywhere received from the apostles through the succession of the bishops. Like Irenaeus, he employs this argument against the Gnostics:

> Jesus Christ our Lord ... did, whilst he lived on earth, Himself declare what He was ... what the Father's will was ... what the duty of man was ... to his disciples of whom he had chosen the twelve chief ones to be at his side. ... After first bearing witness to the faith in Jesus Christ throughout Judaea, and founding churches (there), they next went forth into the world and ... founded churches in every city, from which all the other churches, one after another, derived the tradition of the faith, and the seeds of doctrine. ... Therefore the churches, although they are so many and so great, comprise but the one primitive church (founded) by the apostles, from whom they all (spring). In this way all are primitive, and all are apostolic, whilst they are all proved to be one, in (unbroken) unity, by their peaceful communion, and title of brotherhood, and bond of hospitality—privileges which no other rule directs than the one tradition of the self-same mystery (*De Praescriptione* xx).[4]

> ... all doctrine which agrees with the apostolic churches [i.e. those which the apostles founded], those moulds and original sources of the faith, must be reckoned for truth, as undoubtedly containing that which the (said) churches received from the apostles, the apostles from Christ, Christ from God (ibid. xxi).

Tertullian, since the church in Carthage could not claim to have been founded by an apostle, is careful to 'tighten up' the doctrine of apostolic succession by claiming that recently founded churches, provided that they 'derived the tradition of the faith, and the seeds of doctrine' from churches founded by the apostles are themselves to be reckoned apostolic.[5] In such churches the substance of preaching and the canon of faith will agree with what is preached and taught in churches founded directly by apostles. This is the test to be applied to the churches which, Tertullian says, are being founded every day. If they hold the same faith as the churches founded by the apostles they are to be accounted no less apostolic than they. The churches of Africa, being founded from Rome, where the apostles Peter and Paul were martyred are, Tertullian asserts, rightly called apostolic.[6]

In answering the Gnostics' claim that their teachings have been handed down from the apostles, Tertullian gives rein to the pungent oratorical style which he had acquired in the law courts:

> Let them produce the original records of their churches; let them unfold the roll of their bishops, running down in due succession from the beginning in such a manner as that first bishop of theirs shall be able to show for his ordainer and predecessor some one of the apostles or of apostolic men (ibid. xxxii).

He is confident that the Gnostics have no such lists. Even if they should forge them it would be of no help to them, for their teachings are so contradictory among themselves, and so diverse from that of the apostles that they are evidently not of apostolic origin. The teaching of the apostles is well known. It is that 'canon of faith' which he summarized in *De Praescriptione* xiii,[7] and which we have already noted[8] as being identical in substance with the 'canon of truth' described by Irenaeus some twenty years earlier and 700 miles to the north, and the 'teaching of the Church' which Origen was to set out twenty years later some 900 miles to the east.

THE APOSTOLIC TRADITION AND THE SCRIPTURES

Nor, Tertullian argues, have the Gnostic heretics any rights in the Scriptures. He sets an imaginary scene in a law court where the question at issue is whether Marcion, Valentinus, and other Gnostics possess the right to use the Scriptures:

> It may be very fairly said to them, 'Who are you? When and whence did you come? As you are none of mine, what have you to do with that which is mine? . . . This is my property. Why are you, the rest, sowing and feeding here at your own pleasure? This (I say) is my property. I have long possessed it before you. I hold sure title-deeds from the original owners themselves, to whom the estate belonged. I am the heir of the apostles. . . . As for you, they have, it is certain, always held you as disinherited' (ibid. xxxvii).

Tertullian, as J. N. D. Kelly notes,[9] was well aware of 'the futility of arguing with heretics merely on the basis of Scripture'. They were masters in twisting it to their own use, and in producing specious reasons for their alterations and omissions.[10] Consequently Tertullian, like Irenaeus, takes the position that the Church in its possession of the 'canon of faith' has a key to the correct interpretation of Scripture. This canon is no more, nor less, authoritative than the written tradition. Neither Irenaeus nor Tertullian exalts it above Scripture. But it is, to use Tertullian's legal metaphor, a title-deed which enables the Catholic Christian to enter by right into the property of the Scriptures and to use them as they were meant to be used. There is no denigration of the Scriptures here. Both in his Catholic and in his Montanist writings Tertullian repeatedly appeals to the Scriptures for support.[11]

Tertullian's 'major premiss remained that of Irenaeus,' writes Kelly,

> viz. that the one divine revelation was contained in its fulness both in the Bible and in the Church's continuous public witness. If he stressed the latter medium even more than Irenaeus, elaborating the argument that it was inconceivable that the churches could have made any mistake in transmitting the pure apostolic doctrine, his reason was that in discussion with heretics it possessed certain tactical advantages.[12]

THE MONTANIST IDEA OF THE CHURCH

Thus far Tertullian reproduces in a more emphatic manner the ecclesiology of which we have traced the development from Clement of Rome and Ignatius of Antioch to Irenaeus, namely that the unity of the Church, indeed its very being, consists in agreement in that doctrine which is contained in Scripture and which is expressed in a 'canon' of truth, or faith, of which the official guardians and teachers are the bishops who occupy their sees in a succession traceable back to the apostles. But when Tertullian became a Montanist (c. 207) the eloquent defender of this ecclesiology became its equally articulate critic at several points.

Montanism arose in Phrygia about the middle of the second century, taking its name from Montanus. He and two women companions claimed to be instruments of the Holy Spirit and the recipients, during ecstatic trances, of divine revelations. These revelations were put into the form of brief epigrammatic oracles, to which their followers began to attach an authority higher than that of Scripture. The Montanist prophets taught a rigoristic discipline. They allowed no forgiveness for post-baptismal sin, inculcated a strict rule of fasting and other ascetic exercises, and taught that those who would be perfect should refrain from marriage and that martyrdom, while not to be sought, was to be welcomed as the one death by which Christ was most truly glorified.[13] Despite the non-fulfilment of their prophecy that Jerusalem would descend from heaven on a certain date near Pepuza, the movement won many adherents. The bishops of Asia Minor complained that the churches were being emptied.

At a time when laxity was creeping into the Church—and there is evidence that this was so in Rome and elsewhere—the Montanist insistence on a costly discipline and a courageous attitude towards persecution was doubtless attractive to stouter spirits in the Christian ranks. These were the aspects of Montanism which drew Tertullian. He was also impressed with the phenomenon of ecstatic speaking with tongues which the Montanists practised.[14] But it is doubtful whether he accepted the more extravagant claims put forward by some Montanists, for example that Montanus was a divine incarnation.

Tertullian now sees the Church in a different light, in which the ministry of inspired prophets overshadows that of the bishops, presbyters, and deacons, although the latter does not completely disappear from his view. He sees the Montanist movement which he calls the 'New Prophecy'[15] as the fulfilment of the prophecies in John 14–16 that the Paraclete will bear witness to Christ and reveal necessary truths:

> The integrity of His [i.e. the Paraclete's] preaching commands credit for these (revelations) albeit they be 'novel', inasmuch as they are now in course of revelation . . . (they are revelations) however of none other than Christ who said that He had withal 'other many things' which were to be fully taught by the Paraclete (*De Monogamia* II).

The era of Montanism, therefore, represents the Church's maturity:

> Righteousness . . . was first in a rudimentary state, having a natural fear of God: from that stage it advanced, through the Law and the Prophets, to infancy; from that stage it passed, through the Gospel, to the fervour of youth: now through the Paraclete, it is settling into maturity (*De Virginibus Velandis* I).

Tertullian now, therefore, defines the Church as a society of the Spirit, and its true members are spiritual men. In a tract in which he discusses authority to remit serious sins after baptism[16] he writes:

> The very Church itself is, properly and principally, the Spirit Himself, in whom is the Trinity of the One Divinity—Father, Son, and Holy Spirit. (The Spirit) combines[17] that Church which the Lord has made to consist in 'three'. And thus, from that time forward, every number (of persons) who may have combined together into this faith is accounted 'a church', from the Author and Consecrator (of the Church). And accordingly 'the Church', it is true, will forgive sins: but (it will be) the Church of the Spirit, by means of a spiritual man, not the Church which consists of a number of bishops (*De Pudicitia* XXI).

R. C. Moberly, in commenting on this passage, says[18] that 'while Tertullian's main positive is a truth immovable and of priceless value, his negative inference is an exaggeration and an untruth'. By the 'positive' he means the concept of the Church as the creation of God the Father through the Son in the power of the Holy Spirit to be the Body of the Spirit's presence. By 'negative inference' he means Tertullian's apparent conclusion that the ministerial structure of bishops, presbyters, and deacons has no place in the Church. Such an inference, Moberly rightly says, is so to affirm Spirit as to deny Body. Spirit must always express itself through bodily organisms.

But Moberly is wrong to conclude that Tertullian repudiates the episcopal system. It is as a Montanist that he appealed to the principle of apostolic succession against the teaching of Marcion.[19] In another Montanist work in which he stresses the priesthood of the whole Church, he nevertheless speaks of the distinction between the 'clergy' and the 'laity' as being established by the authority of the Church, and as marked with honour by the allotment of a 'special bench'— presumably in places of worship.[20] It is true that in the same passage he allows the right of all to 'offer' (i.e. to celebrate the eucharist) and baptize, but this is in cases of necessity in the absence of clergy. There is no outright denial of a proper, even a necessary, place within the Church for an ordained ministry. Tertullian, we may conclude, was protesting not so much against the idea of ministerial order as such as against the failure of bishops, whether by laxity or by officialism, to be what they should have been. Such protests have been needed, and that of Tertullian and the Montanists was the first of many.

2 HIPPOLYTUS (*c.* 170–236)

A contemporary of Tertullian in Rome, Hippolytus also attacked what he believed to be the lax discipline in the Church of his day. It is curious that, despite his forthright opposition to contemporary bishops of Rome, and although it seems (though the evidence is far from clear) that for a period he set himself up as an 'anti-pope', Hippolytus came to be canonized.

THE CHURCH AS THE HOLY SOCIETY OF THE RIGHTEOUS

Hitherto the sins of adultery, murder, and apostasy committed by baptized persons had been regarded as incapable of remission. Callistus, Bishop of Rome, 217–23, introduced a less rigorous discipline in restoring to communion after due penitence Christians who had committed the sin of adultery. According to Hippolytus (*Refutation of All Heresies* IX, xii.22 ff) he justified this from the parable of the tares among the wheat, and the account of unclean, as well as clean, beasts being received into Noah's ark. For Hippolytus, however, the Church is 'the holy society of those who live in righteousness' (*Commentary on Daniel* I, 17). He stands with Tertullian for the Church as a community of saints which must exclude sinners. It is an ecclesiology which, in different ways, was to be championed by the Novatianists thirty years later, by the Donatists in the fourth century, and was to reappear constantly in the history of the Church. Christian theology generally has resisted it. While acknowledging fully the Christian's vocation to saintliness, it has conceived of the Church as a 'school for sinners' which cannot exclude those who sincerely acknowledge their sins and will to amend their lives.

THE CHURCH'S HIERARCHY

Hippolytus compiled a 'Church Order' known as *The Apostolic Tradition*. It gives an account of the services of ordination, the testing and instruction of candidates for baptism, the baptismal ceremonies, the times of prayer, and of other liturgical and devotional practices. The book was part of Hippolytus' campaign of recalling the church of Rome from its laxity to the stricter discipline of his youth. It is therefore evidence, although the text is not always reliable, for practice in Rome in the last quarter of the second century.

In this work we have our earliest information about how a bishop was consecrated:[21]

> Let the bishop be ordained (being in all things without fault), chosen by all the people. And when he has been proposed and found acceptable to all, the people being assembled on the Lord's day together with the presbytery and such bishops as may attend, let (the choice) be generally approved.
>
> Let the bishops lay hands on him and the presbytery stand by in silence. And all shall keep silence, praying in their heart for the descent of the Spirit. After this one of the bishops present, at the request of all, laying his hand on him (who is ordained bishop), shall pray thus. . . . (*Apostolic Tradition* I, ii).

The prayer which follows asks:

> Now pour forth that Power which is from Thee of 'the princely Spirit'

which Thou didst deliver to Thy Beloved Child Jesus Christ, which He
bestowed on Thy holy Apostles ... grant upon this Thy servant whom
Thou hast chosen for the episcopate to feed Thy holy flock and serve as
Thine high priest, that he may minister blamelessly by night and day, that
he may unceasingly (behold and) propitiate Thy countenance and offer to
Thee the gifts of Thy holy Church. And that by the high priestly Spirit he
may have authority 'to forgive sins' according to Thy command.... (ibid.
I, iii).

The newly consecrated bishop then celebrates the eucharist.

Two points need careful notice. First: while the bishop is to be
chosen and ordained with the active consent of all the people of the
local church, it is other bishops alone who lay hands on his head. The
presbytery had no part in this action. This implies that, apart from
questions of inward calling and the enabling grace of God, the authority to exercise a bishop's office must officially be imparted by those
who already hold that office. This is the first clear evidence for this
procedure, which rapidly became universal. As we have seen, evidence
is lacking about the mode of appointment of the monarchical bishop
up to this time.[22] Whatever the previous practice had been, Hippolytus
insists that only a bishop possesses the authority to consecrate
another bishop. Indeed, Hippolytus sees the bishop as alone having
authority to ordain presbyters and deacons.

To be noted secondly is Hippolytus' equation of the bishop with the
Aaronic high priest in respect of his functions of offering the 'gifts' of
the Church and remitting sins. It is an equation which some, almost
certainly incorrectly, have seen in 1 Clement.[23] Tertullian not infrequently speaks of the bishop as *summus sacerdos* or *sacerdos*,[24] as
does Cyprian of Carthage thirty years later. The implication of this
language is that the bishop's office is analogous with that of the
Aaronic high priest. The bishop is the Church's principal liturgical
officer. He is the chief celebrant of the eucharist, wherein the Church
offers to God the sacrifice made available by Christ, together with its
own offerings of alms, bread and wine, with thanksgiving and praise.
He is also the principal penitential and disciplinary minister of the
local church. There is, indeed, a certain analogy here with the functions of the Aaronic high priest as described in Leviticus 16. Whether
or not this justified the use, which became increasingly common, of
the terms 'high priest' and 'priest' for the bishop and presbyter may
perhaps be considered a question which in itself raises no important
theological issue. But it is otherwise with the application to the bishop

of the Levitical conception of the high priest as one who propitiates God on behalf of the people.[25] This was to introduce a new idea of the Christian ministry, and one which endangered the teaching of the N.T. that the sacrifice of Christ alone is the sufficient redemptive act on man's behalf.[26] This view of the ministry, as it gained acceptance, doubtless aided by the common use of sacerdotal terminology,[27] inevitably led to a new ecclesiology which sees the Church as essentially a hierarchical body. The concept of the Church as the whole people of God lost ground, and the distinction between clergy and laity was highly sharpened as the latter were relegated to the role of passive dependants. This ecclesiology was to come under formidable attack in the sixteenth century.

Hippolytus' *Apostolic Tradition* presents the bishop as the sole ordaining officer. It is true that in the ordination of a presbyter the other presbyters present lay on hands (I, viii.1). We are told that this is 'because of the similar spirit (which is) common to (all) the clergy' (I, ix.6):

> For the presbyter has authority only for this one thing, to receive. But he has no authority to give holy orders. Wherefore he does not ordain (a man) to orders but (by laying on hands) at the ordination of a presbyter he (only) blesses while the bishop ordains (I, ix.7–8).

In the ordaining of a deacon, the bishop alone lays on hands (I, ix.1) because, says Hippolytus,

> he is not ordained for a priesthood, but for the service of the bishop that he may do (only) the things commanded by him. For he is not (appointed to be) the fellow-counsellor of the (whole) clergy but to take charge (of property) and to report to the bishop whatever is necessary (I, ix.2–3).[28]

The development of this ecclesiology, which places so much emphasis on the monarchical bishop as guarantor of the Church's continuity with the apostles and of the purity of the Church's teaching, as the focus of unity, the chief minister of the sacraments, and the sole ordainer, comes to its peak in Cyprian of Carthage. But we shall first take note of two eminent Alexandrians whose writing activity covered much the same period of time as that of Irenaeus, Tertullian, and Hippolytus.

3   CLEMENT OF ALEXANDRIA (*c.* 150–*c.* 215)

Clement of Alexandria taught at the catechetical school in Alexandria to the headship of which Origen was to succeed him in 203. Clement was a cultivated man who had a wide knowledge both of Greek literature and the Scriptures. He believed that Greek philosophy often supported the claims of Christianity. The strength of the Platonist influence upon him is revealed in his emphasis on the intellect: 'The perpetual exertion of the intellect is the essence of an intelligent being' (*Stromateis* IV, xxii). Against Gnostic claims he produces an apologetic very different from that of Irenaeus or Tertullian. His argument is that it is the Christian who is the true Gnostic. In his trilogy[29] he endeavours to show that the Word of God (the *Logos*), who brought enlightenment to ancient Israel and to the Greek philosophers, has now, in Jesus Christ, come in a new way to bring the saving knowledge of God to all men. He pleads with his readers to take Christ as their tutor. He will first exhort them. Then, after their conversion, he will train them with a salutary discipline, and lead them from the first rudiments of discipleship, through fear to hope, on to disinterested love and to knowledge which is now desired for its own sake, the knowledge of God.

THE EMPIRICAL CHURCH AND THE CHURCH ON HIGH

Clement's ecclesiology was undoubtedly influenced by Plato's doctrine of Forms, that is, the conception that each empirical thing has its perfect pattern and its true reality in the eternal world. He distinguishes between the Church on earth and 'the Church on high', between the historical and empirical Church and the Spiritual Church.

This is not to say that he denigrates the Church as an institution. On the contrary, he tells us[30] that he delights to think of it as at once 'virgin and mother—pure as a virgin, loving as a mother'. This mother has no milk, but nourishes her children with the Word, Jesus Christ, whose flesh and blood are given for their strengthening. There follows a discussion of the eucharist in which, with his usual intellectualizing tendency, he interprets the 'flesh and blood' of Christ as meaning the Spirit and the Word. Nevertheless Clement is here speaking of the Church as an institution, with its preaching, sacraments, and teaching. The same is true in the following passage:

> It is my opinion that the true Church, that which is really ancient, is one, and that in it those who according to God's purpose are just, are enrolled. . . . [It is] an imitation of the one first principle. . . . In substance and idea, in origin, in pre-eminence, we say that the ancient and Catholic Church is

alone, collecting as it does into the unity of the one faith . . . those already ordained, whom God predestinated, knowing before the foundation of the world that they would be righteous.

But the pre-eminence of the Church, as the principle of union, is in its oneness, in this surpassing all things else, and having nothing like or equal to itself (*Stromateis* VII, xvii).

This is the Church, he tells us, which heretics and schismatics try to tear asunder. Yet in the same book he can present the Church as a spiritual entity, 'the Church on high'. Its members are the true Gnostics who have given themselves to the unending contemplation of God, rising above earthly concerns. These are the true presbyters and deacons, whether or not they hold such office in the empirical Church (*Strom.* VI, xiii–xiv). 'The earthly Church is the image of the heavenly', and therefore Christians pray that God's will may be done on earth as it is in heaven (ibid. IV, viii). Clement's distinction is one way, and a natural way for one who shared the Platonic outlook, of interpreting the tension which we observed in the N.T. between the idea of the Church as complete and perfect and the Church as it exists in the process of growth and sanctification, having among its members many who have obviously not proceeded very far on the road to sanctity.

The distinction which Clement makes is to be distinguished from that of Tertullian between the Church of the Spirit and the Church of the worldly. Whereas for Tertullian the sign of the member of the spiritual Church is moral rectitude, for Clement it is intellectual apprehension of the truth which issues in the unceasing contemplation of God. Moreover, while Tertullian would have had grave doubts about the salvation of worldly Christians, Clement believed in the eventual salvation of all men (universalism). His ecclesiological distinction does not, therefore, point to an ultimate distinction between the redeemed and the damned. We shall discuss this matter further in connection with Origen who makes a distinction similar to that of Clement.

4 ORIGEN (*c*. 185–255)

Clement was succeeded by the more famous Origen as head of the catechetical school of Alexandria. Like his predecessor, Origen also distinguished what he spoke of as 'the true Church'[31] from the Church as an historical institution, of which, however, he remained a loyal member until his death which was hastened by sufferings undergone in prison during the persecution under the Emperor Decius.

THE CHURCH AS HISTORICAL INSTITUTION

His many works, theological, e.g. *De Principiis*; apologetic, e.g. *Contra Celsum*; commentaries on the Scriptures; and homilies (his sermons taken down and later published by disciples) contain numerous references to the organization of the Church, its ministry, and the responsibilities of all its members. This Church is the guardian of the teaching of the apostles which has been handed down through the apostolic succession:

> Let the Church's teaching, handed down from the apostles through the order of succession and which continues in the churches to the present day, be preserved (*De Prin.*, Preface 2).[32]

In the Preface to *De Principiis* he goes on to summarize this 'teaching of the Church', which as already noted[33] is strikingly similar in substance to the 'canon of truth' as given by Irenaeus and the 'canon of faith' of Tertullian, although Origen's version is greatly expanded.

THE MINISTRY

This Church is an organized community with a properly constituted ministry of priests, to whose appointment the local congregation must give consent, and at whose ordination 'the presence of the people is required, so that they may all know and be certain that the man elected to the priesthood stands out from all the people in learning, holiness, and eminence in every kind of virtue'.[34] Origen has much to say of the responsibilities of the Church's ministers. The bishops who like Peter have received the keys of the Kingdom, the disciplinary authority to bind and loose, must themselves be men of Peter's quality such that Christ may build the Church upon them.[35] Those pastors who are appointed to examine and instruct candidates for baptism have exacting responsibilities which Origen describes in more than one place.[36]

THE PRIESTHOOD OF THE WHOLE CHURCH

But every member of the Church has a priesthood. 'Do you not know', Origen writes, 'that the priesthood is given to you also, that is to the whole Church of God, the people who believe?' All, therefore, 'must offer to God sacrifices of praise, prayers, pity, purity, righteousness, and holiness'.[37] 'All, whoever have been anointed with the ointment of the holy chrism [i.e. the baptized] have been made priests.'[38]

THE SHORTCOMINGS OF THE EMPIRICAL CHURCH

Origen fully recognizes the defects of the Church and its members. Commenting on 'The Lord has opened his treasury and has brought forth vessels of his wrath' (Jer. 1.25 in the LXX version), he says:

> I can confidently say that the treasury of the Lord is his Church, and in that treasury ... there often lurk men who are vessels of wrath ... chaff with the grain, and fish which have to be thrown out and destroyed together with good fish which have all come into the net (*Homilies on Jeremiah* xx, 3).[39]

In another homily he uses the parable of the tares and wheat in a similar way: 'It is impossible for the Church to be entirely purified while it is on earth.' Open sinners may be excommunicated, but there remain those whose sins are secret.[40] More than once he declares that not all who have been baptized have been 'washed unto salvation'.[41]

THE TRUE CHURCH

Thus Origen was led to distinguish between the empirical Church and the spiritual. The latter is 'the true Church', which the Epistle to the Ephesians describes as 'without spot or wrinkle ... holy and without blemish'.[42] It is the assembly of the saints or perfect ones,[43] whereas the empirical Church is the 'assembly of believers'.[44] This 'true Church' is also 'the heavenly Church', and like Hermas, II Clement and Clement of Alexandria, Origen holds that it existed before the creation of the world. He argues that this is implicit in what is said about the Church in the Epistle to the Ephesians:

> You must please not think that she is called the Bride or the Church only from the time when the Saviour came in flesh: she is so called from the beginning of the human race and from the very foundation of the world—indeed, if I may look for the origin of the high mystery under Paul's guidance, even *before* the foundation of the world. For this is what he says: ... 'as He chose us in Christ before the foundation of the world, that we should be holy and unspotted in His sight' (Eph. 1.4) (*Commentary on the Song of Songs* ii, 8).[45]

Origen goes on to note that Paul (Eph. 2.20) says that the Church is built on the foundation of the prophets as well as the apostles. He interprets 'prophets' as meaning those of the O.T. among whom he includes Adam.[46] Moreover, Ephesians 5.25 ff also implies the pre-existence of the Church, for how could Christ have loved his Church if it did not already exist?

> Undoubtedly he loved her who did exist; she existed in all the saints who have been since time began. . . . They themselves were the Church whom He loved to the intent that He might increase her in multitude and develop her in virtue and translate her through the love of perfectness from earth to heaven (ibid.).

The Platonic doctrine of Forms (that earthly entities and institutions are imperfect copies of heavenly realities) has undoubtedly influenced Origen's ecclesiology, but his appreciation of the importance which the O.T. and N.T. alike attach to human history has transformed that doctrine. The last sentence quoted above shows that his distinction between the Church on earth and the true or heavenly Church is not precisely the Platonic distinction. Rather he seems to envisage the Church on earth as the historic community in which men, by participation in Christ, become fitted to be members of the heavenly Church. The distinction is more akin to the popular medieval distinction between the Church Militant and the Church Triumphant. This statement, however, must be qualified, because there are passages in Origen which indicate his belief that within the membership of the visible Church there are some who must even now be accounted members of the true Church, those within the body

> who are called eyes, doubtless because they have the light of understanding and of knowledge, and others ears, to hear the word of teaching, and others hands to do good works and to discharge the function of religion (ibid. II, 7).

Nor must Origen's distinction be confused with that which we shall find in Augustine[47] and the sixteenth-century Reformers, between the visible Church which includes impenitent sinners who will be damned and an invisible Church which contains only the elect. Such a distinction could not have been the intention of Origen or of Clement, his predecessor. They were both universalists, and for them there could be no question of any contrast between actual and ideal, or between visible and invisible which suggests that any will fail to obtain final salvation.

PROBLEMS IN ORIGEN'S ECCLESIOLOGY

Origen's doctrine of the Church is, therefore, difficult to interpret. His universalism raises the question what more essential place the Church, and indeed the incarnation, can have in his theological system than as aids to hasten the recovery for some men of that state of unity with God which they lost in a pre-cosmic fall, a state which, in his view, all will in the end regain. Yet Origen clearly believes that the incarnation of the *Logos* in Jesus Christ and the life of the Church are integral to the divine plan for universal salvation. We must assume, though he himself is not explicit, that he held that the healing work of Christ in the Church proceeds in those 'aeons' (worlds, or stages) which he envisages beyond this life. When, therefore, he says 'let no man persuade and deceive himself: outside this house, that is, the Church, no man is saved'[48] he is not excluding from salvation those who in their earthly lives are outside the Church. In another sermon he likens these to the humbler household vessels of 2 Timothy 2.20. By God's mysterious and merciful dispensation they will yet have their place in 'the great house'.[49] The phrase 'outside the Church' is Origen's own, but he seems to see these 'humbler vessels' as members of the Church in a nascent sense. In yet another sermon, in commenting on the Pauline phrase 'body of Christ', he says that this body 'is all mankind—rather perhaps the totality of every created thing'. Referring to 1 Corinthians 15.28, he reminds his hearers that it may not properly be said that Christ is subjected to God so that God may be all in all, while any one of those who are Christ's members are not, because of their sin, themselves subjected to God.[50] But at the consummation all men will be subject to Christ, all creation restored through Christ to its primal unity, and God will be all and in all.[51]

5

Cyprian of Carthage

The ecclesiology of Cyprian (Bishop of Carthage 248–58) is the basis of the doctrine of the Church which prevailed in the West throughout the Middle Ages. Compared with the ecclesiology of his older contemporary, Origen, it shows the marks which are usually said to be characteristic of western theology generally. It was practical, legalistic, and logical. Cyprian, like Tertullian whom he spoke of as 'the master', had been trained in Roman law. Throughout his episcopate he was faced with urgent pastoral problems. In his ecclesiology there is tension between the rigorist disciple of Tertullian and the sensitive pastor.[1]

Shortly after Cyprian's election as Bishop of Carthage, the persecution of Christians inspired by the Emperior Decius occurred. Being terminated on Decius' death in 251 it was not of long duration, but it was prosecuted fiercely, especially in Rome and North Africa. Under threat of death many Christians had yielded to the demand to throw incense into braziers before the statues of the gods of Rome or of the Emperor (whose deification was claimed). When the persecution ceased, the question of readmitting the lapsed to communion was vigorously discussed. In the church in Carthage one party demanded their readmission with little or no discipline. Another party demanded the rigorous application of the ancient rule of the Church that apostates be and remain excommunicated. Cyprian ruled that the question should be decided by a council of North African bishops to be called as soon as possible. Meanwhile he admitted to communion penitents who were on the point of death and bade others give strict heed to their penitential exercises. The eventual decision was to judge each case on its merits and, after due discipline, to admit those who were sincerely penitent, although lapsed clergy were inhibited from exercising their ministry.

In Rome, a rigorist party opposed the bishop, Cornelius, who favoured a policy similar to that of Cyprian. It was led by a presbyter, Novatian, and went into schism when he was elected Bishop of Rome in opposition to Cornelius by his supporters who obtained his consecration at the hands of sympathizing bishops. The schism takes its name from Novatian. In Carthage likewise the rigorist party and the laxist party each set up a bishop in opposition to Cyprian. Carthage thus had three men, each claiming to be the legitimate holder of the see. It is not surprising that Cyprian's main theological concern was the unity of the visible Church.

When renewed persecution was threatened in 252 Cyprian permitted readmission to communion of all who were under discipline, that as communicant Christians they might prove their loyalty in the coming trial. This removed the *raison d'être* of the laxist party, but Novatianist opposition increased.

NOVATIANIST ECCLESIOLOGY

Upholding the full rigour of the Church's ancient disciplinary rule of no absolution for apostasy, the Novatianists argued that a church which included lapsed persons or was willing to receive them to communion ceased to be a church because it lacked the mark of holiness. Apostasy corrupts the Church to the point of extinction.

This ecclesiology, then, finds the essence of the Church in its holiness, and its holiness is determined by its members. The Church is seen as the 'Congregation of the Holy'. The vulnerability of such an ecclesiology lies in the difficulty of setting a standard of holiness. The Novatianists placed the emphasis on freedom from apostasy, and appeared to be unconscious of the seriousness of other forms of unholiness of which many of them were certainly guilty themselves: jealousy, ambition, intrigue, and lack of charity. Against them Cyprian and Cornelius used the same arguments by which Pope Callistus[2] had defended his moderating discipline towards adulterers: the appeal to the parable of the tares, etc. It is God who will separate the tares from the wheat. Novation is usurping God's prerogative of judgement.[3] And of the Novatianist schism, Cyprian says:

> This is a worse crime than that which the lapsed seem to have fallen into, who nevertheless, standing as penitents for their crime, beseech God with full satisfactions. In this case, the Church is sought after and entreated; in that case the Church is resisted . . . on the one hand, he who has lapsed has only injured himself; on the other, he who has endeavoured to cause a

heresy or a schism has deceived many by drawing them with him ...
while the lapsed has sinned but once, he sins daily (*De Unitate Ecclesiae*
19).[4]

THE CHURCH'S UNITY

The Novatianist schism raised a new problem in connection with the
doctrine of the unity of the Church. The Novatianists who had wilfully
separated themselves from the Catholic Church were theologically
orthodox; they accepted the 'canon of faith'. It was no longer
sufficient, then, to insist that the basis of unity was the orthodox faith,
the teaching of the apostles. Cyprian now maintains that the principle
of unity is the episcopate.

But the Novatianists claimed to have the episcopate. Their bishops
had been consecrated by bishops who themselves had been validly
consecrated. Nevertheless it was Cyprian's contention that they were
not bishops. The bishop's throne in Carthage was not vacant when the
Novatianist Maximus was set up as a bishop in opposition. Nor was
that of Rome vacant when Novatian's consecration took place.
Cyprian himself and Cornelius respectively held these sees.[5] Neither
Novatian nor Maximus had succeeded to a vacant see, and consequently they were not bishops. It is to be noted that Cyprian is
working here with the concept that the succession of a bishop is to be
traced not through the bishops who consecrated him, but through his
predecessors in office. It is a concept which excludes the possibility of
a bishop who has no properly constituted see.

Having disposed of the Novationist claim to have bishops, Cyprian
insists that it is the possession of the episcopate which gives unity to
the Church:

> Our Lord ... describing the honour of a bishop and the order of His
> Church, speaks in the Gospel and says to Peter: I say unto thee, that thou
> art Peter; and upon this rock will I build my Church. . . . Thence, through
> the changes of times and successions, the ordering of bishops and the plan
> of the Church flow onwards; so that the Church is founded upon the
> bishops, and every act of the Church is controlled by these same rulers
> (*Ep.* xxvi,1; [xxxiii]).[6]

> You ought to know that the bishop is in the Church, and the Church in
> the bishop; and if any one be not with the bishop, that he is not in the
> Church. . . . The Church, which is Catholic and one, is not cut or divided
> but is indeed connected and bound together by the cement of priests

[*sacerdotes*, i.e. bishops][7] who cohere with one another (*Ep.* LXVIII, 8 [LXVI]).

From this clearly enunciated principle of 'No bishop, no Church' Cyprian drew the logical conclusion that the ecclesiastical acts of Novatianists had no validity whatever. A bishop alone has authority to ordain; he is the proper minister of the sacraments, and he alone can delegate their celebration to others. Consequently Novatianists, having no bishops, have no ordinations, baptisms, absolutions, eucharists. When Novatianists sought admission to the Catholic Church, Cyprian's practice was to baptize them, counting their Novatianist baptism as no baptism at all. Several of his letters deal with this subject. The following extracts summarize his position:

> Baptism is therefore one, because the Church is one, and there cannot be any baptism out of the Church. For since there cannot be two baptisms, if heretics truly baptize, they themselves have this baptism. ... But we say that those who come thence are not re-baptized among us, but are baptized. For indeed they do not receive anything there, where there is nothing (*Ep.* LXX, 1 [LXXI]).

Novatianist orthodoxy, moreover, is quite irrelevant to this question:

> If any one objects, by way of saying that Novatian holds the same law which the Catholic Church holds, baptizes with the same symbol [i.e. creed] with which we baptize, knows the same God and Father, the same Christ the Son, the same Holy Spirit, and that for this reason he may claim the power of baptizing, namely that he seems not to differ from us in the baptismal interrogatory ... they lie in their interrogatory, since they have not the Church (*Ep.* LXXV, 7 [LXIX]).

Cyprian thus meets the Novatianist claim that there is one true Church, namely the Church of the holy (interpreted as those who have no dealings with the lapsed) with the equally blunt claim that there is indeed one true Church, but it is the Church which does not depart from the bishops who have lawfully succeeded in the established sees. This is the Church of which he writes,[8] 'outside the Church there is no salvation'.

CYPRIAN AND STEPHEN, BISHOP OF ROME

On the subject of baptizing heretics and schismatics Cyprian found himself fighting on yet another front. Cornelius had been succeeded as

Bishop of Rome by Stephen in 254. Although he held heretics and schismatics to be outside the Church as strongly as did Cyprian, he opposed the latter's practice of baptizing converts who had already received baptism in schismatic churches. He held that baptism outside the Church was valid provided that it was administered with water in the name of the Trinity. Stephen tried to impose his views on the North African Church, and threatened excommunication.[9] A council of North African bishops gave Cyprian strong support, and a protest was sent to Stephen.[10] The severing of communion between Rome and Carthage was averted by Stephen's death in 257. His successor, Xystus, did not attempt to press the Roman practice outside his own sphere of authority.

In this controversy logic appears to have been on Cyprian's side, but the consensus of the Church has supported Stephen. Canon 8 of the representative (though not judged ecumenical) Council of Arles (314) laid down that members of heretical or schismatic bodies who seek reconciliation should be required to recite the creed. If they had already been baptized in the triune name they should be received by the laying on of hands. This principle, which was to be important for Augustine's ecclesiology, has been generally followed in the Church.[11]

CYPRIAN'S POSITIVE DOCTRINE

It is in *De Catholicae Ecclesiae Unitate*[12] that Cyprian presents his conception of the Church positively, and despite the rhetorical style, systematically. The argument is that the Church *is* one. When the 'enemy' deludes some to claim 'the title of the Christian name', and invents heresies and schisms to 'subvert the faith ... corrupt the truth ... divide the unity',[13] it is a question of discovering where the true Church is. Cyprian finds the substance of the answer in Matthew 16.18–19 and John 20.20–23:

> The Lord speaks to Peter, saying, 'I say unto thee, that thou art Peter; and upon this rock I will build by Church....' And although to all the apostles, after his resurrection, He gives an equal power, and says, 'As the Father hath sent me, even so send I you ...;' yet, that he might set forth unity, He arranged by His authority the origin of that unity, as beginning from one. Assuredly the rest of the apostles were also the same as was Peter, endowed with a like partnership both of honour and power; but the beginning proceeds from unity.... Does he who does not hold this unity of the Church think that he holds the faith? Does he who strives against and rends the Church trust that he is in the Church ...? (*De Unitate* 4).[14]

Cyprian then alludes to Paul's witness to the oneness of the Church in Ephesians 4.4–6, and claims that this unity, first given to the Church in Peter and the apostles, is now manifested in the episcopate. As the apostles formed a college or corporate body, so also does the episcopate:

Episcopatus unus est, cuius a singulis in solidum pars tenetur.[15]

The literal translation of the Latin is: 'The episcopate is one, of which a part is held by individual bishops in solidarity.' *In solidum* is a legal phrase used of joint ownership in a property in which each party is not regarded as possessing a *share*, but rather as possessing rights in the *whole*, and as accountable for the whole. Cyprian's concept, then, is of a corporation or college of bishops, with each in his own person and within his own sphere of jurisdiction exercising the whole authority of the episcopate. The concept appears frequently in Cyprian.[16] J. N. D. Kelly points out[17] that it is a rider to this doctrine 'that each bishop is entitled to hold his own views and to administer his own diocese accordingly, and that the principle of charitable respect for each other's opinions must be maintained'. In the letter to Stephen in which he explains his practice in the matter of baptizing schismatics, Cyprian writes:

> We neither do violence to, nor impose a law upon, any one, since each prelate has in the administration of the Church the exercise of his will free, as he shall give an account of his conduct to the Lord (*Ep.* LXXI, 3 [LXXII]).

In *De Unitate* Cyprian goes on to assert that whoever separates himself from the Church whose unity is thus constituted in the episcopal college, separates himself from the promises of Christ to the Church:

> He is a stranger; he is profane; he is an enemy. He can no longer have God for his Father, who has not the Church for his mother (*De Unitate* 6).

THE 'PAPAL' TEXT OF *DE UNITATE*

Another version of the fourth chapter is extant, known as the 'Papal' or 'Primacy' text. It asserts that the 'primacy is given to Peter', that Christ set up 'one throne', and asks whether 'he who deserts the throne of Peter, on which the Church is founded' is confident that he is in the Church. The two versions have occasioned much controversy.

Some have argued that the 'Papal' version is original and provides evidence that the primacy of the Bishop of Rome was acknowledged in the third century. Others have seen the 'Papal' version as the result of later insertions into the manuscripts in the interests of the papal theory. R. H. Bettenson, who gives a brief summary of the issue in his *Early Christian Fathers* says that the 'dominant view at present seems to be that the "Primacy Text" was altered by Cyprian to the *Textus Receptus* as a result of the controversy about baptism with Stephen, Bishop of Rome'.[18]

The 'Papal' text does not very explicitly assert that the Bishop of Rome has jurisdiction over all other bishops. Cyprian was, no doubt, prepared to accord the Bishop of Rome a primacy of honour, but his views on that bishop's right to control policy within the jurisdiction of other bishops may be judged from his resistance to Stephen on the baptismal question. Moreover, for Cyprian to have admitted that the Bishop of Rome had any such right would have contradicted what is clearly his main thrust—that the unity of the Church resides in the consensus of the collective episcopate.

THE PERSON AND OFFICE OF THE BISHOP

Cyprian has much to say about carefulness in the choice of bishops. Several of his letters deal with the subject. There must be a public election, and general consent must be sought. Writing to the church in Spain he says:

> You must diligently observe and keep the practice delivered from divine tradition and apostolic observance, which is also maintained among us, and almost throughout all the provinces; that for the proper celebration of ordinations all the neighbouring bishops of the same province should assemble with the people for which a prelate is ordained. And the bishop should be chosen in the presence of the people, who have most fully known the life of each one, and have looked into the doings of each one as respects his habitual conduct (*Ep.* LXVII, 5).

In a letter to Cornelius he speaks of the choice of a bishop as the result of 'the divine judgement, after the suffrage of the people, after the consent of the co-bishops'.[19] We are given no details of how elections were conducted. It appears that the choice was made by the bishops, but that the people had a definite power of veto. Presbyters seem to have had no more influential part in an election than the laity.

There are passages where Cyprian appears to suggest that once a bishop is consecrated he is without fault: 'To believe that they who are ordained are unworthy and unchaste, what else is it than to believe that his priests (*sacerdotes*) are not appointed in the Church by God, nor through God?'[20] But unhappily, unworthy and even immoral bishops are not unknown, and elsewhere Cyprian shows himself well aware of this. Of them he uses words which might have been used by a Novatianist: 'A people obedient to the Lord's precepts, and fearing God, ought to separate themselves from a sinful prelate, and not to associate themselves with the sacrifices of a sacrilegious priest (*sacerdos*), especially since they themselves have the power either of choosing worthy priests, or of rejecting unworthy ones'.[21] Cyprian's insistence on great care in episcopal elections is no doubt prompted by his realization that unworthy bishops exist.

Here is a weakness in an ecclesiology such as Cyprian's. What is the Christian's duty if his bishop, properly elected and validly consecrated, lives a scandalous life which is tolerated by his brother bishops, and makes demands which are unreasonable and against conscience? In the course of the Church's existence many have felt that they must refuse obedience and form a separated Christian community. Christian disunity occurs not only when men depart from obedience to the college of bishops in the pride and obstinacy which was undoubtedly characteristic both of the Novatianist and laxist schismatics of Cyprian's day, but also when they do so for motives of high Christian principle. The problem of the Church's unity is a more difficult one than Cyprian saw, or perhaps could possibly see in his day.

Cyprian, as we have seen, frequently speaks of the bishop as *sacerdos*. Tertullian had done so before him, and both Tertullian and Hippolytus had also referred to the bishop as 'high priest'.[22] Cyprian consolidates this tendency to draw a close parallel between the Christian ministry and the hierarchical Aaronic priesthood and its sacrificial functions. While for Cyprian himself the pastoral function of the bishop is clearly of the utmost importance, the way is being prepared for a conception of the bishop's office in which his teaching and pastoral duties are overshadowed by his liturgical functions, the most important of which he performs as the chief celebrant of the eucharist which comes increasingly to be thought of in sacrificial terms.[23] Cyprian himself foreshadows later medieval teaching in a passage like the following:

For if Jesus Christ, our Lord and God, is Himself the chief priest of God the Father, and has first offered Himself a sacrifice to the Father, and has commanded this [i.e. the eucharist] to be done in commemoration of Himself, certainly that priest (*sacerdos*) truly discharges the office of Christ, who imitates that which Christ did, and he then offers a true and full sacrifice in the Church to God the Father, when he proceeds to offer it according to what he sees Christ himself to have offered (*Ep.* LXII, 14 [LXIII]).

SUMMARY

Cyprian's concept of the Church and its ministry is a fuller development of what we found in Ignatius of Antioch, Irenaeus, the earlier Tertullian, and Hippolytus. Although significant new emphases were to be introduced by Augustine, it is true to say that Cyprian's hierarchical and sacerdotal view of the Church was to dominate western Christianity for centuries.

Cyprian does not follow the Alexandrians into speculations about an ideal Church whose essence is conceived in an other-worldly sphere. It is the empirical, geographically extended Church which is his concern. In this domain its essential nature and unity must be realized and maintained. This unity is indeed fruitful of great variety, as he argues in *De Unitate*. He illustrates this by the sun and its many rays, the tree and its many boughs, the fountain and its many streams. The Church is also the fruitful mother of Christians.[24] But she is also 'the spouse of Christ (who) cannot be adulterous. She knows one home. . . . She appoints the sons whom she has borne for the kingdom . . . .'[25] The passage ends with the well-known words, previously quoted, 'He can no longer have God for his Father, who has not the Church for his mother.'

Cyprian also uses the Noah's ark image, but in a distinctly new way. The image had often been used to assert the mixed nature of the Church (the clean and unclean animals) against the doctrine of the Church as an exclusive society of the perfect. Cyprian however fastens on the thought that only those inside the ark were saved: 'If any one could escape who was outside the ark of Noah, then he also may escape who shall be outside of the Church.'[26]

His doctrine of the Church may be aptly summarized by the use he makes of the episode of Christ's seamless robe (John 19.23–4):

This sacrament of unity [i.e. the Church], this bond of a concord inseparately cohering, is set forth where in the Gospel the coat of the Lord Jesus Christ is not at all divided nor cut. . . . That coat bore with it a unity that came down from the top, that is . . . the Father, which was not to be at all rent by the receiver and the possessor.... By the sacrament and sign of His garment, He has declared the unity of the Church (*De Unitate* 7).

Thus, for Cyprian the Novatianists, the schismatic bodies of laxists or any other group which, for whatever reason, separates itself from the Church which coheres in the corporate episcopate, are not parts *of* the Church. They are outside the Church altogether and outside the possibility of salvation. A question mark has often been put against this stark doctrine.[27] There are, as we shall see, passages in Augustine where the shape of that question begins faintly to emerge.[28]

6

The Fourth and
Early Fifth Centuries

During the fourth century and the first half of the fifth theologians were chiefly engaged upon the doctrines of the Trinity and of the Person of Christ. It was the period of the Arian, Apollinarian, Macedonian, Nestorian, and Eutychian controversies. Yet important contributions to ecclesiology were made.

1 ORGANIZATION

First it should be noted that this was the period when the administrative structure of the Church took the shape which, apart from the non-episcopal reformed churches, it retains today. It was modelled, understandably enough in view of the Emperor Constantine's conversion, on the administrative structure of the Roman Empire. The major ecclesiastical regions were now made to coincide with the civil provinces or 'eparchies'.[1] In the majority of cases the capital city of eparchy became the see city of the bishop who had primacy over other bishops within the eparchy. Such a bishop was known as a metropolitan (from the Greek *mētēr*, mother, and *polis*, city). The primacy which the bishops of certain sees had long been accorded over an area much larger than a single eparchy, notably the bishops of Rome, Alexandria, and Antioch was, however, preserved.[2]

The canons of Church councils frequently dealt with matters of jurisdiction. Canon 6 of the Council of Nicaea (325) ratified the Bishop of Alexandria's jurisdiction over the bishops of Egypt, Libya, and Pentapolis, and that of the Bishop of Antioch over the bishops of neighbouring eparchies, and noted that there was a similar custom in the case of the Bishop of Rome. The Council of Constantinople (381), in Canon 3 enacted that 'the Bishop of Constantinople has seniority of honour after the Bishop of Rome because Constantinople is new Rome'. Constantinople, formerly the comparatively unimportant

Byzantium, had quickly grown in size and importance since Constantine designated it his imperial city in 326. A new see was created there, whose bishops began to claim jurisdiction over the churches in a wide area. This was resented by bishops of Alexandria, whose see hitherto had been regarded as the most influential of the East. The *status quo*, however, was maintained at the Council of Ephesus (431), apart from granting independence from the Bishop of Antioch to the bishops of Cyprus (Canon 8). But the Council of Chalcedon (451) in Canon 28 gave the Bishop of Constantinople jurisdiction over the Church in the civil dioceses or exarchies of Pontus, Asia,[3] and Thrace, 'rightly judging that the city which was honoured by the Imperial presence and the Senate and which enjoyed equal privileges with ancient imperial Rome, should also, like Rome, have greater importance in ecclesiastical matters, as being second to it'.

The Bishop of Jerusalem had always been accorded a precedence of honour, and was counted among the patriarchs (a title which came into use in the sixth century) with the bishops of Rome, Constantinople, Antioch, and Alexandria. The patriarchal powers included the right to consecrate the metropolitans within their sphere of jurisdiction, to try them if accused of misdemeanours, and to hear appeals against their decisions. The adoption of the hierarchical administrative system of the Roman Empire as a model was clearly a departure from that notion of a collegiate episcopate for which Cyprian had contended.

2   THE EAST

CYRIL, BISHOP OF JERUSALEM (*c.* 315–86)

In his *Catechetical Lectures* (*c.* 350), to candidates for baptism,[4] Cyril of Jerusalem devotes one section of Lecture XVIII to the doctrine of the Church. After his rejection by the Jews the Saviour 'built out of the Gentiles a second Holy Church, the Church of us "Christians". It is of this Church that he promised it would not fail' (*Cat.* XVIII, 25). He enlarges on the meaning of the word 'Catholic'. The Church is called 'Catholic' because

> it extends over all the world ... and because it teaches universally and completely one and all the doctrines which ought to come to men's knowledge ... and because it brings into subjection to godliness the whole race of mankind, governors and governed, learned and ignorant; and

because it universally treats and heals the whole class of sins ... and possesses in itself every form of virtue which is named, in deeds and words, and in every kind of spiritual gift (*Cat.* xviii, 23).[5]

The candidates are warned to mark the difference between the Catholic Church and sects which call themselves churches:

If ever thou art sojourning in cities, inquire ... not merely where the Church is, but where is the Catholic Church. For this is the peculiar name of this Holy Church, the mother of us all, the spouse of our Lord Jesus Christ (ibid. xviii, 26).

THE MYSTICAL BODY

Cyril's instructions on the meaning of the successive stages in Christian initiation serve to introduce a concept of the Church which is implicit in St Paul's teaching on baptism and the body of Christ,[6] and which was now to become basic to the understanding of the Church both East and West. This is the idea of the mystical body (*corpus mysticum*) of Christ. The word 'mystical' is derived from the Greek *mueomai*, 'to be initiated'. The reference is primarily to the initiatory ceremonies by which a person becomes a member of the Church. The elements of initiation, it is to be noted, are instruction, the renunciation of evil, the confession of the Church's faith in the words of the Creed, immersion in water, 'sealing' with the Holy Spirit (symbolized by anointing with oil), and receiving the body of Christ in the eucharist. That this is what is meant by Christian initiation, and not water baptism alone, is clear not only from Cyril, but also from the much earlier *Apostolic Tradition* of Hippolytus. The mystical body of Christ, therefore, is the company of those who have become his members by initiation. The reference is not to a Church of the intellectually or spiritually élite, nor to an invisible Church whose members are known to God alone, but to the visible Church on earth of the Christian congregations with their bishops, presbyters, and deacons, the Church of the Scriptures and the sacraments.

As he expounds the initiatory ceremonies Cyril teaches that those 'who have been found worthy of divine and life-giving Baptism'[7] have entered into union with Christ through the Holy Spirit. At the first anointing (before their immersion) they were 'made partakers of the good olive tree, Jesus Christ', for the oil symbolizes participation in Christ's richness.[8] After the immersion they were anointed again with chrism,[9] the symbol of the Holy Spirit, and were made christs, 'because you are images of Christ'. The chrism given to them is 'the anti-type of that wherewith Christ was anointed' when the Holy Spirit rested on him after his baptism in Jordan.[10] So they have been 'made partakers and fellows of Christ'.[11] They can now be called Christians, a title to which they had no real claim before.[12] The candidates' first participation in the eucharist, which immediately followed the anointing with chrism, is what makes them 'of the same body and blood with Christ':[13]

> For in the figure of Bread is given to thee His Body, and in the figure of Wine His Blood; that thou by partaking of the Body and Blood of Christ mayest be made of the same body and the same blood with Him. For thus we come to bear Christ in us, because His Body and Blood are distributed through our members; thus it is that, according to the blessed Peter, 'we become partakers of the divine nature' (*Cat.* xxii, 3).

This text (2 Peter 1.4) is the scriptural basis of a salvation doctrine which is typical of the eastern Fathers of this period. This is the doctrine of *theosis* ('deification') of the Christian in virtue of his participation in Christ: 'The Word was made man in order that we might be made divine',[14] words of Athanasius written early in the fourth century, are often quoted in illustration of it. The concept of the Church as Christ's mystical body is closely interwoven with it.

GREGORY OF NYSSA (c. 330–c. 395)

likewise speaks of the incarnation as a conjoining of the divine nature with human nature 'in order that our nature might ... itself become divine'.[15] This 'conjoining' is extended in the Church: 'All being conjoined to the one body of Christ by participation, we become his one body.' In the consummation, therefore, Christ will be subjected to the Father 'mingled with his own body which is the Church'.[16]

CYRIL OF ALEXANDRIA (d. 444)

The idea of the Church as the mystical body of Christ is presented in several passages by Cyril, Bishop of Alexandria. He does so at some length in his *Commentary on St John's Gospel* in a section which expounds John 17.21, 'that they may all be one, even as thou, Father, art in me, and I in thee'. The passage is given here at some length since it represents the doctrine of the Church which has predominated in the eastern Churches ever since. It will be noted that the idea of the Church as the fellowship of the Spirit is not neglected.

In the foregoing [an expounding of the doctrine of the Trinity] we said, and not without reason, that the mode of the divine unity, the identity of substance of the Holy Trinity and the complete coinherence (of the Three Persons) must be copied in the unity of believers through their unanimity of heart and mind. But now I want to show that there is what we might call a unity of nature by which we are bound to one another and are all bound to God. ...

The Mystery[17] which has to do with Christ is established, as it were, as a beginning and a way of our participating in the Holy Spirit and in union with God. ... The Only-begotten, through the wisdom which is his and through the counsel of the Father, found and wrought a means by which we might come into unity with God and with one another—even we ourselves, although by our differences we are separate individuals in soul and body. For by one body, and that his own he blesses those who believe in him by a mystical communion and makes them of one body with himself and one another. ... For if we all partake of the one loaf, we are all made one body; for it is not possible that Christ be divided. Therefore the Church is called 'Body of Christ' of which we are individually members, according to Paul's understanding. For we are all united to the one Christ through his holy body, inasmuch as we receive him who is one and undivided in our own bodies. ...

Now if we are all of one body with one another in Christ, and not only with one another but with him who assuredly is within us through his own flesh, clearly we are all one, both in one another and in Christ. For Christ, who is both God and man in one person, is the bond of unity.

With regard to union in the Spirit ... we shall say again that we have all received one and the same spirit, namely the Holy Spirit, and are, so to speak, mingled with one another and with God. For though Christ makes the Spirit of the Father who is also his own Spirit to dwell in each of us individually, many as we are, yet the Spirit is one and undivided; and in that individuality which is his by nature he holds together in unity those spirits which are separated from unity one with another, showing them all to be as one in himself. For as the power of the holy flesh makes those in whom it may come to dwell to be of one body, in the same way, I hold, the one indivisible Spirit dwells in them all and binds them all into spiritual unity (*Comm. in Joannem* XI, 10).

These Greek Fathers, then, present a doctrine of the Church as the mystical body of Christ, the faithful baptized in and with their Lord, nourished, vivified, and unified by and in his eucharistic body and by and in his Holy Spirit.

3   THE WEST

HILARY, BISHOP OF POITIERS (315–67)

It was the Donatist schism, beginning early in the fourth century, which caused the next wave of urgent concern with the doctrine of the Church's nature on the part of western theologians. But first the ecclesiology of Hilary of Poitiers, who was not directly concerned with the Donatist question, must be mentioned.

Hilary speaks of the Church as the fellowship of the faithful, the bride of Christ and his body. The Church is one in that it holds the apostolic and Nicene faith. This unity is much deeper than the holding of ideas in common. In his *De Trinitate* he argues against those who hold that the unity of the Church consists merely in being 'of one heart and soul' (Acts 4.32). The unity of the Church indeed comes through faith. But those who are one 'through faith' are one 'through the nature of faith', and thus have 'a natural unity'. This is given in baptism, by which those who acknowledge one God, one Lord, and one hope become 'one by regeneration into the same nature'.[18] Hilary thus begins to sketch a doctrine of the mystical body which becomes clearer when a little later he speaks of the Church's unity being manifested in the eucharist:

> Now how it is that we are in Him through the sacrament of the flesh and blood bestowed upon us, He Himself testifies, saying, '. . . because I live ye shall live also; because I am in My Father, and ye in Me, and I in you'. If He wished to indicate a mere unity of will, why did He set forth a kind of gradation and sequence[19] in the completion of the unity, unless it were that, since He was in the Father through the nature of Deity, and we on the contrary in Him through His birth in the body, He would have us believe that He is in us through the mystery of the sacraments? (*De Trinitate* VIII, 15).

Hilary proceeds to speak of the eucharist as 'the sacrament of this perfect unity', and concludes:

> I have dwelt upon these facts because the heretics [Arians] falsely maintain that the union between Father and Son is one of will only, and make use of the example of our own union with God, as though we were united to the Son and through the Son to the Father by mere obedience and a devout will, and none of the natural verity of communion were vouchsafed us through the sacrament of the Body and Blood; although the glory of the Son bestowed upon us through the Son abiding in us after the flesh, while we are united in Him corporeally and inseparably, bids us preach the mystery of the true and natural unity (ibid. VIII, 17).

The idea of the mystical body of Christ was, then, being developed in the West while Athanasius and Cyril of Jerusalem were developing it in the East. This ecclesiology is characterized by its emphasis on the sacraments. The unity of the body is a mystical unity because men enter into it through baptism in which 'all were born again to innocence, to immortality, to the knowledge of God, to the faith of hope'.[20] Since there is but one God, one hope, and one baptism they enter into a unity of nature which finds its climax in the eucharist which, it is to be remembered, is integral to Christian initiation. Nothing is further from the minds of exponents of this ecclesiology than that a catechumen would participate in the baptismal eucharist and then cease to be a communicant. They see the Church as a eucharistic community whose life is maintained by continuing and faithful participation in the sacramental body and blood of Christ.

DONATISM

There are many points of similarity between Donatism and Novatianism. Both schisms originated in the aftermath of persecution, both denied that the Church should have any dealings with the lapsed, both stood for the idea of the Church as the Congregation of the Holy, and both flourished in North Africa.

One of the objects of the severe persecution initiated by the Emperor Diocletian in 303 was the destruction of Christian books. Under threat of death some bishops and others who had charge of copies of the Scriptures, service books, and other Christian writings had handed them over to the Roman authorities. They were known as *traditores*.[21] When the persecution ceased some Christians, like the Novatianists some sixty years before, insisted that the Church must dissociate itself from all *traditores*. In particular they objected to the consecration of Caecilian as bishop of Carthage (311) on the ground that one of his consecrators was a *traditor*. A *traditor* is unholy, they argued, and cannot be a member of the holy Church. Those who have dealings with a *traditor* themselves lose sanctity and cease to be members of the Church. Those who are thus outside the Church cannot perform ecclesiastical functions. If they claim to have the sacraments the claim is false, for the validity of the sacraments depends on the worthiness of the minister. Hence they held that Caecilian was not a bishop and set up a bishop of Carthage of their own, Majorinus, succeeded in 313 by Donatus, from whom the schism is named.

The Donatists baptized the converts they received from the Catholic Church. This was logical since, in their view, the Catholic Church by its recognition of Caecilian had ceased to be the Church and to possess the sacraments. It is to be noted that the Donatists did not teach an ecclesiology of the invisible Church. For them the empirical Church on earth must be holy. Their standard of holiness was that of having no dealings whatsoever with *traditores* as being apostates whose reconciliation was impossible. Donatism, like Novatianism, ignored other dimensions of holiness. It was 'a fanatical brand of puritanism'.[22]

The accusation against Caecilian's consecrator was proved to be unfounded after an exhaustive inquiry instituted by the Emperor Constantine. In 314 the western Council of Arles, summoned by Constantine to settle dissensions which had arisen from the persecution, enunciated the principle that ordination by an unworthy minister is not invalid (Canon 13). Nevertheless, the schism persisted, aided by the nationalist feeling of the native Berbers, whose opposition to any institution supported by imperial Rome could be counted on. During the fourth century Donatists gained possession of many North African churches, often by violence or its threat. Bishops were set up, and since these were consecrated by sympathizers among the episcopate, and in some cases installed in sees which were vacant, they could present a plausible claim to be in the apostolic succession. The Donatists also claimed the authority of Cyprian for one of their main positions, for Cyprian had taught that sacraments are invalid outside the one true Church.[23] The Donatist schism, therefore, raised unprecedented problems of ecclesiology which demanded new theological answers.

OPTATUS (fl. 370)

Optatus, Bishop of Milevis in North Africa, wrote seven books on the schism of the Donatists, directed against Parmenian, the Donatist Bishop of Carthage. His points were to be taken up and developed by St Augustine (see Chapter 7), and are therefore only summarized here with brief comments.

(1) The Church's sacraments derived their validity not from the worthiness of the minister but from God.

If this argument stood by itself it would appear to allow for the recognition of the sacraments of any dissident and separated group of

Christians, and to undermine any concept of Church order. It is, however, but one point in Optatus' chain of argument. It is a reminder to the Donatists that no man, however holy, gives the grace of the sacraments he administers. God is the giver, and as St Thomas Aquinas was to insist, the true minister of all the sacraments is Jesus Christ.[24] The principle enabled Optatus to meet the uncharitable intransigence of the Donatists' refusal to acknowledge sacraments outside their own body with an assurance of his readiness to recognize the validity of their sacraments.

(2) The holiness of the Church depends not on the moral character of its members, but on the endowments it has from God. These endowments include the Trinitarian creed, the chair of Peter, the faith of believers, Christ's teaching, and the sacraments. The parable of the tares shows that Christ wills to have sinners within his Church until the final judgement. It is impossible for man, who does not see with the eyes of God, to separate the good from the bad.

(3) Catholicity and unity are also important marks of the true Church. As for catholicity, taken in its geographical sense alone, the Donatists were confined to North Africa, but a small part of the world. The Church's unity was outwardly manifested by communion with the see of Rome, whose first occupant was Peter, the apostle whom Christ, for the sake of unity, placed before all the others.[25] But the Donatists did not have communion with the see of Rome. By their own act they had severed themselves from the Church, and like branches broken off from a tree they are cut off from the source of life.

7

Augustine and Jerome

When Augustine became Bishop of Hippo[1] in 396 his diocese had long been split by the Donatist schism. Both the practical and the theological implications of the schism claimed his attention as a bishop in this strife-torn part of the Church, and many of his writings deal with the nature of the Church and its unity. As a presbyter he had written *A Psalm Against the Donatists*, designed to give a simple explanation of their tenets. His major works on Donatism are *On Baptism, Against the Donatists* (in seven books, 400–401), *Against the Writings of Petilian the Donatist* (400–402), *A Letter to Catholics on the Unity of the Church* (402), *Against Cresconius the Donatist* (406), and *On One Baptism Against Petilian* (410). Many passages of his *Expositions on the Book of Psalms* and a number of his sermons and letters deal with the same issues.

THE MYSTICAL BODY

Basic to Augustine's ecclesiology is the idea of the Church as the mystical body of Christ. Scripture, he contends,[2] speaks of the one Christ with three points of reference: as the eternal Word, equal to the Father, as the Mediator between God and man, and as the Church. Among instances of the last he several times cites the words of Christ (Acts 9.4) to the persecutor of the Church: 'Saul, Saul, why do you persecute me?'[3] 'The head of the Church is Christ, and the Church is the body of Christ';[4] but also 'Head and body are one Christ: not because he is not whole without the body, but because he has also deigned to be whole with us, who even without us is whole and entire.'[5] In view of this integral unity of head and body Augustine speaks in various passages of the Church as 'the whole Christ', 'one man', 'entire man', 'one person', 'perfect man'.[6]

In one of his sermons Augustine in graphic language speaks of the eucharist as that which expresses the unity into which the Christian has entered through the ceremonies of initiation:

> If you wish to understand the body of Christ, hear what the Apostle says to the faithful: 'Now you are the body of Christ, and his members' (1 Cor. 12.27). Therefore if you are the body and members of Christ, it is your mystery which is set forth on the Lord's table, and which you receive. To that which you are you answer 'Amen',[7] and in so answering you declare your assent. You hear the words 'body of Christ', and you answer 'A-men'. Then *be* a member of the body of Christ, that your 'Amen' may be true. What then is the significance of the loaf? Let us bring to this question no answers of our own, but listen once more to the Apostle. When speaking of this sacrament he says 'we, the many, are one loaf, one body' (1 Cor. 10.17). . . . 'The many are one body.' Remember that a loaf is not made of one grain, but of many. When you were exorcized you were, so to speak, ground. When you were baptized you were, so to speak, moistened. When you received the fire of the Holy Spirit you were, so to speak, baked. Be what you see [upon the table] and receive what you *are*. This is what the Apostle meant about the loaf. . . . So also of the wine. There are many grapes hanging in the cluster, but their juice is mingled in a unity. Thus the Lord Christ has put his mark upon us, willed us to belong to him, and consecrated the mystery of our peace and unity upon his table (*Sermon* 272).[8]

THE FELLOWSHIP OF THE SPIRIT

In developing the image of the Church as the body of Christ, Augustine does not neglect the N.T. idea of the Church as the fellowship of the Holy Spirit. As the human body is indwelt and quickened by the soul so the Holy Spirit indwells and quickens the mystical body. 'The spirit by which every man lives is called the soul: you see what the soul does in the body. It gives life to all its members. . . . What the soul is to the body of a man, the Holy Spirit is to the body of Christ, the Church.'[9] Now it is fundamental to Augustine's theology that the Holy Spirit is the bond of love, both in the life of the Divine Being[10] and in human relationships. Therefore it must be said that the quickening principle of the Church is love. Here we have one of Augustine's firmest convictions. The Church is a fellowship of love, a fellowship created by the Spirit who is love and a fellowship of those who love both God and the sons of God in Christ:

> Nor can any love the Father except he love the Son . . . by loving he becomes himself a member, and comes through love to be in the frame of

the body of Christ, so there shall be one Christ, loving Himself. For when the members love one another, the body loves itself (*Homilies on 1 John* x, 3).

Thus Augustine holds closely together the ideas of the Church as the body of Christ and as the creation, the temple, and the fellowship of the Holy Spirit.

THE UNITY OF THE CHURCH

From this concept of the Church as the fellowship of the Holy Spirit of love, Augustine deduces the nature of the Church's unity. Those who do not love God or their fellow-Christians sever themselves from the one Church. For Augustine true unity and charity are synonymous, and consequently schism and lack of charity are closely linked. The schismatic actions of the Donatists, their antagonism to that body of which the love of God and man is the very soul, betray their failure in charity. And since the Holy Spirit is the giver of charity he concludes that the Donatists do not have the Holy Spirit:

> He who has the Holy Spirit is in the Church, which speaks with the tongues of all men. Whoever is outside this Church does not have the Holy Spirit. The Holy Spirit deigned to reveal himself in the languages of all nations precisely so that when a man is contained within the unity of the Church which speaks with all languages, he may know that he has the Holy Spirit (*Sermon* 268.2).[11]

Augustine was prepared to allow to the Donatists what Cyprian would not grant to the Novatianists, that their sacraments were valid. But he held that they could not be effective for salvation unless and until the recipient was received into the Catholic Church, when the Holy Spirit would make them efficacious and fruitful.

> If a member is cut off from the body it may still be recognized for what it is, finger, hand, arm, ear. Apart from the body it has form, but no life. It is the same with a man who is separated from the Church. You ask him about the sacrament? You find it there. Baptism? You find it. The Creed? You find it. But it is only the form. Unless you live inwardly by the Spirit, it is vain to boast outwardly about the form (ibid.).

The point is made more explicitly in the following:

> All things [i.e. the sacraments] were indeed theirs before, but profited them nothing, because they had no charity. For what truth is there in the profession of Christian charity by him who does not embrace Christian

unity? When, therefore, they come to the Catholic Church, they gain thereby not what they already possessed, but something which they had not before—namely that those things which they possessed begin then to be profitable to them. For in the Catholic Church they obtain the root of charity in the bond of peace and in the fellowship of unity (*Letters* LXI, 2).

Although he differs from Cyprian about the technical validity of the sacraments of schismatic bodies, Augustine agrees with him that there is no salvation outside the Church.[12] Schismatics have not the Holy Spirit, they are without love and outside the unity of the Church.

Yet some have discerned in Augustine a certain reluctance to draw the conclusion that the Donatists were in no sense with the Church. Cyprian had spoken of the seamless robe of Christ as incapable of being rent,[13] implying that the schismatics of his day had not torn the Church into pieces, but had departed from it, leaving it entire and undivided in itself. But Augustine speaks of the Donatist schism as a rending of the seamless robe and a tearing of Christ's body.[14] and this language implies, it is suggested, that though the Church is thereby divided, the sundered parts still belong to the Church.[15] His use of the seamless robe metaphor cannot be pressed too far, but Augustine's willingness to allow that Donatist sacraments were valid lends support to the suggestion that he was unwilling to regard the Donatists as utterly separated from the Church. Cyprian's position, that the Novatianists were outside the Church, was the more logical. For Augustine, perhaps we may say, pastoral concern overcame logic. He ardently desired to open a way for Donatists to enter into communion with the Catholics, and so to enter into the sphere of the spirit of charity in which alone, he believed, they could find salvation.

If Augustine's ecclesiology discloses some ambiguity, it also raises some formidable theological objections. A doctrine that the Holy Spirit is effectively active among men nowhere but within the boundaries of the visible Catholic Church seems forgetful of the biblical doctrine of the Spirit of God as the giver of life in all its dimensions. Augustine's argument seems also to imply that a separated body of Christians, and a member of a separated body, can express or experience *nothing* of the love of God, of Christ, and of neighbour.

The distinction which Augustine makes between the 'sacrament' and 'the effect or use of the sacrament'[16] is fraught with problems for sacramental theology. That a sacrament administered by a Donatist presbyter should lie dormant until, perhaps years later, the recipient is reconciled to the Catholic Church, when it will at last produce its fruits of grace, suggests a mechanical view of the sacraments. Optatus' declaration[17] that the sacraments belong to God implies a sacramental theology different from this.

THE HOLINESS OF THE CHURCH

Holy Scripture clearly supports the concept of a 'mixed' Church. But it also speaks of the Church as holy, 'without spot or wrinkle'. How could this be said of the Church of which Augustine was a member, which, as he well knew, included many unworthy men among its members? He found a solution of this difficulty in a distinction, which at first appears to have affinities with that made by Clement of Alexandria and Origen, between the empirical and the essential.[18] There are, he admits, within the Church 'the covetous, and defrauders, and robbers, and usurers, and drunkards, and the envious'. But the true members of the Church are 'the holy and just'. They are the 'garden enclosed, the fountain sealed, a well of living water, the orchard of pomegranates with pleasant fruits' of which the Song of Solomon speaks.[19] At this point Augustine's doctrine of predestination exerts its influence. The true members of the Church are 'the fixed number of the saints predestined before the foundation of the world'.[20] Among this number, Augustine says,

> there are some also who as yet live wickedly, or even lie in heresies or the superstitions of the Gentiles, and yet even then 'the Lord knoweth them that are His'. For, in that unspeakable foreknowledge of God, many who seem to be within yet really are without (*On Baptism* v, 27 (38)).

A distinction between the Church as inclusive of both worthy and unworthy members and the Church's righteous core has given way to a distinction between the visible Church and an invisible Church consisting of a fixed number of people, known to God alone and predestined by him for salvation from before their creation, a doctrine which, J. N. D. Kelly contends, means that 'the notion of the institutional Church ceases to have any validity'.[21]

Augustine did not imitate the Donatists in setting up a criterion by which true members of the Church might be distinguished. This was God's prerogative. Moreover, out of his own experience he knew that God's grace could effect conversions which confounded the judgement which one man might make about another's worthiness. And it was with the visible Church, its unity, its life and well-being, that he was chiefly occupied throughout his long episcopate, as the pastoral concern, so clearly documented in his sermons and letters, shows. He believed that those who were destined by God for salvation must before death find their way by baptism into the fold of the Catholic Church. For this he laboured, and this explains both his eventual reluctant agreement to the use of force by imperial officers to compel Donatists into the Church, and his opposition to the death penalty for those who refused.

THE CATHOLICITY OF THE CHURCH

In his controversy with the Donatists, Augustine uses the credal adjective 'catholic' in its geographical sense. How, he asks, can the party of Donatus claim to be the Church when it exists in North Africa alone?[22] Alluding to the accusation that communion between Catholics in North Africa and *traditores* contaminates the Catholic Church throughout the world, he speaks of the folly of 'pronouncing the whole world defiled by unknown crimes of Africans, and the heritage of Christ destroyed through the sins of these Africans by the maintenance of communion with them' (*Letters* LIII, 6). The catholicity of the Church consists in communion with the see of Rome and with the universal Church.[23] The Church is the *Ecclesia Catholica*, and Augustine, especially in his anti-Donatist writings, frequently designates it by the one word *Catholica*.

For Augustine, however, the universality of the Church is extended not only geographically, but also in time.[24] The body whose head is Christ is co-extensive with all who by grace live in righteousness, 'from Abel to the last elect person'.[25]

THE APOSTOLICITY OF THE CHURCH

Augustine takes from Irenaeus and from his North African predecessors, Tertullian and Cyprian, their doctrine that the apostolic faith and life of the Church is guaranteed by an unbroken succession of bishops in the sees founded by apostles, and in their daughter sees. He makes the point that it is futile for Donatists to claim apostolicity for their 'party' since there has never been a Donatist among the successive bishops of Rome which he regards as the outstanding example of an apostolic see. It appears, then, that he conceives of apostolic succession in the same way as his predecessors: a bishop succeeds to a vacant see, and traces his succession through his predecessors in that see. But Augustine's admission that Donatist bishops were validly bishops, who could therefore validly consecrate other bishops, points to another way of interpreting episcopal succession; namely, that a bishop traces his succession through his consecrators (of whom the Council of Nicaea had laid down that there should be at least three). This interpretation came increasingly to be taken for granted in later centuries. The consecrating bishops are seen as bringing the new bishop into the apostolic succession and providing authority for his sacramental ministry.

This interpretation of apostolic succession, if accepted, must be applied to others than the Donatist bishops whom Augustine hoped to reconcile to the Catholic Church. It means that any man who has received consecration at the hands of validly consecrated bishops must be regarded as capable of conferring orders even though he becomes a heretic or schismatic. It is an interpretation which has in fact ministered to great confusion, and to the proliferation of numerous splinter episcopal 'churches'.[26] The doctrine of apostolic succession relates to Church order, and if a particular interpretation leads to confusion it must be inadequate. The older doctrine which interprets the succession as that of those who have been chosen with the full concurrence of the Church, duly consecrated and installed in a recognized sphere of pastoral, sacramental, and juridical authority, has greater merit.

THE CHURCH AS MOTHER

Augustine frequently used the metaphor, previously employed by Tertullian and Cyprian, of the Church as the mother who gives birth and nourishment to Christians and provides a safe home for her children: 'You are safe who have God for your Father and His Church for your mother.'[27] She gives birth through baptism, and Augustine argues[28] that it is she who gives birth to Christians baptized in Donatist churches: 'It is the Church that gives birth to all, either within her pale ... or beyond it.'[29] This is because these schismatics have retained the sacraments which belong essentially to the Catholic Church alone. Therefore, 'the generation ... proceeds from the Church, whose sacraments are retained', not from the sect as such, which, if it were to abandon what it has 'retained of the essence of the Church' would 'lose the power of generation'.[30] In line with his doctrine of the Church as a 'mixed society' Augustine acknowledges that many of the children whom this mother brings forth prove to be sinners. Repentance is always possible, and reconciliation always offered ('we ought to despair of no man').[31] But there is no second baptism; the sinner 'is purged by faithful discipline and truthful confession'. He returns to his mother.

The concept of the Church as mother, bringing to birth, nursing, caring for, and agonizing over both her wayward and her exemplary children, has had a continuing attraction.[32] Its appropriateness, however, only becomes credible when the Church, through its pastors and people, in fact exercises this self-sacrificing care.[33] Augustine himself set a shining example.

In several passages[34] Augustine develops a saying of St Ambrose: 'Mary is the type of the Church.' He draws out the similarities and dissimilarities between Mary, the mother of Christ who is the Head, and the Church which gives birth to the members. In view of the mystical union between Head and members the Virgin Mary typifies the Church. Yet, sanctified and saved as she is through her Son, she is but one member among many, and the Church is greater than she.

THE CITY OF GOD AND THE CHURCH

Augustine's best known work, after his *Confessions*, is his *De Civitate Dei*, 'On the City of God'. It was written primarily to give an answer to the accusation that the calamity of the fall of Rome to the Goths (410) was caused by Rome's desertion of its old gods in favour of Christianity. In providing it Augustine found himself obliged to present what amounts to a history of the world interpreted as the progress of two 'cities', the heavenly City of God, and a city which revolts from God. The creation of the angels originates the City of God, and the angels form a large part of it. The foundation of the city which opposes God is laid by the wilful disobedience of the angels who fell. With the creation and fall of man the two cities became established in this world. History is interpreted as the intermingling, sometimes the co-operation, sometimes the enmity and always the tension between these two cities, the earthly and the heavenly, both constituted by love, the former 'by the love of self even to the contempt of God, the heavenly by the love of God, even to the contempt of self'.[35]

Augustine undoubtedly identifies the City of God with the Church:

What is the city of God, but the Holy Church? For men who love one another, and who love their God who dwelleth in them, constitute a city unto God. Because a city is held together by some law; their very law is Love; and that very Love is God; for openly it is written, 'God is Love'. He therefore who is full of Love is full of God; and many, full of Love, constitute a city full of God (*Expositions on the Psalms* xcviii, 4).[36]

But in what sense of the word 'Church' is this identification to be understood? To this question various answers have been given:[37] the empirical Catholic Church; the Church as the mystical body, or bride of Christ; the invisible Church of the elect. Identification of the City of God with the empirical Church is made difficult in that the latter is a 'mixed society' within which are some who are not predestined to salvation. Complete identification with the mystical body is made difficult in that angels are said to be the first citizens of the City of God[38] while Augustine never speaks of them as members of Christ's body. A probable conclusion is that the City of God is indeed the Church whose extent and membership are invisible to man, which in its celestial part 'is made up of the holy angels',[39] and in that part 'which wanders as a stranger on the earth'[40] consists of those members of the Catholic Church who are the 'congregation of the saints', persevering in faith and love and predestined at the consummation of all things to enter into the peace and blessedness of God's eternal city. It must not be forgotten that for Augustine membership of the Catholic Church by baptism is a *sine qua non* of final salvation.

Augustine's theological influence has been immense. R. W. Battenhouse has written:

> The civilization of medieval Christendom was to owe more to him than to any other of the Church Fathers. Gregory the Great turned to him for scriptural commentary and theology, Charlemagne for political theory, Bonaventura for mysticism, and Aquinas for elements of scholastic philosophy. Later, with the coming of the Reformation, Luther and Calvin became his disciples and, after them, Pascal—each gathering from the bishop of Hippo fresh stimulus for revitalizing Christian piety.[41]

In ecclesiology Augustine's doctrine of the mystical body governed the thinking of the medieval Church. His teaching that the unity of the Church is secured by communion with the see of Rome gave influential support to the mounting claims of that see to primacy and supremacy. His arguments against the Donatists provided a ready arsenal whenever a sect arose to insist that the Church must dissociate itself from sinners and to claim that it alone was the Church of the Holy. His doctrine of the Church as the invisible company of the elect was to be taken up again by Calvin in the sixteenth century.

JEROME (340–420)

We quote here two passages from Augustine's famous contemporary, Jerome, biblical scholar and translator, traveller, presbyter, and monk of Bethlehem. The first suggests an origin of episcopacy different from that which was generally accepted in his day:

> A presbyter, therefore, is the same as a bishop, and before ambition entered into religion by the devil's instigation and people began to say: 'I belong to Paul, I to Apollos, I to Cephas' (1 Cor. 1.12), the churches were governed by the council of the presbyters, acting together. But after each began to think that those whom he had baptized were his, not Christ's, it was unanimously decreed that one of the presbyters should be elected and preside over the others, and that the care of the Church should wholly belong to him, that the seeds of schism might thus be removed (*Commentary on the Epistle to Titus* I, 6–7).[42]

From the time of Irenaeus it had been generally assumed that the apostles appointed bishops, and that in each of the important centres of Christianity a succession of bishops could be traced back to apostles. Jerome suggests that in the earliest times oversight of the churches (*episkope*) was exercised by a college of presbyters, and that the practice later arose by which the presbyters delegated this oversight to one of their number, who then became known as *the* bishop (*episkopos*).

Jerome's jealousy for his reputation for orthodoxy is well known; he cannot have intended to write anything which could draw the accusation of unorthodoxy. As a biblical student he may have seen his theory as an implication of the N.T. passages which equate *episkopos* and *presbyteros*, some of which[43] he cites in the same commentary. This theory of the origin of the episcopate receives some support from evidence that in Alexandria until 230 *episkope* was regarded as residing in the college of presbyters. Alexandria certainly had bishops before this date, but they were elected and consecrated by the presbyters.[44] Jerome himself mentions this in *Epistle* CXLVI, 1. He travelled extensively (Gaul, Syria, Egypt, Italy, Palestine) and it is possible that he found local traditions elsewhere which supported his theory.

The second passage, from a letter to Pope Damasus who had sponsored his Latin version of the Bible (Vulgate), is one of the clearest declarations of the primacy of the Bishop of Rome made in the first four centuries:

Following no one as leader except Christ, I associate myself in communion with your Beatitude, that is, with the see of Peter. I know the Church was built on that rock. Whoever eats a lamb outside this house (Exodus 12.46) is profane. Any who is not in Noah's ark will perish when the flood prevails (*Epistle* xv).

The ecclesiology which declares not only the primacy of the bishop of Rome, but also his supremacy in all ecclesiastical affairs to be essential to the idea of the Church will be the major topic in the following chapter.

Part 3

THE MEDIEVAL PERIOD

8

The Church
as Papal Monarchy

Throughout the long and turbulent period known as the Middle Ages there was one, and only one continuing institution, the Christian Church. These centuries saw changing economic systems and social structures, political innovations, and new cultural expressions. The Church influenced all these movements, and was influenced by them, but itself, in the eyes of most, stood out above them as having made good the claim to everlastingness once claimed for ancient Rome.

The medieval Church of western Europe was a highly structured organization centred on the papacy, for which increasingly the claims of primacy and supremacy were made. We have already noted passages in some of the early Fathers which accord to the see of Rome a primacy of honour[1] and have been thought by some to acknowledge more than this. But it is extremely unlikely that even those who admit the most (Optatus, Jerome, Augustine) ever envisaged the total *magisterium* over all bishops which was soon to be claimed for the papacy, still less its temporal claims.

'The real framers and promoters of the theory of the Roman primacy were the popes themselves,' writes J. N. D. Kelly.[2] Men like Damasus (366–84), Siricius (384–99), Innocent I (402–17), and their successors not only strove to advance it on the practical plane, but sketched out the theology on which it was based.

LEO I

Pope Leo I, the author of the *Tome* which was accepted at the Council of Chalcedon, 451, as an orthodox expression of the doctrine of Christ's Person, drew together and systematized pronouncements of his predecessors, and provided what may be called a firm first draft for the doctrine of the papacy. The bases of the doctrine are:

(1) that Christ chose one man, Peter, and gave him precedence

over all the apostles and all the Fathers of the Church, so that, although there are many bishops and pastors among the people of God, Peter properly rules all those whom Christ originally also rules (*Sermons* IV, 2).

(2) that the words of Christ in Matthew 16.18 ('upon this rock') refer to Peter himself, and not to his faith (ibid. IV, 3).

(3) that Peter was in fact the first Bishop of Rome, and that his precedence over the whole Church devolves upon the successive bishops of Rome, who are therefore 'vicars of Peter', and his heirs.

(4) that just as the authority given to Peter by Christ was conveyed to the other apostles through Peter,[3] so the authority of the bishops is derived, not immediately from Christ, but through the Bishop of Rome.

(5) that, therefore, the Bishop of Rome has the plenitude of power, *plenitudo potestatis*, in the Church, whilst other bishops have only a share in his responsibility, *pars sollicitudinis* (*Epistles* XIV, 1).[4]

Such claims are to be found in many of the extant sermons and letters of Leo. Their most systematic treatment is in *Sermon* IV and *Letter* XIV to which reference is made above.

GELASIUS, BISHOP OF ROME, 492–6

Towards the end of the fifth century, Pope Gelasius wrote a letter to the Emperor Anastasius which contained the following passage:

> There are two powers, august Emperor, by which this world is chiefly ruled, namely the sacred authority of priests and the power of kings. Of these, the responsibility of the priests is the heavier in that in the divine judgement they will have to give an account even for kings. For you know, most dear son, that you are permitted rightly to rule the human race, yet in things divine you devoutly bow your head before the principal clergy and ask of them the means of your salvation. . . . In these matters, as you know, you are dependent on their judgement, and you have no desire to compel them to do your will. And if it is proper that the hearts of the faithful be in submission to all priests everywhere who exercise their divine ministry aright, how much more is obedience to be given to the bishop of that see whom the Most High God willed to be pre-eminent over all other bishops? (*Ad Anastasium Imperatorem*).[5]

Apart from the reiteration of the papal claim to be the vicar of Peter, this statement on the surface seems to be no more than a reminder from an influential bishop to a Christian ruler of his Christian responsibilities. But it is pregnant with larger claims which were soon to be made explicit. Meanwhile the papal claim to be vicar of Peter was by no means generally admitted. The Church in the East was well aware that no General Council had ever granted the Bishop of Rome jurisdiction over other metropolitans, or over other bishops outside his own metropolitical sphere. And in the West explicit and universal admission of the papal claims was slow in coming.

GREGORY I, THE GREAT, BISHOP OF ROME, 590–604

But several factors contributed to the eventual recognition in the West of the pope's primacy in much more than an honorific sense. The centre of imperial administration had long been in Constantinople. In the West the Roman bishop gained in prestige. In a society increasingly under the attack of barbarian tribes, he represented an institution dedicated to peace and order. This prestige was enhanced by the character and energy of the popes themselves, many of whom were active in providing the protection and promoting the welfare services for the distressed which the emperors would not or could not give. Of particular importance was the work of Pope Gregory I.

His ecclesiology was predominantly Augustinian. He followed his predecessors in maintaining that the see of Rome is 'the Church of the blessed Peter', and that its bishops were the heirs of the 'prince of the apostles' from whom they had inherited the power to bind and loose. But he saw authority as to be exercised only in humility and service; and the more so, the greater the authority might be. He laboured incessantly to protect Rome from the invading Lombards; he fought plague and famine; he promoted missions for the conversion of the northern barbarians; and in all this displayed a high order of political wisdom, administrative ability, and pastoral concern. 'In such a man the might of the papacy stood more erect than any claims to Petrine singularity could ever have predicted.'[6] By the year 700, says R. W. Southern, 'no one in the West denied that the pope possessed all the authority of St Peter over the Church'.[7] This is not to say that the doctrine was everywhere vigorously promoted. For example, as Yves Congar notes,[8] the writings of the Venerable Bede (d. 735), whose ecclesiology is based on Augustine and Gregory the Great, contain no mention of a primacy of the pope. Yet he clearly shares the devotion to St Peter which was characteristic of the age. The theological arguments which linked papal primacy to the apostle Peter were often simply taken for granted.

'THE DONATION OF CONSTANTINE'

It is possible to read into the letter of Gelasius to the Emperor Anastasius[9] a hint of claims over temporal rulers which were not confined to matters ecclesiastical. Circumstances during the eighth century led to the venture of attempting to transform this hint into reality. The benefits of collaboration between the papacy and the ambitious Frankish chieftains became clear to both parties. Charles Martel and his son, Pepin the Short, were greatly impressed with the civilizing success amongst Germans east of the Rhine of the missionary work of Boniface, the emissary of Pope Gregory II (715–31). Pepin was named King of the Franks, and anointed by Boniface, now Archbishop of Mainz, in 751. His son, the able Charles the Great (Charlemagne), found it possible to promote the military and political ambition of the Franks, and Christian missions at the same time. According to his biographer,[10] St Augustine's *De Civitate Dei* was Charlemagne's favourite reading. It is possible that he believed himself called to establish the City of God on earth by a revival of the ancient Roman Empire, but if there was any connection in his mind between this and *De Civitate* he clearly mistook Augustine's intention. On Christmas Day 800, Charlemagne was crowned Emperor of the Romans by Pope Leo III in the basilica of St Peter in Rome. His biographer tells us that this was unexpected, and that he agreed with reluctance, but papal records represent it as a well-planned occasion. It is unlikely that Charlemagne and the Pope saw precisely the same significance in the ceremony.

The papal interpretation of this coronation was that it simply recognized the status and privileges of the Bishop of Rome as set forth in the 'Donation of Constantine'. This was a document of unknown authorship which appeared during this period, and probably in the late eighth century. It was one of those documents, of which history provides many examples, 'in which the theories of the present were represented as the facts of the past'.[11] It purports to be a letter from the Emperor Constantine to Sylvester I, Bishop of Rome (314–35). Its contents are conveniently summarized by R. W. Southern:[12]

> ... a long account of Constantine's conversion, baptism, and cure from leprosy at the intercession of Pope Sylvester. It then goes on to record the Emperor's gifts to the vicar of St Peter: the grant of pre-eminence over the patriarchal sees of Antioch, Alexandria, Jerusalem, and Constantinople, and all other churches; the gift of the imperial insignia, together with the

Lateran palace in Rome; and finally the transfer to the pope of the imperial power in Rome, Italy, and all the provinces of the West.

Thus the pope is seen, not only as supreme over the Church, but as supreme in the West in temporal affairs. The coronation of Charlemagne by the Pope was a recognition of this, not to be forgotten; but the endeavour to make the claim effective was to be the work of centuries.

THE CHURCH IN THE WESTERN WORLD

Effective government in the West was, however, short-lived. Such centrality of government as Charlemagne had achieved was soon to be broken in internecine struggles between powerful feudal lords, the dukes, some of whom would make good a claim to be 'king' over a certain territory, a few of whom aspired to, and were accorded, the title of Emperor of the Romans. The feudal system, into which were built elements from both the Germanic and Roman world, tended to exacerbate and prolong the conflicts. The system, by no means identical in all places, was hierarchical. Each man, from the serf working on an estate and the local lord of the manor to the more powerful dukes and the king, was a vassal, bound in allegiance to his overlord. Theoretically, the emperor was at the head of this hierarchy. Allegiance entailed payments in money, kind, or service, including military service when required. Each of the great lords could expect, for the lives and livelihood of their vassals depended on it, the provision of fighting men whenever they were engaged, as they frequently were, in struggle with a neighbour. These were not times in which popes, however able, could effectively exercise temporal lordship.

It was hardly less difficult for them to exercise the vicariate of Peter in the spiritual affairs of western Europe. It was impossible to convene general councils. Papal letters might or might not arrive at their destination; if they did, the pope had no means of enforcing his wishes.

The Church, perhaps inevitably, became part of the feudal system. Its leaders, the bishops and abbots, were overlords in respect of those who worked in their service, and vassals in respect of the dukes and kings from whom the Church received gifts of land. The writer of the Epistle to Diognetus[13] had spoken of Christians as sharing all things as citizens whilst knowing that their true citizenship is in heaven, and of obeying the established laws whilst outdoing those laws by their lives. It is possible to see the feudal period as one in which the Church was attempting to work out such a programme. An alternative might have been, ignoring the dominical 'ye are the salt of the earth', to attempt to withdraw from society, prepared to accept whatever might come, even though it be extinction. Its choice was, however, to live in the world, and that world was the feudal world. How successfully it manifested the ideal of the Epistle to Diognetus, and provided salt for the feudal world is a matter for debate.[14] On the one hand one notes the careers of such men as the warlike Odo, Bishop of Bayeux, who was devoted to the cause of William the Conqueror, and distinguished himself at the Battle of Hastings. On the other hand there is much evidence that many bishops and abbots strove to reduce warfare, to protect the weak, and to promote good husbandry on their estates.

In these confused times the bishop and the abbot in most places in the West were the two persons who were the leading representatives of the oldest existing institution, one which was acknowledged to have not only divine sanction, but also long experience in effective and beneficent administration. They, and their clergy and monks, were more often than not fully deserving of the confidence and affection which the common people gave to them. It is certain that the great feudal lords were alive to the advantages of co-operation with bishops and abbots. So important did they believe this to be that they claimed, and not infrequently exercised, the right to appoint bishops. Pope John XI in 921 protested sharply against its exercise by a local duke, while admitting 'the ancient custom' that a Christian king might present a bishop for consecration. Nevertheless the bishops and the abbots were to be the pope's men in the controversies with monarchs which were later to develop.

TRENDS IN ECCLESIOLOGY, NINTH AND TENTH CENTURIES

THE MYSTICAL BODY OF CHRIST

The basic emphasis remains the Augustinian concept of the mystical body. The incarnate body of Christ, the eucharistic body, and the body which is the Church are three realizations of the same mystery. The words of Haymo of Halberstadt (d. 891) are typical:

> Just as that flesh [which the Word of God assumed] is the body of Christ, so this bread becomes the body of Christ. Nor are there two bodies, but

one body ... and as that bread and blood [*sic*] become the body of Christ, so all those in the Church who worthily partake of it are one body of Christ. ... Yet that flesh which he assumed, and this bread, and the Church as a whole do not make three bodies of Christ, but one body (*Commentary on 1 Corinthians* x).[15]

PAPAL PRIMACY OR SUPREMACY?

Despite the now official interpretation at Rome of Matthew 16.18 as supporting papal supremacy, elsewhere the interpretation of Cyprian[16] who, taking the text in conjunction with Matthew 18.18 and John 20.22–3, read them as pointing to a collegial episcopate, persisted strongly. Bede (d. 735) and Paul the Deacon (d. *c.* 800) had so interpreted them in the eighth century; Haymo of Halberstadt and Rabanus Maurus (d. 856) followed suit in the ninth, and Rathier of Verona (d. 974), and Gerbert of Aurrilac who became Pope Sylvester II (d. 1003) in the tenth.[17] 'Everybody in the West acknowledged the Roman primacy, but not everybody did so in the sense that had been given to it at Rome since St Leo.'[18]

Hincmar, Archbishop of Rheims (845–82) in particular resisted the claims of successive popes to override metropolitan bishops by judging in the first instance matters concerning bishops. He maintained also that the college of bishops is more than merely a passive instrument under the absolute authority of the pope; it must play an active part in regulating the life of the Church. Hincmar recognized the primacy of Rome as of divine institution, but declared that papal decisions must be in accordance with the Scriptures and the canon law which derives from the acknowledged ecumenical councils. It is in such Catholic councils that the mind of the Church is expressed, and the episcopal college plays its rightful role therein. Only when a bishop, even a pope, judges or decides in accordance with canons derived from conciliar decisions, can he be sure that the whole Church judges and decides with him.[19]

THE CHURCH 'WHICH ESPECIALLY CONSISTS OF THE CLERGY'

In this period the distinction between clergy and laity was accentuated. Yves Congar writes:[20]

The faithful no longer understood Latin. From the end of the eighth century the Canon of the Mass was said in a low voice, the priest celebrated with his back to the people, the faithful no longer brought their offerings to the altar, private masses became frequent in the monasteries; at the beginning of the ninth century, instead of the simple phrase 'who offer to thee' (i.e. in the third person) we find 'for whom *we* offer to thee or who offer to thee' in the Canon. . . . From this period one could begin making a list of passages which imply that the Church consists principally in the clergy.

He offers as examples: 'the Church which especially consists of the clergy' (Florus of Lyons, d. 860);[21] 'for the Church is nothing other than the faithful people, although the word particularly designates the clergy'(? John VIII, Pope 872–82).[22]

Here the idea of the Church as the congregation of the faithful is in danger of being lost, and the great majority of Church people in process of becoming passive nonentities.

TRENDS IN ECCLESIOLOGY, ELEVENTH AND TWELFTH CENTURIES

LEO IX, POPE 1049–54

R. W. Southern, in the book already cited several times, bids us pay attention, if we would understand the increased papal claims of the latter part of the eleventh century, to the activity of Leo IX. He mentions: 'the political alliance with the Normans; the exacerbation of relations with the Greeks;[23] the reform of papal administrative machinery; the beginning of a consistent plan of government through legates, councils, and a vastly increased correspondence'.[24] He gathered round him a group of able men, among them two monks: Hildebrand, and Humbert who was appointed cardinal-bishop of Silva Candida in 1049. Canon law, into which the Donation of Constantine was incorporated, was revised. The idea of the Church, first sketched by Leo I and briefly exemplified by Gregory the Great, was brought to the fore. The Church was seen as 'a unique kingdom under the papal monarchy in whose universal responsibility and power the bishops had only a partial share'.[25] The Roman Church is the see of Peter. In relation to the rest of the Church it is 'head', 'mother', 'hinge', 'fount', 'foundation'. It cannot err in the faith. Long-needed reforms were taken in hand, in particular against simony (the granting of ecclesiastical offices in consideration of bribes). Humbert wrote a treatise 'Against Simoniacs', in which he asserted that ordinations by simoniacal bishops were invalid.

GREGORY VII (HILDEBRAND), POPE 1073–85

Building on the success of this reactivation of the papal claims and of the practical activities which supported them, Hildebrand, himself one of Leo IX's most able advisers, when he became Pope Gregory VII some twenty years later was ready to extend them both by words and action. The words are to be found in brief notes, known as the *Dictatus Papae* ('The Dictations of the Pope'). Whether they were actually dictated by Gregory is disputed. They appear among the collection of his letters, and certainly belong to his pontificate.[26] There are twenty-seven notes, but they may be summarized under four heads:

1 The Roman Church

The *Ecclesia Romana* was founded by God alone; its bishop is rightly called universal. It has never erred and never will. Nobody is a Catholic who does not agree with it.

2 Papal power over the Church

The Bishop of Rome can ordain anyone from any part of the Church. He alone can depose, reinstate, or transfer bishops to another see. A papal legate, even though of lesser ecclesiastical rank, presides over bishops in council. The pope alone can make new laws, create new episcopal sees or unite existing ones. He alone can call a general council; actions of synods are not canonical without his authority. His decrees can be annulled by no one, but he can annul the decrees of anyone. All important ecclesiastical disputes must be referred to him.

3 Papal authority in relation to emperors and kings

The pope has the power to depose emperors. On appeal to the pope no one shall be condemned in any other court. The pope may permit or command subjects to accuse their rulers, and may absolve subjects from their oath of allegiance to wicked rulers.

4 The papal status

The pope alone may use the imperial insignia. All princes shall kiss his foot alone. He can be judged by no one. A pope who has been canonically ordained is made a saint by the merits of St Peter.

These words, describing the pope's all-embracing authority over the whole of Christendom, emperors and kings and their affairs no less than the officers of the Church and theirs, were dramatically translated into action in 1076 when Gregory deposed and excommunicated Henry IV of Germany, heir to the imperial throne. He conceived himself to be acting as vicar of Peter, to whom he addressed the deed of deposition and excommunication:[27]

> ... I now declare in the name of the omnipotent God, the Father, Son and Holy Spirit, that Henry, son of the Emperor Henry, is deprived of his Kingdom of Germany and Italy; I do this by thy authority and in defence of the honour of thy Church, because he has rebelled against it.'

Henry submitted, and did penance at Canossa in 1077, whereupon Gregory withdrew the deposition and lifted the excommunication.

The ecclesiology which is implied in all this is apparent. It may be described as a doctrine of the Church as a papal monarchy. The Bishop of Rome is supreme not only over ecclesiastics and ecclesiastical affairs, but over emperor and rulers and the affairs of civil government. The Church is seen as coterminous with the empire, a notion which in theory, and often in practice, denied the privileges of citizenship and even protection to those who were not in communion with the see of Rome, not only heretics and schismatics, but groups like the Jews. It is a doctrine of the Church which, for its implementation, demanded a tight structure of papal legates in every country, emissaries to the courts of every king, prince, or baron, and an elaborate court of political experts in Rome to keep a finger on the whole. Beneath this new hierarchy the authority of metropolitans and bishops in their own provinces and dioceses was often reduced to vanishing-point.

REACTION

There was no lack of protesting voices. Gregory was accused of treating the bishops as a large landowner treats his farmers.[28] The German bishops at a synod at Worms in 1076 charged him with pride and ambition. He had 'introduced worldliness into the Church'; 'the bishops have been deprived of their divine authority'; 'the Church of God is in danger of destruction' through Gregory's presumption.[29]

The papal claim to temporal supremacy met with opposition from every ruler powerful enough to make his influence felt. They received support from some theologians and canonists,[30] who took up again the dictum of Gelasius: 'There are two powers by which this world is chiefly ruled. . . .'[31] More radical opposition was also forthcoming. An unknown writer, the so-called 'Anonymous Norman' (*c.* 1000) contends that the Church is to be defined as 'the Christian people', 'the congregation of faithful Christians living together in the house of God in one faith, hope and love'. It is a royal and priestly people. Its only head is Christ. Priesthood is related to the temporary humiliation of the Word in the incarnation, while kingly rule derives from his divinity. Kings then are vicars of God, priests only of Christ in his humanity. From this it follows that kings have a sacred power of government in ecclesiastical matters, and authority over bishops, and that kings properly invest bishops with their authority.[32]

The first stages of the long-drawn-out struggle between popes and rulers were fought on the investiture issue. A compromise was reached between Callistus II (Pope 1119–24) and the Emperor Henry V at the Concordat of Worms in 1122. Elections of bishops were to be the free prerogative of the Church. Bishops would be invested with the ring and crozier, representing their spiritual authority, by the pope or his deputies, while the emperor would invest them with their temporal authority and possessions and receive their homage.

BERNARD OF CLAIRVAUX, 1090–1153

The founder and first abbot of the Cistercian monastery at Clairvaux was both a supporter and a critic of the papacy. His sermons on the Song of Solomon present a doctrine of the Church as the mystical body, and at once the spouse of Christ. The sense of the need for deep personal religion inspires his writing. The union in the mystical body is the spiritual union of souls with Christ in Love. He can use the phrase: 'The Church or the soul which loves God'.[33] The Church is the Saviour's spouse, but every soul also is the spouse of Christ insofar as it shares individually in the love for Christ of the one and only spouse.

Bernard preached the ideal of poverty, and was deeply critical of the imperial style of life which the papacy had assumed, and which was likely to present the pope to the world as the successor of Constantine rather than St Peter.[34] He warned Eugenius III (Pope 1145–53), his former pupil and a Cistercian monk, against involving himself in a continuous round of secular and litigious business.[35] While he did not doubt that the pope possessed *plenitudo potestatis*,[36] it was not appropriate that he should do all that he had the power to do.[37] If the Church is to be the Church of God, who according to Scripture is Love, not Honour or Dignity,[38] it must not confine itself within the structures of power and juridical authority.

TRENDS IN ECCLESIOLOGY, THIRTEENTH CENTURY

INNOCENT III, POPE 1198–1216

The high point of the papal claims and of the ability to translate them into action was reached in the pontificate of Innocent III, who was elected after a long campaign on his behalf by members of the influential Conti family from which he came.[39] His aim was to display the papal *plenitudo potestatis*, interpreted now not merely in relation to the *pars sollicitudinis* of other bishops, but as supremacy in all the affairs of men. He built up an efficient organization of legal and financial officers in Rome. His legates and other emissaries penetrated to every part of western Europe. His own knowledge of canon law, and the skill of the canonists whom he enlisted, enabled him to make effective use of the papal appeal court.

FOURTH LATERAN COUNCIL, 1215

Innocent was a competent theologian, and it was by his inspiration that the Fourth Lateran Council in its first canon set out a summary of Christian doctrine (the Trinity, the Incarnation, the Church, and the Sacraments). It defined the eucharistic presence of Christ in terms of transubstantiation, a doctrine to which the development of medieval theology had been leading.[40] The Council laid down rules for the administration and reception of the sacraments.[41] A programme of education of the faithful was proposed. The checking of abuses, such as the superstitious use of relics, was promised.[42] Plans were approved for a new crusade against the Saracens (never to be undertaken, although Innocent devoted much attention to its preparation during his last months).

The Council also forbade the creation of new monastic Orders, whose recent proliferation alarmed Innocent. It was perhaps reluctantly that he had sanctioned the rule of St Francis of Assisi. The two Orders of friars, Franciscan and Dominican, which had their beginnings during Innocent's pontificate, were, however, to prove strong pillars of papal power.

PAPAL AUTHORITY IN ACTION

Among the many ways in which Innocent demonstrated his authority over bishops was his restriction of their power to grant indulgences, which effectively diverted income to the papacy. He was the first to *require* bishops to grant benefices to his own nominees. The later growth of this practice was a chief cause of national resentment against the popes.

His exercise of temporal supremacy was illustrated by the episode of the excommunication of King John of England in 1209, of John's capitulation and the surrender of his territories 'to God, and to Saints Peter and Paul His apostles and to the Holy Roman Church our mother, and to our lord Pope Innocent III and his Catholic successors',[43] receiving them back as the Pope's vassal for the payment of 1,000 marks annually. In his dealings with the imperial throne, Innocent was less successful. At the beginning of his pontificate there were several claimants. After a long period of political activity, carefully documented in the papal registry of letters, Innocent was able to secure the election of the man of his choice, Otto IV. Otto, however, proved to be a broken reed, and in 1211 Innocent successfully promoted the election of his youthful ward, Frederick II. Frederick's extraordinary career was to provide manifold difficulties for Innocent's successors, and to make clear that the papal claim to temporal lordship was incapable of fulfilment.

THE VICAR OF CHRIST

Canon 1 of the Fourth Lateran Council, among its doctrinal statements, affirms simply that 'there is one universal Church of the faithful, outside of which there is absolutely no salvation'. How Innocent himself interpreted this is made clear in his letter to King John of England (1215). Jesus Christ who is both King of kings and eternal Priest has established both his kingdom and his priesthood in the Church. The Church, therefore, is both a priestly kingdom and a royal priesthood. Christ has set one, the Bishop of Rome, as his vicar on earth over all. As every knee should bow to Jesus, so obedience is required of his vicar. Consequently, unless kings venerate and serve this vicar they must doubt whether they are reigning properly. Kingdom and priesthood, for the benefit of each, are to be united in the person of the vicar of Christ.

'The vicar of Christ', not now the vicar of Peter. 'We are the successor of the Prince of the Apostles,' Innocent admitted, 'but we are not his vicar, nor the vicar of any man or Apostle, but the vicar of Jesus Christ himself.'[44] To be 'vicar of Peter', indicating merely authority over the successors of the apostles, was a title no longer adequate to indicate the temporal claims of the pope.

GREGORY IX (POPE 1227–41) AND INNOCENT IV (POPE 1243–54)

Innocent III's successors, although hindered by the defiance of the Emperor Frederick II until his death in 1250, hammered in a little more deeply some of the nails which he had placed. Gregory IX consolidated the canon law, and sponsored the School of Bologna as a centre for its study and dissemination. He initiated a practice designed to bring the Italian sees firmly under papal control, by appointing the very able but youthful Ottaviano degli Ubaldini as his agent, with the title of archdeacon, in the diocese of Bologna during a deliberately maintained interregnum. Innocent IV made Ottaviano a cardinal and appointed him his legate in northern Italy, equipped with practically full papal power. His influence, in fact, extended far beyond Italy. He became a kind of shadow pope, distrusted and feared by almost all. His relationship with the papal enemy, the excommunicated Frederick II, was ambiguous. Dante placed him (*il cardinale*) with the Emperor in hell.

BONIFACE VIII (POPE 1294–1303)

The beginning of the fourteenth century saw the publication, 1302, of Boniface's Bull, *Unam Sanctam*. It is an important document which gives classical expression to the papal concept of the Church as it was understood after eight and a half centuries of theoretical and practical development upon foundations laid by Leo I. It must be quoted at some length:[45]

> ... There is one holy Catholic apostolic Church ... outside of her there is no salvation or remission of sins, as the Bridegroom says in the Song of Solomon: 'My dove, my undefiled is but one. . . .' (Song 6.9); which represents the one mystical body, whose head is Christ. . . . In the time of the flood there was only one ark, that of Noah, prefiguring the one Church ... all things on the earth outside of this ark were destroyed. This Church we venerate as the only one, since the Lord said by the prophet: 'Deliver my soul from the sword; my darling from the power of the dog' (Ps. 22.20). He prayed for his soul, that is, for himself, the head; and at the same time for the body; and he named his body, that is, the one church, because there is but one Bridegroom,[46] and because of the unity of the faith, of the sacraments, and of his love for the church. This is the seamless robe of the Lord which was not rent but parted by lot (John 19.23). Therefore there is one body of the one and only church, and one head, not two heads, as if the church were a monster. And this head is Christ and his vicar, Peter and his successor; for the Lord himself said to

Peter: 'Feed my sheep' (John 21.16). And he said 'my sheep', in general, not these or those sheep in particular; from which it is clear that all were committed to him. If therefore Greeks or anyone else say that they are not subject to Peter and his successors, they thereby necessarily confess that they are not of the sheep of Christ. For ... there is one fold and only one shepherd (John 10.16). By the words of the Gospel we are taught that the two swords, namely the spiritual authority and the temporal are in the power of the church.[47] For when the apostle said 'Here are two swords' (Luke 22.38)—that is in the church, since it was the apostles who were speaking—the Lord did not answer 'It is too much', but 'It is enough'. Whoever denies that the temporal sword is in the power of Peter does not properly understand the word of the Lord when he said: 'Put up thy sword into the sheath' (John 18.11).[48] Both swords, therefore, the spiritual and the temporal, are in the power of the church. The former is to be used by the Church, the latter for the church; the one by the hand of the priest, the other by the hand of kings and knights, but at the command and permission of the priest.

Boniface goes on to show why the temporal must be subject to the spiritual authority. He quotes Romans 13.1 which declares that all existing powers are ordained by God, and takes 'ordained' in the sense of 'arranged in order'. He then calls to his aid the authority of Dionysius the Areopagite[49] to support the proposition that a hierarchical order of things is of divine origin, and that it is a law of the universe that the lower is given its due order, and thereby enhanced, by the higher. He adds that it is necessarily to be admitted that the spiritual power surpasses any earthly power, and with some naivety claims that the truth of this is evident from the fact that men pay tithes to and receive benediction from the spiritual power:

> Thus the prophecy of Jeremiah concerning the church and the ecclesiastical power is fulfilled: 'See, I have this day set thee over the nations and over the kingdoms, to root out, and to pull down, and to destroy, and to throw down, to build and to plant (Jer. 1.10).

First Corinthians 2.15 is then quoted to show that the spiritual power will rightly judge the temporal, itself being subject to the judgement of no man, but of God only. The familiar Matthew 16.18–19 is used to show that

> this authority, although it is given to man and exercised through man, is not human, but divine. For it was given by the word of the Lord to Peter, and the rock was made firm to him and his successors, in Christ himself whom he had confessed.

Finally, Boniface alludes to Romans 13.2: 'Therefore he who resists the authorities resists what God has appointed, and those who resist will incur judgement.' He ignores the plural 'authorities', and assumes that the authority of which St Paul speaks is that of the Bishop of Rome:

> We therefore declare, say, and affirm that submission on the part of every man to the bishop of Rome is altogether necessary for his salvation.

It should be noted how the papal doctrine of the Church is impressed upon the old scriptural and patristic images of the Church, many of which are present in this document: the bride, the dove of Solomon's Song, the ark, the body, the seamless robe. To be noted too is the ingenious combination of symbolic and literal interpretation of the Scriptures. It is a document which Innocent III could have signed, although he would probably have eliminated its ambiguities[50] and exegetical infelicities. Leo I would probably have applauded it—and marvelled that the time should have come when such a document could be published. One can only guess that Clement I in 96 would have been thoroughly puzzled by it. Does its ecclesiology represent a legitimate or divinely ordered development? The events of the fourteenth century were strongly to suggest a negative answer.

In the year after the publication of the Bull, Boniface died. His Bull *Clericis Laicos* of 1298, which forbade secular rulers to impose any taxes whatsoever upon clerics without papal permission, and threatened the excommunication of rulers who exacted or clerics who paid such unauthorized taxes, thoroughly antagonized Edward I of England and Philip IV of France. The latter sent an expedition of French soldiers to attack the papal palace at Anagoni, and Boniface died as a result of the violence and insults he received. So ended a period of cordial relationship between the papacy and kings of France which had lasted nearly 200 years. In 1309 Pope Clement V moved to Avignon. The minor scandal of the removal of the centre of government of the successor of Peter from the city of which the apostle had been the first bishop and where he was martyred was ended sixty-nine years later when Gregory XI returned to Rome, only to be succeeded by the greater scandal of the 'Great Schism'. Between 1378 and 1449 there were only seventeen years when there were not at least two popes claiming to have been duly elected by the cardinals. Secular rulers were not slow to take advantage of a situation in which the first half of a *divide et impera* policy was actually provided for them. To play one pope off against another was as easy as it was obvious. The number of acts designed to limit papal temporal jurisdiction multiplied in the statute books of many countries. Voices of protest from churchmen, appeals for reform and for new definitions of the order and function of the Church, though they had not been lacking in the thirteenth century, now became more frequent and persistent. We shall consider these in Chapter 10.

9

The Ecclesiology
of the Schoolmen

The thirteenth century has been described as the golden age of scholasticism, that is the theology of the scholars (scholastics or schoolmen) who taught at the universities. The universities arose during the twelfth century. Their beginnings were in the schools of learning established by monastic Orders and, in the thirteenth century by the Franciscans and Dominicans, in the larger cities of Europe. Anselm, Archbishop of Canterbury (d. 1109) is often called 'the Father of the Schoolmen', but perhaps Peter Lombard (1100–1160), who taught at the School of Notre Dame in Paris, has a better claim to the title, for his *Sentences* became a standard textbook of theology, and commentaries on them were written by most of the later schoolmen of consequence, including Albertus Magnus, Thomas Aquinas, and Bonaventure.

The schoolmen in their commentaries on the *Sentences*, and their *Summae*, treated the whole range of theology. Yves Congar notes[1] that 'none of the great scholastics undertook a special treatise on the Church'. Professor Hans Küng[2] also remarks that the medieval period produced much less writing on the theology of the Church than canonical material on questions of ecclesiastical constitution and authority. The ecclesiology of these writers is for the most part to be found in the context of their Christology and their doctrines of grace and the sacraments. Perhaps the fullest treatment of the doctrine of the Church is that of Thomas Aquinas in his *Expositio super Symbolo Apostolorum* ('An Exposition on the Apostles' Creed').

The scholastic theologians of the twelfth and thirteenth centuries employ the biblical and patristic images and symbols of the Church, and in the main follow the lines of St Augustine. As we look briefly at the ecclesiology of some of them we shall, however, note a new development in a tendency to make a certain distinction between 'Church' and 'mystical body of Christ'.

HUGH OF ST VICTOR, 1096–1141

Hugh taught at the school of the abbey of St Victor in Paris. The Church, he maintained, is the body of Christ. Its principle of unity is faith, confirmed by the baptism by which we are incorporated into Christ.[3] The Church is at once the body of Christ and the creation of the Holy Spirit: 'Just as the spirit of a man comes down by the mediation of his head to give life to all his members, so the Holy Spirit comes to Christians through Christ.'[4] 'When you become a Christian, you become a member of Christ, participating in the Spirit of Christ.'[5]

Congar notes[6] that in the twelfth century the 'birthday' of the Church is less frequently identified with Pentecost, than with the flowing of water and blood from the side of Christ on the cross (John 19.34). This notion occurs several times in Hugh. The reference to the sacraments of baptism and the eucharist is clear. The Church is seen as the sphere where the sacramental grace which flows from Christ's humanity operates. There is a tendency here, which will be more pronounced in the thirteenth century, towards a doctrine of the Church which is 'essentially Christological, not pneumatological'.[7]

ALEXANDER OF HALES, 1170–1245

Alexander of Hales, a Franciscan who studied and taught in Paris, the author of a commentary on Peter Lombard's *Sentences* and a *Summa*, presents two points of interest. The first is reminiscent of Jerome's equation of the presbyter with the bishop.[8] The ecclesiastical orders may be considered either from the point of view of sacramental power, or of power in relationship to the Church. In the first case, the order of the priesthood, which has the power to celebrate the eucharist, stands at the head of the hierarchy. But from the point of view of the total needs of the Church, which include the ordination of priests and pastors, the episcopate must be added.[9]

Secondly, in Alexander we find a distinction between the members of the Church and the members of Christ. For membership in the Church faith[10] is sufficient, but for membership in 'the body of the Church' or the mystical body of Christ charity, or faith which has been formed (*fides formata*), is necessary. By receiving the sacrament of faith (baptism) one can be a member of the Church in point of number (*numero*), i.e. as merely one of a number. But by faith which has been formed one is not only a member of the Church, but a member of Christ,[11] and this in point of merit (*merito*), i.e. deservedly.

BONAVENTURE, 1221–74

Bonaventure, a Franciscan who taught in Paris and a commentator on the *Sentences*, whose doctrine of the Church is basically Augustinian, makes a distinction similar to that of Alexander, whose pupil he was. Here and there he identifies 'Church' and 'mystical body', but introduces a distinction when he considers the status of sinners. Unrepentant sinners are 'within the Church',[12] even members of the Church. But they are not members of the mystical body, unless one can say that they are 'dead and rotten members'.[13] Congar sums up Bonaventure's position thus: 'It is clear that for him "Church" denotes the body in and by which salvation is at work, and one can be a member of it merely as one of a number (*numero*); while the "mystical body" implies union with Christ by charity and living fellowship. Its members are those who are members of the Church deservedly (*merito*).'[14]

Bonaventure was a strong supporter of the concept of the papal monarchy, but expressed himself cautiously on the question of the political power of the pope. But he has no doubt that the pope possesses plenitude of power over the Church. It is a 'triple' power, because (a) 'he alone has the whole plenitude of authority which Christ conferred upon the Church'; (b) 'he possesses it everywhere in the churches'; and (c) 'all authority flows from him throughout the Church to all the lower ranks'.[15] 'If everything in the Church were destroyed, and he alone remained, he could restore it all.'[16] The pope's authority is both juridical and doctrinal: 'It is recognized that at the time when truth and grace were revealed the plenitude of power was conferred upon the vicar of Christ, and consequently it must be said that to assert anything in a matter of faith or morals which is contrary to what he has defined is an evil in no way to be tolerated.'[17] This is close to an assertion of papal infallibility.

ALBERTUS MAGNUS, 1206–80

The Dominican, Albertus Magnus,[18] who also taught in Paris, writes frequently of the mystical body. He treats it in close relationship with the eucharist. Incorporation with the mystical body is through the eucharistic body which he thinks of as the extending to all of the union which the Word of God effected with human nature in the incarnation. Yet for him the Holy Spirit is the principle of unity of the body of

Christ, and the sanctifier of the Church.[19] His pupil, Thomas Aquinas, was to develop this pneumatological aspect of the Church, which was not prominent among the scholastics.

Albert, like Alexander of Hales and Bonaventure, distinguishes between the 'Church' and the 'mystical body'. The mystical body means something more than 'the congregation of faithful people'—charity is necessary. Yves Congar remarks that 'Albert says the same about the Church, which strictly would lead to the unacceptable idea of a Church composed only of saints.'[20] But elsewhere he makes a distinction between belonging to the communion of grace and belonging to the society of the means of grace, between being a member of the Church *merito* and a member *numero*.[21]

The pope's plenitude of power is acknowledged;[22] jurisdiction descends from the pope. But Albert ascribes to him neither absolute monarchy nor infallibility. He speaks of indefectibility (based on Luke 22.32, 'that thy faith fail not') rather than infallibility, and he refers it to the 'see of Peter and his successor', not to the pope personally.[23]

THOMAS AQUINAS, 1225–74

The life span of St Thomas Aquinas fell between the pontificates of Innocent III and Boniface VIII, and thus coincided with the period when popes and canonists were mounting their largest claims for papal supremacy, both spiritual and temporal. Thomas, an Italian of noble family, was a Dominican friar, a pupil of Albertus Magnus, and taught in Paris.

THE MYSTICAL BODY

The ecclesiology of Augustine dominates Thomas's doctrine of the Church. It is the mystical body of which Christ is the head. He draws an analogy with the human body of which the head is the centre of order, perfection, and power (all the senses are centred there). The analogy, however, he warns must not be pressed; it is a question of resemblance rather than exact correspondence.[24] The analogy is inadequate in that the members of a human body are all joined together at one time, but 'the members of the mystical body are not all together . . . since the body of the Church is made up of the men who have been from the beginning of the world until its end.'[25] In the same passage (in which he is commenting on 1 Timothy 4.10: 'the Saviour of all men, especially of those who believe') he says that Christ is the Head of all mankind, but not of all men in the same way:

> First and principally, He is Head of such as are united to Him by glory; secondly, of those who are actually united to Him by charity; thirdly, of those who are actually united to Him by faith; fourthly, of those who are united to Him merely in potentiality, which is not yet reduced to act, yet will be reduced to act according to Divine predestination; fifthly, of those who are united to Him in potentiality, which will never be reduced to act; such are those men existing in the world, who are not predestined, who, however, on their departure from this world, wholly cease to be members of Christ, as being no longer in potentiality to be united to Christ.

Thomas's strong doctrine of predestination brings him close here to a doctrine of the invisible Church.

THE CHURCH AS THE CREATION OF THE HOLY SPIRIT

Thomas takes up again[26] the theme that the Church on earth derives its existence from Christ's passion: 'From the side of Christ, sleeping on the cross, the sacraments flowed—namely, blood and water—on which the Church was established.'[27] This is in line with the Christologically centred doctrine of the Church which is typical of western medieval theology. Yet he acknowledges the constitutive activity of the Holy Spirit in the life of the Church:

> As in one single human being there is one soul and one body but many members, so the Catholic Church has one body but many members. The soul animating this body is the Holy Ghost.[28] Hence the Creed, after bidding us believe in the Holy Ghost, adds, 'the Holy Catholic Church' (*Exposition on the Apostles' Creed* 9).[29]

It is the Holy Spirit who anoints the Church, just as the faithful Christian receives an anointing for his sanctification,[30] and who is the ultimate principle of its unity.[31] But, as Congar says:[32] 'It must be admitted that Thomas has hardly gone into detail in this regard. His theology of habitual grace[33] led him to think chiefly of Christ as the communicator of grace.'

THE CHURCH A MIXED SOCIETY

Although he frequently speaks of the Church as *societas sanctorum* (a society of saints), he clearly does not conceive of it as a society of the perfect. Quoting Ephesians 5.27, 'a glorious Church, not having spot or wrinkle', he says that this must be understood of the goal to be achieved through Christ's passion, that is, 'in heaven, and not on earth, in which "if we say that we have no sin, we deceive ourselves" (1 John 1.8).'[34]

THE CONGREGATION OF THE FAITHFUL

In one section on the Church in his *Exposition on the Apostles' Creed* Thomas says that 'church' means 'congregation', and defines Holy Church as 'the congregation of believers of which each Christian is a member', citing Ecclesiasticus 51.23: 'Draw near to me, ye unlearned; and gather yourselves together into the house of discipline.' Here again, the Church is seen as a mixed society, the school of sinners and the ignorant, rather than a society of the perfect. Hans Küng[35] draws special attention to the frequency with which Thomas speaks of the Church as the *congregatio fidelium*. This definition, or description of the Church, seemingly at variance with the tendency of medieval ecclesiology to emphasize the hierarchy, was never quite submerged. It was not forgotten even by the canonists,[36] whose concern for the most part was to support the idea of the Church as a hierarchy under the papal monarchy, and it was to be the basis of the conciliarists' argument for the superiority of a general council over the pope.[37]

The *Exposition* goes on to comment on the four credal marks of the Church. The tone is devotional, rather than dogmatic.

One

The Church is one. The Song of Solomon 6.9, 'My dove, my perfect one, is only one', supplies Thomas's text.[38] This unity has a triple cause in the agreement of faith, hope, and charity: of faith, because all who belong to the body of Christ hold the same truths; of hope, because they have the same confidence of receiving eternal life; of charity, because all are bound together in the love of God and one another. He recognizes that this is not always so (again the admission that the Church is a mixed society) in the words which follow: 'The genuineness of this love is shown when the members of the Church care for one another and are compassionate together.'

In this context of the unity of the Church he employs the ancient image of the ark of Noah, but not with the polemical and exclusive intent we have noted in others.[39] That the Church is like Noah's ark 'outside of which nobody can be saved' is a reason for gentle treatment of weaker brethren: 'Nobody should be despised, nobody should be treated as an outcast.'

Holy

The Church is holy. Here he uses the biblical image of the temple: 'Ye are the temple of God' (1 Cor. 3.16). When a sacred building is consecrated it is washed and anointed. So the members of the Church have been washed by the blood of Christ and have received the anointing of the Holy Spirit for their sanctification. The Church, therefore, is holy. 'Moreover, the Church is holy by the indwelling of the Blessed Trinity.' Neither here nor elsewhere does he work out the possibilities of this pregnant theological assertion.[40] That members of the Church are not always holy he recognizes in adding: 'Let us guard against defiling our souls with sin: "for if any man violate the temple of God, him shall God destroy" (1 Cor. 3.17).'

Catholic

The Church is catholic, or universal, in three ways. First, with regard to place. It extends to every nation as it obeys the commission to go into the whole world and preach the gospel to all men (Mark 16.15). Moreover, it extends to heaven and to purgatory, where saints and waiting souls are its members.[41] Second, with regard to human beings. No one is rejected, from whatever race, class, or sex (Gal. 3.28). Third, it is universal in time. It began with Abel, and will endure to the end of the world, 'and even after, for the Church remains in heaven'.[42]

Apostolic

The principal foundation of the Church is Christ; secondary foundations are the apostles and their teaching. This is why the Church is called apostolic. With such foundations the Church stands firm. Peter, the Rock, represents this strength. The Church will never be overthrown, despite persecutions, errors, and other attacks of the devil. While there are regions where the faith has been lost or greatly weakened, the Church of Peter, 'to whose lot fell all Italy when the disciples were sent out to preach', has always stood firm, and 'still flourishes in faith and free from heresy'. This is not surprising, for Christ said to Peter: 'I have prayed for thee that thy faith fail not' (Luke 22.32).

The Papacy

Thomas, therefore, accepts the papal interpretation of St Peter's confession of faith at Caesarea Philippi and of Christ's commission to

Peter (John 21.15 ff). Peter was made supreme pontiff, and the pope succeeds him. He accords to the pope plenitude of power over the Church in spiritual matters, but this power is not to be used capriciously. He may dispense from ecclesiastical regulations in matters of human law, but 'in matters of the Natural Law, the articles of faith, and the sacraments, he cannot dispense, and any claim to such power is not authentic, but a pretence'.[43] Thomas also declares the pope to have a supreme teaching authority in matters of faith, even to the extent of publishing a new creed:

> A new edition of the symbol [i.e. creed] becomes necessary in order to set aside the errors that may arise. Consequently to publish a new edition of the symbol belongs to that authority which is empowered to decide matters of faith finally, so that they may be held by all with unshaken faith. Now this belongs to the authority of the Sovereign Pontiff: 'I have prayed for thee, Peter, that thy faith fail not, and thou, being once converted, confirm thy brethren.' The reason for this is that there should be but one faith of the whole Church . . . this could not be secured unless any question of faith that may arise be decided by him who presides over the whole Church, so that the whole Church may hold firmly to his decision. Consequently it belongs to the sole authority of the Sovereign Pontiff to publish a new edition of the symbol, as do all other matters which concern the whole Church, such as to convoke a general council (*Summa* IIa–IIae, 1, 10).

It is to be noted that Thomas asserts that the pope alone has power to summon a general council. This assumption, understandable in the heyday of the success of papal claims, was to be challenged by the conciliarists.[44]

Thomas, however, gave no support to the papal claim to supreme temporal authority:

> Spiritual power and secular power both derive from divine power. Consequently the secular power is subject to the spiritual power only to the extent that it is so subordinated by God, namely, in matters relating to the soul's salvation, where the spiritual power is to be obeyed before the secular. In matters of political welfare, however, the temporal power should be obeyed before the spiritual: 'Render to Caesar the things that are Caesar's.' That is the rule, unless historically it happens that secular power is joined to spiritual power, as in the Pope, who occupies the peak of both powers, according to the dispensation of Christ, who is both priest and king (IV *Sentences* XLIV, iii. 4).[45]

Of the apparent exception to the rule in favour of the pope, Gilby justly remarks[46] that the reference is probably to the pope's power within the papal estates. It does not mean that Thomas shared the political view of thirteenth-century canonists.

In matters of faith, however, Thomas evidently regarded the pope as possessing the authority which in earlier centuries was thought to reside in a general council. Cyprian's teaching that the unity of the Church in the apostles' faith is guaranteed by the whole episcopate acting as a collegiate body is left far behind.

10

Opposition to the
Papal Concept of the Church

THE ALBIGENSIANS

The most overt opposition to the papacy and the hierarchy came from a sect, known as the Albigensians, which appeared in the Albigeois region of Aquitaine during the twelfth century. Its strongholds were the cities of Albi and Toulouse. They are also known as the Cathari (the Pure Ones), a term used also, however, for similar sectarian groups in other parts of Europe. The Albigensians taught a Manichaean dualism and an exaggerated asceticism set within a semi-Christian framework.[1] From the Manichaean premiss that there are two gods, they concluded that there were two churches: that of the good God, the Father of greatness and the source of all light, founded by Jesus Christ, which they identified with their own community; and that of the evil god, or Satan, identified with the Church of Rome which they described in such terms as 'the mother of fornication', 'Babylon the Great', 'sanctuary of the devil', 'synagogue of Satan'. In keeping with the Manichaean doctrine of matter as evil, their Christology was docetic, and the ceremonies which they substituted for the Catholic sacraments were given a purely spiritual interpretation. There were two classes of adherents, the 'perfect', from whom their ministers were chosen, and 'believers' who were regarded as not yet capable of perfection. A rigid asceticism was demanded. Marriage was forbidden to the 'perfect'; all were required to refrain from eating flesh, cheese, milk, and eggs. The taking of oaths was forbidden. The requiring of oaths and the application of sanctions against the nonconformists by secular powers were regarded as wicked. The endurance of suffering and persecution even to death was demanded.

The Albigensians drew numerous converts from those who were affronted by the wealth and laxity of the Church and were attracted and challenged by the demand for 'spiritual' perfection. The majority were peasants who cannot have understood that the basic dualism of the Albigensian teaching undermined the foundations of Christian faith. The papacy, however, saw clearly that here was heresy; and heretics must be made to recant or be extirpated. Pope Innocent III first tried to convert them by missions, but in 1209 launched a crusade against them under the leadership of Simon IV de Montfort. The conflict was lengthy and had disastrous and long-lasting results for the economy of a large area of southern France. Pope Gregory IX (1227–41) set up a tribunal (the Inquisition) under the Dominican friars with wide powers to root out the heretics, and by the middle of the thirteenth century the task was completed. This ruthless harrying of misguided peasants is one of the greatest blots in the history of the medieval Church.

THE WALDENSIANS

Simultaneously with the rise of the Albigensians another protest movement developed. The Waldensians took their name from Peter Waldo (*c.* 1140–1217), a wealthy merchant of Lyons who relinquished his riches and gave himself to a life of preaching in 1173. Waldo and his followers in their early days accepted Catholic doctrine and order, and believed themselves to be loyal members of the Church. They renounced worldly goods and preached a gospel of poverty. Waldo called his disciples 'the Poor Ones of Lyons'. Catholic opposition, however, was aroused by their preaching without ecclesiastical licence and their use of unauthorized vernacular translations of the Scriptures. Their asceticism linked them in Catholic minds with the Cathari, with whom they were often confused, despite the documented fact that the Waldensians regarded the Cathari as Manichaean heretics. They received the same treatment as the Albigensians. Eighty were burned at the stake in Strasbourg. The survivors began to scatter to other parts, and also to move to an independent position in ecclesiology and sacramental doctrine which anticipated the sixteenth-century reformers. A Waldensian catechism of disputed date[2] has these questions and answers on the Church:

Q. Do you believe in the holy Church?
A. No, for it is a creature, but I believe that it exists.
Q. What do you believe regarding the holy Church?
A. I say that the Church must be thought of in two ways; one in terms of its substance or nature, the other in terms of the ministry. As for its sub-

> stance, the holy Catholic Church is made up of all God's elect, from the beginning to the end who have, according to the grace of God by the merits of Christ, been gathered together by the Holy Spirit and previously ordained to eternal life, their number and names being known only to the one having chosen them. . . . But the Church with regard to the ministry comprises the ministers of Christ with the people submitted to them, profiting from the ministry of faith, hope, and charity.[3]

Here is the idea of the invisible Church of the elect who are known only to God. Yet the Church as a visible institution is not rejected as a mere human contrivance. Faithful ministry within the institution builds people up in faith, hope, and charity. Preaching, sacraments, and prayer help to deepen the Communion of Saints. The Waldensian communities appointed their own ministers, of whom an exemplary life was required. Their duties were to preach the gospel and to administer properly the sacraments of baptism and the eucharist. The improper administration of the sacraments is described as

> . . . when the priests do not understand the mind of Christ and, not knowing his purpose in the sacraments, say that grace and truth are bound up with external ceremonies alone, thus leading men to receive these same sacraments without the truth of faith, hope, and charity (ibid.).

Although this catechism is to be dated later than originally thought, there is no doubt that the early Waldensians protested against the idea of the mechanical operation of the sacraments which was popularly held in the medieval Church. Their prohibition of anything in Christian worship, discipline, and life which was not enjoined in the Scriptures was a protest against the multiplication of ecclesiastical observances, ceremonies, and devotions in the medieval Church.

In the sixteenth century there were Waldensian communities in north-west Italy and the neighbouring parts of France. Friendly contacts were made with Reformation leaders. In recent years the Waldensians in Italy have increased in numbers, and have become active in missionary work.

ROBERT GROSSETESTE, BISHOP OF LINCOLN, *c.* 1175–1253

There were also individual clerics (and we have noted that Bernard of Clairvaux was among them) who, while remaining loyal to the papacy, could also be outspoken in their criticism. Such was the forthright Robert Grosseteste, Bishop of Lincoln (1235–53), during the pontificates of Gregory IX and Innocent IV. From the beginning of his episcopate he vigorously undertook the reformation of his own diocese, the largest in England. To the consternation of the lax he travelled round the archdeaconries and rural deaneries, calling the clergy together to meet him. He initiated a programme of evangelism through the agency of the Franciscans. He defined the duties of archdeacons and rural deans, arranged for the periodic visitation of monasteries and parish churches and provided an exhaustive question-naire for use on these occasions. He was not a man who laid himself open to the criticism he levelled against others.

In a memorandum[4] he wrote of the evils of the times, widespread unbelief, the state of schism in the Church, the prevalence of heresy and vice. Avaricious and immoral clergy have, he admits, a good deal to do with this. But, although he declares he fears to say it, the primary cause is in the papacy. The occupant of the holy see is peculiarly the representative and vicar of Christ, pledged to work for the coming of the Kingdom of God; yet the Roman court does little to combat the evils.

Grosseteste particularly attacked papal 'dispensations', by which acts or states of life were permitted which were strictly against canon law, and papal 'provisions', by which the pope or his legates secured, over the head of legitimate patrons and bishops, benefices for their own nominees. These were usually foreigners who had little sense of the pastoral needs of their flocks. As often as not, these 'provided' rectors were absentees who secured a priest to perform the minimal duties for a pittance. But it is not enough to provide a priest to ad-minister the sacraments and to recite the daily offices—and even these things, he says, are rarely done by these 'mercenaries'. Pastoral care consists also of teaching the truth of God, rebuking vice and punishing it when necessary, things which absentee rectors cannot, and their ill-paid deputies dare not do. Pastoral care includes also ministering to the hungry, clothing the naked, giving hospitality, visiting the sick and prisoners, things again which absentee incumbents cannot do and poorly paid 'hirelings' have not the resources to do. Grosseteste clear-ly sees the papal practice of 'provision' as the direct cause of the deterioration in the life of many parishes. He goes on:

Those who preside in this see (of Rome) are in a special degree the representatives of Christ, and to that extent are entitled to be obeyed in all things. If, however, through favouritism or on other grounds they command what is opposed to the precepts and will of Christ, they separate themselves from Christ and from the conception of what a Pope should be, they are guilty of apostasy themselves and a cause of apostasy in others. God forbid that such should be the case in this see! Let its occupants, therefore, take heed lest they do or enjoin anything which is at variance with the will of Christ.

These are strong words. Whether or not the memorandum from which they are quoted ever came to the notice of the Pope, it was made clear in Rome that Grosseteste had strong opinions about what a pope might do in 1253 when he refused Innocent IV's demand that a canonry in Lincoln cathedral be given to his nephew.

JOHN OF PARIS, b. 1240–64(?), d. 1306

During the latter part of the thirteenth century and in the fourteenth, criticism of the papal view of the Church, and especially the claim to all-inclusive temporal power, grew steadily.

John of Paris, a Dominican friar, in his *On the Power of Kings and Popes*[5] argues that while the spiritual or priestly power excels the temporal or kingly power in that it is directed towards man's ultimate end, it is not greater in all respects. The temporal power is not derived from the spiritual. Each is derived from a higher power, the divine. Temporal power, therefore, has its own autonomous sphere, namely in temporal affairs. Even so, since the spiritual power is greater than the temporal, it must be conceded that in an absolute sense the priest is greater than the prince.

In his definition of the spiritual power, John of Paris anticipates the later conciliarists. Authority in the Church is derived from God and rests in the whole Church, the body of Christ. The authority of bishops and pope, while it comes from God, comes also indirectly from the Church, through its electing and consecrating representatives. The pope, then, is not an absolute monarch, but essentially 'servant of the servants of God', a title which Pope Gregory VII had used. Christ is the head of the Church; the pope may only be so described in the sense that he is the first among its ministers. The faith, moreover, is the faith of the Church, and the pope cannot define it without a general council. A general council represents the authority of the Church more fully, and its convoking is necessary in the event of papal heresy of maladministration. The possibility of the deposition of a pope is envisaged.

MEISTER JOHN ECKHART, *c.* 1260–1327

The teachings of John Eckhart,[6] known as the *Meister* (Master), a German Dominican, imply a different kind of criticism of the highly institutionalized Church of the later Middle Ages. Eckhart ardently desired for himself and his readers and hearers a consciousness of the presence of God and union with him. This is not an end to be attained necessarily by living as a hermit or monk, or by busying oneself with ecclesiastical practices and devotions. It is a question rather of an inward poverty and solitude. Man's only part is to attain a state of sheer nothingness. This opens the soul to God, and God then fills it as he wills. When this happens a man knows God everywhere, in the streets as much as in church or in a monastic cell; he has learned to penetrate things where they are and find God, for God is everywhere.

Out of their context some of Eckhart's words suggest that the outward practice of religion lacks all value. So he was understood by many, and this was among the reasons for the condemnation of his teaching, shortly after his death, by Pope John XXII (1329). He seemed to be undermining the Church as a papal and hierarchical institution by inculcating an individual search for God in the ordinary walks of life.

DANTE ALIGHIERI, 1265–1321

In his *De Monarchia*, written probably between 1309 and 1317, Dante takes up the arguments of John of Paris, sharpening them on his sense of outrage at ecclesiastical politics of which he had first-hand experience during his early political life in Florence. He was appalled that the papal powers were so often used to promote the careers and fortunes of members of the pope's family.

Dante declares that papal and imperial power are each derived immediately from God, the one that men may be led to eternal life, the other that men may be led to the temporal beatitude which can minister to spiritual welfare. Emperors and kings do not hold their authority from the pope. They have their own responsible sphere in the temporal which they are charged to administer for the spiritual blessedness of their subjects. He grants that the pope's spiritual authority does extend over much of man's temporal life, since mortal felicity is to be subordinated to immortal felicity. There is a sense, then, in which the Roman prince is subject to the Roman pontiff, and Caesar should pay to Peter the reverence due from a son to a father. But what is most needed is the collaboration of the spiritual and temporal powers, and in this lies the hope of human peace and happiness which Dante so greatly desired.

Dante always remained a loyal and orthodox Christian, but he ceased to trust the leadership of popes. In the *Divina Commedia* Boniface VIII, together with his predecessor and successor are placed in the *inferno* among those guilty of simony: 'You have made a god of gold and silver for yourselves: wherein do you differ from the idolater?'

MARSILIUS OF PADUA, *c*. 1275–1342

Far more radical is Marsilius of Padua, who in his *Defensor Fidei* ('The Defender of the Faith')[7] presents a scheme which may fairly be described as a thoroughgoing Erastianism.[8] The book ends with forty-two 'Conclusions',[9] which may be summarized as follows.

There can be only one supreme ruling authority in a state. This is the 'legislator', that is the whole body of citizens, its majority, or the prince who rules by its expressed will. The legislator (the whole body or the elected prince) has jurisdiction over all individuals and groups, lay and clerical, and over their possessions within the state. The legislator, as defined (who is assumed to be a Christian), alone has power to determine the number of churches, and of the clergy to serve them; to control the qualifications for ordination and to promote to orders; to remove from ecclesiastical office; to use ecclesiastical property after the needs of the clergy, the poor, and the expenses of divine worship have been met; to permit or forbid the establishment of religious Orders and houses; to condemn and punish heretics; to permit marriages forbidden by 'human law' (but not those forbidden by the New Testament); to legitimatize children of an illegitimate union; to release from oaths. Excommunication must be authorized by the legislator. He alone can confer or take away 'separable'[10] ecclesiastical offices including those of bishop and archbishop. And only the legislator may convoke a general or local council.

Within the Church a general council is the supreme authority, as representing the whole body of faithful people. It consists of bishops, priests, and laymen and, he says elsewhere, must include those learned in divine law. They are to be chosen from each state, and the legislator has the chief voice in their appointment with coercive power over reluctant appointees. The primary function of a general council is to define ambiguous passages in the Scriptures and decide what articles of faith are necessary to salvation: 'No partial council or single person of any position has the authority to decide these questions.' Its other functions include arrangements of divine worship, the creation of metropolitan churches and bishops, the canonization of saints, the making of disciplinary rules, for example about the marriage of clergy, and dispensation from them. He adds that the council or the legislator alone may prohibit practices, trades, or teachings which divine law permits.

There are some ambiguities here which make it difficult to understand Marsilius' conception of the relation between the 'legislator' and the general council in all respects. For instance, Conclusion 42 gives to the general council alone the power to create a metropolitan bishop; by his definition, this is a 'separable' ecclesiastical office to be 'conferred or taken away only by the authority of the "legislator" ', according to Conclusion 23. Nevertheless the general picture is of a very definite subordination of the spiritual to the temporal power.

The Church, for Marsilius, is the totality of the faithful who believe and call upon the name of Christ. Bishops and priests are essentially equal; differences between them are by the appointment of temporal rulers. He denies the primacy of the papacy:

> All bishops derive their authority in equal measure immediately from Christ, and it cannot be proved from the divine law that one bishop should be over or under another, in temporal or spiritual matters.
>
> The other bishops, singly or in a body, have the same right by divine authority to excommunicate or otherwise exercise authority over the bishop of Rome, having obtained the consent of the 'legislator', as the bishop of Rome has to excommunicate or control them.[11]

It is not surprising that a number of propositions from his teaching were condemned by Pope John XXII (1327) and that Marsilius was declared heretical.

WILLIAM OF OCKHAM, *c.* 1290–1349

Marsilius' younger contemporary, the English Franciscan William of

Ockham, was equally critical of the Church of his day. Martin Luther was frequently to declare his indebtedness to him. Ockham defines the Church as the congregation or community of the faithful: 'the whole congregation of the faithful living at the same time in this mortal life'.[12] The idea of the mystical body plays little part in his ecclesiology. He lays great stress on faith as constitutive of the Church. The Church is essentially a community of 'true and real persons'[13] who profess one faith. Yves Congar writes:[14]

> The great concern of Ockham is to defend the liberty of persons. In this are brought into play at the same time his English outlook with its emphasis on the individual, his philosophy of the concrete individual subject (i.e. nominalism) and finally his Franciscan evangelism which expresses itself in an original affirmation of the liberty of the gospel: 'the liberty of the law of the gospel'. As few rules as possible! It is the first time that a theologian of stature applies this great concept effectively to ecclesiology. Christians are no longer under the old law. There is here, in Ockham, a positive Christian element which is very remarkable. He is an initiator of a new world. ... He had inaugurated for the believer, in place of a world of natures, institutions, and laws, a world of persons and of liberty in the faith.

Ockham's *On the Authority of Emperors and Popes*[15] is his main work in criticism of the papal claims. Christ, he argues, gave no plenitude of power to Peter in temporal matters. Luke 22.25 ('The kings of the Gentiles exercise lordship. ... But not so with you.') and its parallels prove this. Nor did he give plenitude of power in spiritual matters, for this must have included power to impose heavier burdens than those of the old law, which Peter himself said 'neither our fathers nor we have been able to bear' (Acts 15.10). Such a plenitude of power would be contrary to 'the liberty of the law of the gospel'. Consequently neither Peter nor his successors possessed plenitude of power, temporal or spiritual. In particular, for the pope to intervene in temporal affairs is 'to put his sickle into another's harvest'.[16]

In his *Dialogue* Ockham discusses whether a pope who is heretical may be deposed, and if so how. The rule that a general council may not be called without the authority of the pope is normally to be observed. But it is to be interpreted 'sensibly'. A general council may be necessary at a time when it either will not or cannot be called by the pope, namely when the pope is heretical, and when during a vacancy the cardinals have failed to elect. He goes into some detail about the composition of a general council. His suggestion is that representatives be sent from parishes or local communities either to an episcopal council or to the parliament of a secular power, which should then elect its representatives to the general council. Thus the whole of Christendom would be represented.

Ockham was excommunicated by Pope John XXII in 1328, but sought reconciliation towards the end of his life.

JOHN WYCLIF, *c.* 1328–84

Equally radical was the criticism of the papal conception of the Church of John Wyclif, a secular priest,[17] the pioneer of translation of the Scriptures into English. He spent most of his life at Oxford, first as student, and then as lecturer, engaging fully in the theological debates which were a feature of university life in the later medieval period. He was very influential at the University of Oxford, whose authorities tried to protect him when, towards the end of his life, certain theses from his writings were condemned by a synod at Blackfriars, London. He had a powerful supporter in John of Gaunt, the heir apparent to the throne, who saw in Wyclif's teachings a strong weapon against the Avignon popes, and justification of the removal of obstreperous clerics. John of Gaunt presented him to the rectory of Lutterworth where he spent his last years.

Wyclif produced the works which made him famous[18] in the last eight or nine years of his life. It was a time when the proponents of the papal idea of the Church were greatly embarrassed by events. Gregory XI had restored the papal court to Rome from Avignon. His death in 1378 signalled the beginning of the 'Great Schism' which was to last for decades. Gregory's successor, Urban VI, within a few months alienated the cardinals, and the French members of that body declared his election invalid and set up an anti-pope at Avignon.

TRUE LORDSHIP

Central to Wyclif's ecclesiology is the doctrine of 'true lordship'. This depends, not on any right received from an overlord, temporal or spiritual, but is held from God and belongs to those who keep God's law and receive and live by his grace. Lordship over persons and property is forfeited by those who break God's law. In the contemporary Church, Wyclif held, there was no true lordship, and confiscation of church property was justifiable. It was in this kind of teaching that John of Gaunt saw interesting possibilities. Opponents were not slow to attack Wyclif as an anarchist. He would not have agreed that the application of his doctrine of the 'dominion of grace' would produce anarchy. While the temporal *dominium* of the papacy and the hierarchy ought to be abandoned, the authority of the Bible would replace it. The way would be opened for a return to the simple organization and the poverty of the early Church. The magnificence of the papal court and the wealth of cardinals, bishops, and abbots were in scandalous contrast with the Christianity of the New Testament. It was a 'religion of fat cows'. The pope's claim to be the vicar of Christ was to be measured by his imitation of Christ who thrust away worldly lordship.

THE INVISIBLE CHURCH

Wyclif's ecclesiology draws much from Augustine, especially the idea of the invisible Church as the whole body of the predestined. Unlike Augustine, however, he makes a definite identification of the mystical body of Christ with the invisible Church of the elect: 'The Church is truly called the mystical body of Christ because, by the eternal words of predestination, it is joined with Christ its spouse.'[19] This Church is to be distinguished from the Church of 'prelates and priests'. Wyclif, therefore, offers an entirely new interpretation of the mystical body.

THE CHURCH TRIUMPHANT, EXPECTANT, AND MILITANT

In his *On the Church and Its Members* he shows something of a conservative strain, reproducing the accepted threefold partition of the Church as triumphant, expectant, and militant.[20] The first part consists of angels and saints in the bliss of heaven, the second of those who are purging their sins in purgatory (to pray for whom is, however, a cause of many errors), and the third is that of good Christians who will be among the saved. These are they who are 'of the Church'. Others, sinners not predestined to salvation, may be 'in the Church'. In the Church militant we do not know whether we are members of 'holy Church', although the strength of a man's hope may give him grounds for supposing that he is. Thus Wyclif is able to accept the idea of the Church on earth as a mixed society of good and bad, and a great deal of his writing is aimed at its purification and reformation. In such passages it is clear that he does not entirely sweep aside the 'Church of prelates and priests'; but he would have the clergy realize that their office is a ministry, not a lordship.

On the other hand, there is also much to suggest that he did think of the 'Church of prelates and priests' as an altogether different Church from the mystical body. He constantly draws a strong contrast between God's law and canon law; he expresses the opinion that it was the failure of priests which led to the foundation of monasteries, the covetousness of monks which occasioned the rise of the semi-monastic canons, and the laxity of these which made way for the coming of the friars, whose existence in the Church, he suggests, has no divine sanction; and he designates the pope as 'Antichrist' and the 'head vicar of the fiend'. A picture of an anti-church is cumulatively built up. Yet, despite the fulminations, the impression is given that Wyclif would willingly recognize any pope, prelate, priest, monk, or friar who truly exercised the lordship of grace as a sound member of the Church militant. The truth is, as Professor Geddes Macgregor suggests,[21] that Wyclif's ecclesiology is not fully worked out, and leaves some untidy ends.

CHRIST THE HEAD OF THE CHURCH

On one thing Wyclif makes himself perfectly clear. He constantly insists that Christ is the only Head of the Church. Here he applies the Chalcedonian doctrine of the two natures of the one Person of Christ in a novel and over-subtle way. In his *On the Church* he argues that the Church cannot have two heads like a monster. Nevertheless there is a mysterious sense in which it does have two heads. For Christ has two natures. In virtue of his divine nature he has what Wyclif calls 'extrinsic headship' over all men and things, and therefore over the Church and its members. In virtue of the human nature which Christ assumed for man's salvation he has headship over the Church in a second way which is *intrinsic* to the Church, a way in which he forms a living body with his members, continually present with and activating them. Thus the two natures of Christ may be said to give him a twofold headship over the Church, although in view of the unity of his Person there is but one head, the one Christ. This is a forceful expression of the idea of the Church as the mystical body founded in the humanity of the incarnate Christ.[22] It must not be forgotten, however, that for Wyclif the mystical body is the invisible Church of the elect, known to God alone.

Later in *On the Church*,[23] and also in *On the Office of the King*,[24] Wyclif draws another conclusion from the doctrine of the two natures of Christ. Since by his divine nature Christ has headship over all men and things, the authority of secular rulers answers to the divine nature. The authority of the Church corresponds to the human nature. The king is the vicar of Christ's divinity; and since divinity is more glorious and powerful than humanity, the conclusion that the king has supreme authority within his state in much the way that Marsilius of Padua conceived the authority of the 'legislator' can hardly be avoided.

Some of Wyclif's propositions were condemned by Pope Gregory XI in 1377, and by a synod at Blackfriars in 1382, but Wyclif was not excommunicated.

JOHN HUS, *c.* 1369–1415

Wyclif's doctrines were to prove a greater threat to the papacy in Bohemia than in England. There were good communications between the two countries, and especially between the universities of Oxford and Prague. John Hus, a priest and member of the University of Prague, of which he was chancellor in 1409, and other academics, themselves engaged in an attack on the corruption of the Church, adopted much of Wyclif's teaching. Hus translated Wyclif's *Trialogus* into Czech, and incorporated much of Wyclif's material into his own *De Ecclesia*. Professor Matthew Spinka has shown[25] that Hus was by no means Wyclif's slavish imitator, but his ecclesiology was undoubtedly greatly indebted to the English reformer, and we shall not consider it separately here.

The reforming movement in Bohemia coincided with the rise of national spirit among the Czechs. Hus was a leader both in the nationalist and in the reforming movement. He preached and wrote against the corruption of the clergy, and the simoniacal practices of the papacy. He advocated the restoration of the chalice to the laity and a vernacular liturgy. The Archbishop of Prague secured from the pope an order to destroy Wycliffite books in 1410, and the excommunication of Hus in 1411. But Hussite teaching continued to gain acceptance and the movement spread rapidly. When the Council of Constance gathered late in 1414, both anti-papalists like Gerson and d'Ailly,[26] and conservatives, were determined to stamp it out. Hus was summoned before the Council, being promised safe conduct by the Emperor Sigismund. Hus, who had expected a theological debate on his views, was, however, arrested. He was tried, condemned as a heretic, and handed over to the secular authorities for burning. The Council now condemned 267 propositions in Wyclif's works, ordered all copies to be burned, and his body to be removed from consecrated ground.

THE CONCILIARISTS

Mention of the Council of Constance necessitates some account of the 'conciliarists'. Several writers already mentioned in this chapter present the idea that authority in the Church is given to the congregation, or whole body, of the faithful (*congregatio*, or *universitas fidelium*), and that this authority can be expressed through a general council. The medieval Church never entirely lost sight of this concept of authority in the Church. Even the 'decretists', the lawyers who worked upon the body of canon law, and did so mainly in the interests of papal authority, did not reject the concept of the Church as the *universitas fidelium*. The idea persisted in the canon law itself, alongside the idea of the Church as a hierarchical body of clerics with the pope as its head. One of the decretists, Huguccio, Bishop of Pisa, in his *Summa* (c. 1190) asserted that it was to the Church in the sense of *universitas fidelium* that preservation from error was promised. The decretists discussed such questions as the relation of the pope to a general council and the necessary procedures if a pope fell into heresy, which Gratian in his *Decretum* (c. 1150) maintained was possible. But these were as yet hypothetical questions, learnedly discussed with a view to reconciling discrepancies in the rapidly increasing *corpus* of canon law.[27]

The state of the Church during the Avignon papacy and the subsequent 'Great Schism' led to an open demand for a general council. The term 'conciliarists' denotes the canonists and others who worked for this end during the latter part of the fourteenth century and in the early fifteenth. Among the most influential were Conrad of Gelnhausen (c. 1320–90), Henry of Langenstein (1340–97), Francis Zabarella (1360–1417), Dietrich of Niem (c. 1340–1418), Pierre d'Ailly (1350–1420), Jean Gerson (1363–1429), Nicholas of Clémanges (1367–1437) and Nicholas of Cusa (c. 1400–1464).

These men approached the question of authority in the Church from different angles, 'so that there is no body of conciliarist doctrine that might be set down as common to them all'.[28] But they agreed that a distinction, which in no way necessarily diminishes the *proper* authority of the papacy, must be drawn between the Church as *congregatio fidelium* and the Church understood as personified in the pope who possesses *all* the authority of the Church and exercises it through the papal curia.

They argue that authority resides in the whole body of the faithful. For the most part they do not dispute that it may be given to one man, the pope, but they hold that if so given it is not irrevocably given. If it is abused it can be withdrawn. There are occasions (and they include papal heresy and a disputed papacy) when the *congregatio fidelium* must resume the exercise of its inherent authority. This was to be done through a general council, and some argued that such a council possessed an authority superior to that of a pope, being more broadly representative of the Church than a single person.

PIERRE D'AILLY (1350–1420)

The notion that the body of the Church has the authority to take action on behalf of its unity and welfare through a general council without convocation by a pope can be well illustrated by summarizing the principles drawn up by Pierre d'Ailly shortly before the Council of Pisa in 1409. The document is known as *Propositiones Utiles*, from its first words: 'Useful propositions for ending the present schism by a general council'.[29]

Because 'Christ is the head of the Church' and 'we are all one body in Christ', the unity of the mystical body of the Church depends completely on the unity of Christ. The pope may 'in a certain way' be called head of the Church, but its unity does not depend on or originate from him. It remains even when there is no pope. The Church has its authority immediately from Christ, and with it the power to assemble, or to call a general council to represent it, especially to protect its unity. Christ promised his presence where two or three are gathered in his name, not in the name of Peter or the pope. This power of the Church is supported also by natural law, because every natural body summons up all its members and powers to resist partition.

D'Ailly notes that James and not Peter presided at the Council of Jerusalem (Acts 15.13). Canon law had restricted the calling of councils to the pope, partly to honour the apostolic see, and partly to prevent heretics and schismatics from persuading secular rulers to convoke councils in support of their errors. But positive laws cannot completely remove from the Church what belongs to it by divine and natural laws. The positive law of those canons which give the pope authority to convoke councils was introduced for the good of the Church; but there are circumstances in which this law can harm the Church, namely the occurrence of heresy or persecution during a papal vacancy, if there should be a mad or heretical pope, and (as in 1409) if there should be rival popes.

The canon law on this point must, therefore, be interpreted sensibly (*civiliter*, literally, in a civilized manner).[30] The document finally asserts that the present crisis of the Church justifies the calling of a council without the pope's authority, either by the cardinals or by any faithful Christian who is influential enough to secure it.

THE COUNCILS OF THE FIFTEENTH CENTURY

What the conciliarists had worked for came to pass with the convoking of the Council of Pisa in 1409, the first of a series held during the next forty years. The details of their successes and failures do not concern us here. Hopes were considerably higher than achievement. At the conclusion of the Council of Pisa there were three instead of two rival claimants to the papacy, and not until 1449 could it be said that there was an undisputed bishop of Rome. The 'Great Schism' was, however, formally brought to a close by the Council of Constance (1414–18), which received the resignation of one of the three claimants to the papacy, deposed the others, and elected Martin V. Hopes for the healing of the schism between Constantinople and Rome mounted during the Council of Florence (1438–45),[31] but came to nothing.[32]

Special mention must be made of the Council of Constance of which d'Ailly and Gerson were influential members. On its legitimacy and that of its procedure in the matter of the three claimants to the see of Rome, Hans Küng says that 'the legitimacy of Martin V (1417–31) and all other subsequent popes up to the present day depends'.[33] Its decree *Sacrosancta* (1415) declared that the Council was legitimately convoked, represented the Church militant, and held its authority directly from Christ. The decree *Frequens* gave directions about the frequency of future councils: the first should be held five years from the conclusion of Constance, another seven years after the close of the first, and 'for ever thereafter one shall be held every ten years'. The decree *Sacrosancta* declares:

This holy synod of Constance, being a general council, and legally assembled in the Holy Spirit for the praise of God and for the ending of the present schism, and for the union and reformation of the Church of God ... ordains, declares, and decrees as follows: And first it declares that this synod, legally assembled, represents the Catholic Church militant and has its authority direct from Christ; and everybody, of whatever rank or dignity, including also the pope, is bound to obey this council in those things which pertain to the faith, to the ending of this schism, and to a general reformation of the Church in its head and members. Likewise it declares that if anyone ... including also the pope, shall refuse to obey the commands ... of this holy council, or of any other holy council properly assembled, in regard to the ending of the schism and to the reformation of the Church, he shall be subject to the proper punishment.[34]

JOHANNES DE TURRECREMATA, 1388–1468

Despite this affirmation of the conciliar idea of the Church, the papal curia worked so successfully for the restoration of the papal authority that by 1460, Pope Pius II could venture to publish the Bull *Execrabilis* which forbade an appeal from the pope to a general council. By this time the papacy had entered into the period of the so-called Renaissance popes, some of whom were more concerned for their literary style than for the welfare of the Church, and the days were closing in towards the more radical and activist protest which was the sixteenth-century reformation. At this point we must take note of a book written in support of the papal idea of the Church in the light of the conciliar activity of the early fifteenth century.

This was the *Summa de Ecclesia* of Cardinal Johannes de Turrecremata (or Juan de Torquemada), a Spanish Dominican, published posthumously in 1489. Early in the work he examines the word *ecclesia*, discovering in it fifteen meanings. The Church is the *congregatio fidelium* considered as a whole, or as gathered for public worship, or meeting in a house for prayer. *Ecclesia* may also mean the local church, the elect, the clergy, or hierarchy. Geddes Macgregor makes the comment[35] that Turrecremata does not explain how these meanings are related to each other: 'He treats them as aspects of the same thing. He finds himself able to consider the aspect of the Church as the company of Christ's faithful side by side with the aspect of the Church as the hierarchically organized institution whose head is the Pope.' The idea of the Church as the *congregatio fidelium* is, however, well to the fore in Turrecremata's ecclesiology, and this is another reminder that the sixteenth-century reformers in using it were not reintroducing an ecclesiology which had been entirely neglected in the medieval period. We have already met it in the conciliarists, in Thomas Aquinas, and even in the twelfth-century decretists. These, however, had seen it as providing one important insight, amongst others, into the nature of the Church. The reformers were to use it much more exclusively as a definition of the Church.

Christ is the efficient cause of the Church and its unifying principle. The Christian must put his faith in Christ, not in the apostles or the Church; nevertheless the Church is Christ's and there is no salvation outside it.[36] Turrecremata's treatment of the Church as the mystical body[37] is Augustinian. Christ unites the faithful to himself by the indwelling of the Holy Spirit and in unity of will. Turrecremata follows Augustine in other respects: his treatment of the four credal notes of the Church; his use of the image of the net to explain why the Church on earth is a society which contains both bad and good; and his argument that Abel was the first member of the Church.[38] He rejects the view of a contemporary (Augustin Favaroni) that Christ became Head of his body, the Church, only by the incarnation.

Turrecremata is in no doubt that the hierarchical structure of the Church is divinely ordained. The distinctions between clergy and laity, and between bishop, priest, and deacon are biblically rooted and intended by Christ. So also was the papacy, which is one of the strongest bonds of the Church's unity. It distinguishes the Church from separated gatherings of heretics and schismatics.[39] Books II and III of the *Summa de Ecclesia* deal with the papacy and councils. The pope is head of the Church not merely in the sense that authority is vested in him by the body of the Church as a whole. He is the vicar of Christ whose power comes immediately from Christ. In this he is the successor of Peter who alone was made a bishop immediately by Christ.[40] The following passage reveals the argument:

> When Peter is said to have received power for all, and more than all, we must not understand that he received it in the way a single agent may receive some gift in the name of certain others . . . but in the way that we say the sun received light from God more than all the stars and for them all. 'More than all', because in greater plenitude than the other stars. 'For them all', because it was so that light might fall upon the rest of the stars from the sun as from a fountain. . . .[41] So it is with Peter who was not merely endowed with authority more than all others, but was made head and the ruler whose influence extends to all others in the body of the Church (*Summa de Ecclesia* II, 22).

Consequently, all jurisdiction within the Church is derived from the pope.[42]

Yet, as Hans Küng points out, Turrecremata was 'in no way espoused to a papal absolutism in everything'.[43] He admits the possibility of an heretical or schismatic pope, and the necessity of a general council in such cases. With regard to heresy he declares that 'by heresy a pope ceases to be pope'.[44] The rock on which the Church is built is faith in Christ,[45] and one who falls away from the faith ceases to be a member of the Church, and cannot be its head. This being so, the council does not depose the pope; rather it declares that he is judged by God not to be pope. On the possibility of a schismatic pope, he says that schism is not only to be understood as separation from the pope. Basically it is separation from Christ, and it is possible for a pope, although he is Christ's representative, to separate himself from Christ by disobedience. In such a case, too, it must not be thought that the council causes the pope to lose office. The judgement of God upon an unfaithful pope causes this; the council declares it and makes it effective. This interpretation of the function of a general council in relationship to an offending pope (which is supported by present-day Roman Catholic canonists)[46] rebuts the claim of the more radical conciliarists that a general council is superior to the pope.

Aside from the situations described above, Turrecremata assigns to the council a definitely subordinate role. It is little more than an advisory body. The pope must consult with men of wisdom, by whom he undoubtedly means the cardinals, on matters of divine law, and it will be sufficient if he has such men at hand in Rome.[47] He does, however, say that in a matter of faith which has not yet been defined the opinion of a general council is to be preferred to that of the pope.[48]

For Turrecremata, therefore, the institutional Church as it existed in the mid-fifteenth century was a development in accordance with the will of God. He recognizes that there may be abuse of power within it, as his discussion of the possibility of an unfaithful pope reveals, but he is strangely silent about many of the matters which not only radical protesters like Wyclif and Hus, but also moderate conciliarists had regarded as abuses. His *Summa de Ecclesia* is important for two reasons in particular. First, it was from this that all subsequent defenders of papal primacy, including Bellarmine, up to the First Vatican Council (1870), drew their arguments. Second, it sets out clearly, close to the beginning of the Reformation, the papal idea of the Church which a large part of Europe was emphatically to reject.

11

Ecclesia in Eastern Orthodoxy

Relations between East and West

Relations between the Church in western and eastern Europe worsened slowly throughout the medieval period. It is not our object to tell the story of this deterioration, but reference to some of the events must be made since they help towards an understanding of the different emphases in ecclesiology.[1]

By the year 700 the expansion of Islam had overtaken the territories of the patriarchs of Alexandria, Antioch, and Jerusalem. Those patriarchates survived, but with little communication with the Church elsewhere. Of the four eastern patriarchates Constantinople alone, the most recent of them, now had any effective voice in the affairs of the Church. Constantinople had no desire to challenge the primacy of the see of Rome, but steadily resisted western attempts to translate primacy into a supremacy over the whole Church. On this issue Constantinople firmly took its stand on those canons of the early general councils which dealt with ecclesiastical jurisdiction.[2] These councils allowed a primacy of honour to the see of Rome. They ratified a certain jurisdiction of the bishop of Rome over other ecclesiastical dioceses in the West, but they did the same for Constantinople, and indeed for Alexandria and Antioch in the East. There was nothing here to justify Rome's claim to jurisdiction over the whole Church.

In the seventh and eighth centuries, despite tensions both of a political and an ecclesiastical nature, there was no question of a split between Eastern and Western Christendom. Indeed there were many expressions of unity and good will. Greek Christian refugees from the Islamic invasions were received hospitably in Rome; papal legates were sent to councils in the East; the Pope himself visited Constantinople in 710. Patriarchs of Constantinople called on the support of Rome against the encroachments of Byzantine emperors into the sphere of doctrine, especially during the long-drawn-out iconoclastic controversy. Iconoclasm (Greek *eikon*, image or picture; *klasma*, smashing), became imperial policy under the Emperor Leo III who in 726 issued an edict for the destruction of icons in all churches. He deposed and replaced Germanus, Patriarch of Constantinople, who resisted the order. Iconoclasm made considerable headway in the East. A council at Hieria (attended neither by the Pope nor by any eastern patriarch) condemned the cult of the icons in 754. In the West a strong resistance was maintained. Pope Gregory III condemned iconoclasm at two synods held at Rome in 731 and excommunicated all iconoclasts. The first phase of the controversy ended in 787 after the death of Leo III's grandson. His orthodox widow, Irene, made possible the convoking of the second Council of Nicaea (the seventh Ecumenical Council), to which Pope Hadrian I sent delegates. It restored icons to the churches and defined the sense in which veneration might be shown to them. The campaign against icons was renewed in 815 by the Emperor Leo V, but, again under an empress, Theodora, the icons were restored in 842.

For the West, the repercussions of this controversy had political consequences. In retaliation for the opposition of the Pope, the Emperor Leo III annexed the papal lands in southern Italy and Sicily. This, in addition to the fact that for decades the Byzantine emperors' interest in the West had been largely financial and that no assistance was forthcoming from them against the encroachment of the Lombards into Italy, led the popes to look towards the Frankish rulers for an alliance. The coronation of Charlemagne as Emperor of the Romans by Pope Leo III in St Peter's, Rome (800), signalled the fact of a politically divided Europe in which for centuries the 'Emperor of the Romans' and western kings and princes were to be engaged in a continual struggle for power, and the Greek (Byzantine) emperor was left to face the still expanding power of Islam.

The ecclesiastical division of Europe still lay in the future. But divisive influences were at work: the difference in language; a growing diversity in ecclesiastical customs; and a mounting contempt, in the West for the effete and dilettante Byzantines, and in the East for the barbarian westerner. Doctrinal difference became an issue over the western addition of 'and the Son' (*filioque*) after the phrase 'the Holy Spirit . . . who proceedeth from the Father' in the Nicene Creed. This unauthorized addition seems to have originated in Spain in the seventh century. Its use spread to France; Charlemagne tried to enforce its universal use. The popes long resisted the innovation, but it was in use in Rome with papal approval by 1030. The Greeks, with good reason, objected to this unilateral insertion into an ecumenical creed. They also objected to the theology of the added phrase. Had an addition been permissible, it should have been 'through the Son'. To say that the Holy Spirit proceeds from the Father *and* the Son implied that there were two sources of being in the godhead. Western theologians denied that it had this intention. But apart from the question of theological adequacy, the Church of the West was not justified in adding to the creed of an ecumenical council.

In the ninth century relations were seriously strained in the pontificate (858–67) of Nicholas I, which occurred during a period when the patriarchate of Constantinople was in dispute between Ignatius and Photius. Nicholas, the most energetic of ninth-century popes in asserting papal supremacy, intervened in the dispute and demanded that the deposed Ignatius and Photius who had replaced him should submit to his arbitration. Photius refused, and was declared deposed by Nicholas at a council held in Rome in 863. Affronted also by western manoeuvring to bring Bulgarian Christians within the jurisdiction of Rome, Photius retaliated in 867 by an encyclical which condemned the Latin intrusion into Bulgaria, denounced the *filioque* clause, and designated those who used it as heretics. In the same year a council at Constantinople declared Nicholas I deposed and excommunicated. A reversal of fortune for Photius and the reinstatement of Ignatius shortly afterwards led to another council at Constantinople in 869 which withdrew the decisions of the previous council. In the West this was reckoned as the eighth ecumenical council. In the East it is usually known as 'the anti-Photian Council'. Photius, however, was restored to the patriarchate on the death of Ignatius in 877. Better relations with Rome were established. Pope John VIII (872–82), much more irenic than Nicholas, recognized Photius as legitimate patriarch of Constantinople. The uneasy peace was not much disturbed during the tenth century which was a period of degeneracy and enfeeblement for the papacy which was in no position to enforce its claims in the East.

It was in the eleventh century at a time which seemed propitious for strengthened relations that the decisive break occurred. The papacy and the Byzantine emperor had a common enemy in the Normans. Pope Leo IX (1048–54) had suffered military defeat at their hands, and they were threatening southern Italy, still part of the Greek emperor's territory. The pope prepared to open negotiations with the

Byzantine emperor. At this time a letter written by the Greek metropolitan of Bulgaria which was highly critical of western ecclesiastical customs, came into the hands of the pope. The papal legates who in 1054 carried Leo IX's proposals for a mutually beneficial alliance to the Greek emperor, also carried letters to the patriarch of Constantinople, Michael Cerularius. They portrayed the Church of Rome as above human judgement, unswervingly orthodox, the Mother whose spouse is God. Constantinople was a disobedient, pleasure-loving, and insolent daughter from whom complete obedience was demanded. The papal point of view was presented in the strongest language. Any nation which disagreed with Rome was 'a confabulation of heretics, a conventicle of schismatics, a synagogue of Satan'.[3] Cardinal Humbert,[4] one of the legates charged with this mission of reconciliation, has been suspected of influencing the language of these letters, if not of composing them himself (Pope Leo IX was a prisoner of the Normans at the time of their dispatch). Further controversy ensued in Constantinople, and the outcome was that the legates placed a Bull on the altar of the Church of St Sophia, excommunicating 'Michael and his followers'. Among the reasons which the document gives for this action is that the Greeks had *omitted* the *filioque* from the creed! The patriarch responded by excommunicating the authors of the 'impious document'. To what extent these excommunications were intended to include the patriarchate of Constantinople and the Church of the West respectively as a whole is a matter of debate. The excommunications were lifted over nine centuries later, simultaneously in Rome and Istanbul in 1965, 'by a courageous act of Christian reconciliation on the part of Pope Paul VI and the Patriarch Athenagoras, who mutually asked each other's forgiveness'.[5]

The breach, however, was not complete. The earlier crusaders were offered and received the sacraments from Orthodox bishops and priests in the countries where they campaigned. There were attempts to effect reconciliation by means of what R. W. Southern[6] calls 'the political package deal'. An example of this in all its simplicity is provided in a letter of Pope Clement IV to the Byzantine Emperor Michael VIII, Palaeologus, in 1267. Its gist is: you attack the Moslems on one side, and the western crusaders will attack them on the other. If you are afraid that the Latins will attack you, 'the answer is simple: return to the unity of the Roman Church and all fears of this kind can be put aside for ever'.[7] Such a fear was not an unnatural one for the Greeks to entertain. In 1204 one of the most disgraceful episodes in ecclesiastical history had occurred when soldiers of the Fourth Crusade attacked Constantinople, sacked the city, and plundered the churches. The 'package deal' was attempted a few years later at the Council of Lyons (1274). The envoys of the Emperor Michael VIII agreed to all the Roman conditions, and reunion was proclaimed. But the Emperor was completely unsuccessful in persuading the clergy and people of Constantinople to accept the agreement, which quickly became a dead letter.

The subsequent century and a half is not without signs of a guilty conscience on the part of Latin Christians for the western share of responsibility for the continuance of the schism. On the Greek side also some appreciation of the value of western theology and respect for Latin concepts of order and discipline were replacing the traditional Greek disdain for the intellectually inferior West. Unhappily the Western Church did not reciprocate with any attempt to understand the theology and life of the Eastern Church. 'This attitude', writes R. W. Southern, 'has run through western history with astonishing consistency.'[8]

We have already noted the demand for a general council which arose in the West at the end of the fourteenth century. Several of the conciliarists, Jean Gerson in particular, and, somewhat later, Nicholas of Cusa, hoped that a general council would end the schism between Rome and Constantinople. The Council of Constance (1414–18) did not reach this subject on its agenda. It had a prominent place on the agenda of the Council of Basle, convoked in 1431. Some years previously the Byzantine Emperor Manuel Palaeologus had appealed to the Pope for help against the Ottoman Turks who were now threatening Constantinople, and received from Pope Martin V in 1422 the now stereotyped reply: military aid was possible only at the price of 'full agreement' with the Church of Rome. Conciliarists like Nicholas of Cusa, however, had the higher and more realistic hope that the unity of Christians might be achieved at a council, representative of Latins, Greeks, and Bohemians (Hussites) in a spirit of dialogue rather than by dictation. But these hopes were to be dashed. Pope Eugenius IV succeeded Martin V, whose views about papal supremacy he fully shared, in 1431, shortly after the Council had begun its work at Basle. He tried unsuccessfully to dissolve it, but nevertheless succeeded in forestalling the desires of the more enlightened canonists and conciliarists. He transferred the Council to Ferrara in 1438 and then to Florence where in 1439 the reunion of

Rome and Constantinople was declared. The size of the Greek delegation had greatly diminished since 1431, and there were few theologians among them. Persuaded by the Byzantine Emperor John VIII to whom assistance against the Turks was all-important, the delegation signed the decree with the single exception of Mark, Metropolitan of Ephesus, whom Professor John Meyendorff describes[9] as the only spokesman for the true Byzantine theology of the time. The decree declared that the *filioque* had been legitimately added to the Nicene Creed, and set forth the papal claims to govern the universal Church although it contained a face-saving clause for the Byzantines: 'without prejudice to the privileges and rights of the patriarchs of the East'.

The agreement at once met with strong opposition from the clergy and people in Constantinople. It was not until December 1452 that it was proclaimed in the church of St Sophia, and then only through the emperor's pressure on a complaisant patriarch. Like the agreement at the Council of Lyons, it became a dead letter almost at once. On 29 May 1453, Constantinople fell to the Turks, the last of the Byzantine emperors having died during the siege. Pope Pius II's offer to the conqueror, Mahomet II, to make him emperor of the Greeks if he would but be baptized, was ignored. Then began the long history of the patriarchate of Constantinople under Turkish rule.

The clear lesson from this melancholy history is that the schisms of the Church are unlikely to be healed under political pressure, or over the heads of the great body of clergy and people.

THE CHURCH IN EASTERN ORTHODOXY

That the ecclesiology of eastern Orthodoxy is treated no earlier than in Chapter 11, may betray my western stance. In the early chapters of this work, however, I was dealing in fact with the ecclesiology of the Church of the East. It is in the Scriptures and in what the ecumenical councils and creeds and the early Fathers have to say about the Church that Orthodoxy finds sufficient material to guide and govern the life of the Church, whose existence it holds to be a mystery. The Church is a mystery, a fact which is given by God. Yves Congar, speaking of ecclesiology in the early medieval period, says:[10]

> There is no more a 'dogma' of the Church in the East than in the West: less indeed, if that is possible. St John Damascene,[11] for example, has no

chapter on the Church in his *On the Orthodox Faith*; only an occasional mention, which suffices, however, to show that for him the Church is the reality which envelops the whole of the Christian life. In the East, even more than in the West, the Church is, in this period, a fact more than a doctrine. A fact which asserts itself as having the same absolute value as that of salvation, that is to say, the divine life acquired in Jesus Christ and communicated by his Holy Spirit; a fact which is lived, and which is the very reality in, by, and according to which one is a Christian and in communion with God.

'A fact which is lived' rather than theologized and dogmatized. Orthodox writers produced nothing comparable to the fairly frequent treatises *De Ecclesia* of western theologians in the Middle Ages, and we look in vain among Orthodox documents for authoritative definitions of the Church such as we find in the confessions of many of the Reformed churches.

THE CHURCH AS 'MYSTERY' AND THE IMAGE OF GOD, THE COSMOS, AND MAN

What we do find, however, in Orthodox writing throughout the centuries are many works which, with an abundant wealth of imagery, treat of the Church as a divine-human mystery. Among these are the 'Mystagogies'[12] (mystical interpretations of the Church and sacraments), commentaries on the liturgy, and descriptions of the Church as a building which draw out the symbolism of its various parts and ornaments. These works make clear that Orthodox ecclesiology holds the earthly and spiritual aspects of the Church closely together. Any sharp distinction between the Church militant and the Church triumphant is foreign to its thought. The Church 'is both *visible* and *invisible*, both *divine* and *human* . . . a single and continuous reality'.[13] On earth the Church is the *eikon* (image) of the heavenly, and Orthodox theology explicates this in terms of the communion of its members in the one faith, its liturgy, and the building in which its members gather for the celebration of the liturgy.

With a rather different nuance Orthodoxy also thinks of the Church as the image of God the Holy Trinity, of the *kosmos* (universe), and of man.

The *Mystagogy* of Maximus the Confessor[14] (*c.* 580–662) is an early, typical, and important example of this literature. The first seven chapters expound the symbolism of the Church as building and the following sixteen explain the meaning of the eucharist and its ceremonies. 'The idea of the Church which stands out', writes Yves Congar, 'is that of a mystery of unity.'[15] The Church is an image of God who is all in all and holds all things together in unity, in that it unites within a single body men of every age, condition, and race. It does this by the grace and power which the energy of God working within it generates.

The Church is also the image of the cosmos. Like the universe it unites things visible and invisible, the visible things of the Church's life (hierarchy, sacraments) being the symbols of invisible, spiritual realities. To illustrate the closeness of the union Maximus uses the figure of the wheels of the chariot of God in Ezekiel 1.16: 'their construction being as it were a wheel within a wheel'. The union of earthly and heavenly is imaged also in the Church as building, the nave representing the earthly and the sanctuary the heavenly, both brought together in the act of worship.

The Church, too, is an image of man as God intends him to be. The nave, the sanctuary, and the altar are the image of the body, soul, and mind (Greek, *nous*) of man who must approach God through his mind, which is represented by the altar.

Maximus also sees the nave and sanctuary as the image of the Old and New Testaments; and the later chapters of the *Mystagogia* interpret the liturgy as symbolically representing the whole saving work of Christ. The Church, then, and the building in which the faithful gather, are seen as what may be called all-embracing images of God the Holy Trinity in the totality of his work in creation, redemption, and sanctification.

This great wealth of imagery is again illustrated a little later in a work commonly, though perhaps mistakenly, attributed to Germanus (*c.* 634–733), Patriarch of Constantinople, and known as 'History of the Church and Mystical Contemplation' (Greek, *Historia ekklesiastikē kai mustikē theōria*).

The Church is God's temple, a sacred enclosure, house of prayer, a gathering of the People, body of Christ, his Name, Bride of Christ, which calls the peoples to penitence and prayer; purified by the water of holy baptism and washed by his precious blood, adorned as a bride and sealed with the ointment of the Holy Spirit. . . . The Church is an earthly heaven wherein the heavenly God dwells and walks; it is an anti-type of the crucifixion, the burial and resurrection of Christ. . . . The Church is a divine house where the mystical living sacrifice is celebrated . . . and its precious stones are the divine dogmas taught by the Lord to his disciples (*Historia Ekklesiastikē*, Intro.)[16]

That the Church is the terrestrial heaven is a frequent Orthodox theme. It follows from the concept of the Church (both as community and building) as the place where the visible and the invisible of the cosmos are brought together, and it is closely connected with the body of Christ image which we consider next. As in the incarnation there was a descent of the invisible into the visible, so in the Church the heavenly descends into the earthly. The idea is dramatically presented to the eye in the typical Byzantine church, in which the great central dome suggests the heavens descending upon the earth, and the huge mosaic of Christ the *Pantokrator*[17] which dominates the ceiling of the dome suggests the presence of him who is both merciful saviour and judge of the world.

THE MYSTICAL BODY

Orthodox theology gives great prominence to the idea of the Church as the body of Christ. The early Fathers who developed the doctrine of the mystical body, Cyril of Jerusalem, Cyril of Alexandria, and Augustine are often quoted, and the body of Christ idea is woven together with that of the deification of man in virtue of his participation in Christ.[18] Anastasius of Antioch (d. 599) provides a typical example:

> (God) assumed our whole race in a single individual, having become the first-fruits of our nature. Hence Christ is called 'the first-fruits' (1 Cor. 15.20, 23). For his purpose was to raise up in its totality what has fallen. Now what had fallen was our whole race. Therefore he mingled himself completely with Adam, Life itself with the dead, in order to save him. He penetrated into the totality of him to whom he was united, like the soul of a great body, vivifying it throughout, communicating life to it wholly in all its perceptive faculties. This is why mankind is called 'the body of Christ and his members in particular' (1 Cor. 12.27)—the body of the Christ who both diffuses himself equally in all together, and dwells individually in each one according to the measure of his faith (*De nostris dogmatibus veritatis*, *Oratio* III).[19]

The Church as the body of Christ is seen as the totality of those who believe in Jesus Christ as Son of God and Saviour, and are united with him, their Head, by participation in the sacraments. Therefore the

Church is, and can only be, one. Orthodoxy speaks of the Church as visible and invisible, but in doing so neither makes the western distinction between the Church militant and triumphant, nor the distinction between an invisible Church of the elect and a visible Church of saints mixed with sinners which the western Reformers took from Augustine and elaborated. It is rather a recognition that the one Church exists invisibly in the departed saints and faithful, *and* visibly in the worshipping community on earth. The distinction is made simply from the human point of view. There is but one Church, invisible and visible, heavenly and earthly: 'The Church, the Body of Christ, manifests forth and fulfils itself in time, without changing its essential unity or inward life of grace. And therefore, when we speak of "the Church visible and invisible", we so speak only in relation to man'.[20]

THE CHURCH AS THE EUCHARISTIC COMMUNITY

Ecclesiologies which present the Church as the mystical body of Christ place great emphasis on the eucharist.[21] So it is in Orthodox theology. Acts 2.42 which describes the life of the Church brought into being by the creative act of the Holy Spirit is an important text for Orthodox ecclesiology: 'They continued steadfastly in the apostles' teaching and fellowship [*koinōnia*], in the breaking of bread and the prayers.' It indicates that worship is essential to the Church's life.

The themes of the Church as body of Christ, as creation of the Holy Spirit, and as eucharistic community are closely integrated in Orthodox theology, as the following words of Professor N. A. Nissiotis[22] make clear:

> Orthodox worship is centred on the Christ event. The real presence of Christ in the midst of the worshipping community is the act of the Holy Spirit . . . upon the invocation of the worshipping community to God the Father. The eucharistic *epiklēsis*[23] to the Father, 'send down thy Spirit on us and on these elements (the bread and wine) . . .' is the climax and focus of all ecclesial worship which, following the biblical revelation, is an enactment of the energy of the Trinitarian God in history.
>
> The action of the Spirit—who is the Lord now in whom alone we can call Jesus Lord, who alone can lead us to the realization of the truth of Christ, who raised Christ from the dead, who set up the Church in history on the day of Pentecost, who gives us the earnest of the final victory of Christ over death according to the Scriptures—is absolutely decisive for Orthodox worship. Again and again, at the most decisive moments during

the Orthodox services, the Spirit is invoked, mentioned or prayed to as the Spirit creating the new situation in history, as the one through whom alone the reality of individual faith and the existence of the one community, the Ecclesia, becomes possible at all times and in all places. . . .

In this eucharistically centred worship, the Church is constantly recreated and recognized. Orthodox ecclesiology is directly affected by the liturgical-eucharistic event. Before the Church can be defined as a sacred institution in scholastic or ontological terms, or as a sociological organization for administering the Word and sacrament, she has to be understood as a charismatic community centred upon the real presence of Christ and enacted by the Spirit. That is why Orthodox ecclesiology emphasizes the 'mystery' aspect of the Church. 'Mystery' here does not signify an obscure and incomprehensible event, but it emphasizes the connection between the Head and the body as it is realized in Word and sacrament and points to the divine-human reality of the Church, as the people of God, united with Christ through the action of the Spirit.

Orthodox theology insists that in the eucharist the community, and each faithful member, is thankfully remembering Christ's work of redemption in the body of his flesh, celebrating his presence as the risen Christ, and anticipating his coming in final triumph as Lord of all. Past, present, and future are brought together in the one act of worship. Moreover, Orthodox obedience to Christ's command, 'do this', at the Last Supper has both an historical and an eschatological dimension; that is to say, the eye of Orthodox faith looks out to the world and its history, but also to the end which is God's purpose for the world beyond the world and its history. Christ is acknowledged as Lord of the Church and of the world, the Lord of history who is also Lord beyond the end of history.

This acknowledgement of the total lordship of Christ[24] makes it impossible for Orthodoxy to understand the sharp distinction which the Western Church and in particular the Protestant churches, have found it so easy to make between Church and world, sacred and secular. This is why the Eastern Church, from the time of Constantine and throughout the Byzantine period, conceived of Church and State (under a Christian ruler) as a single society, governed by two hierarchies, ecclesiastical and imperial, each autonomous, but acting in 'symphony'.[25] This is why Orthodoxy conceives Christian mission as the Church expressing itself in the life of the different regions of the world, committed to the conversion of the people within their own culture. This is why it is the concern of every faithful Orthodox pastor that the community under his care, which in the eucharistic liturgy acknowledges the world as the creation of God and Christ's total lordship over it, should bear active witness to this truth in its life, and the life of all its members. Liturgy as worship and liturgy as mission and service in the world are not to be separated.[26] The Orthodox understanding of the life of the Church in all its spheres, worship, mission, ministry to the needy, is based on the premiss that the Church is a community brought into being and sustained by the Holy Spirit in the eucharist which establishes the communion of the faithful with Christ crucified, risen, triumphant, and reigning Lord of all—the *Pantokrator*.

THE MARKS OF THE CHURCH

Orthodox ecclesiology follows in the main Augustine's interpretation of the credal marks of the Church,[27] but certain special emphases are to be noted. There is insistence that the unity of the Church is inclusive of diversity. This is an implication of the doctrine of the Church as the image of God the Holy Trinity, in whose essential unity are the distinctions of Father, Son, and Spirit. Unity is not conceived in any monolithic sense. Consequently, from the beginning, eastern Orthodoxy has opposed the idea of the supremacy of one ecclesiastical see over all others, has defended the autonomy of the patriarchates, and as its mission expanded[28] encouraged the creation of autocephalous churches creatively involved in the culture of the locality. Likewise, Orthodoxy sees the mystery of unity in diversity exemplified in councils, where under the guidance of the Holy Spirit the Church represented by bishops from many places seeks a common mind.

Catholicity is interpreted much as in the West, but less is made of the purely geographical sense of the word. This is perhaps because the Orthodox sees the local church as no less catholic than a church which is completely worldwide. Orthodox theologians lay great stress on the local church. The Church necessarily manifests itself locally. Appeal is made here to the earliest of the eastern Fathers, Ignatius of Antioch:

> Let that be considered a valid eucharist which is celebrated by the bishop or by one whom he appoints. Wherever the bishop appears let the congregation be present, just as wherever Jesus Christ is, there is the Catholic Church.[29]

Wherever faithful people are gathered round the bishop or his delegate for the celebration of the eucharist, there is the local Church *and* the Catholic Church. Ignatius' point, it is argued, is not that Christ and the bishop are to be equated in some way; rather it is that the local eucharistic community manifests, even explains, the nature of the whole Church of Christ. It is in the worshipping and working life of the local community of the faithful that the Catholic Church has its very being.

With regard to the note of holiness the Orthodox Church knows the tension which we have several times referred to:[30] the conviction that the Church, the body of Christ, is holy, and the knowledge that its members are imperfect and sinful.[31] The frequent litanies for the needs of the Church and the constantly repeated *kyrie eleison* (Lord, have mercy) eloquently dispel any suspicion that Orthodoxy conceives the members of the Church to be a society of perfect ones. Ephraim of Syria (*c.* 306–73) spoke of 'the Church of the penitents, the Church of those who perish'.[32] How can it be that members of the Church are sinners, but that the Church is the image of God, and the communion of saints? 'The mystery of the Church', writes Professor John Meyendorff, 'consists in the very fact that *together* sinners become *something different* from what they are as individuals; this "something different" is the Body of Christ'.[33]

The Orthodox interpretation of apostolicity will be discussed in the next section.

THE MINISTRY AND APOSTOLIC SUCCESSION

For the Orthodox Church 'apostolic succession' has a broader meaning than it bears, at least in the popular mind, in the West. Since the nature of the Church is both manifested in and sustained by the eucharist, continuity with the apostles lies in the succession of eucharistic communities. This is not to say that Orthodoxy minimizes the role of the bishop. It fully accepts the idea that the bishops have continuity with the apostles through their ordination.[34] But, as by Ignatius of Antioch and other early Fathers, the bishop's role as the chief celebrant of the liturgy is emphasized.

Ministry in the Church is Christ's ministry. He alone is truly bishop (1 Pet. 2.25), priest (Heb. 2.17), and deacon (Luke 22.27). The ministry of Christ is distributed in the Church by the Holy Spirit who apportions the gifts of God (1 Cor. 12.11). Bishop, priest, and deacon have their allotted functions in the life of the Church, and particularly in the eucharist wherein the life of the Church is sustained. The fact that the ordination of bishops, priests, and deacons takes place within the setting of the eucharist emphasizes that these are orders of ministry *within* a eucharistic community, and not above or apart from it. The eucharistic community is theologically prior to the bishop and the other orders of ministry. 'The documents at our disposal', writes Professor Meyendorff,[35] 'do not give us any certainty about the existence of a "monarchical episcopate" in all the Churches from the first century. . . . On the other hand, we can assert that there never was a Christian Church where the Lord's Supper was not celebrated.'

Episcopate, priesthood, and diaconate are *orders*. A hierarchy is implied, but not the spiritual superiority or greater importance of one over another. Nor is there implied a 'second-class citizenship' for laymen and laywomen. They are equally members of the eucharistic community. There can be no eucharistic liturgy without the presence of the laity.[36] Without the eucharistic community bishop, priest, and deacon would have no function.

Thus Orthodoxy insists that the Church is essentially the *people* of God, a eucharistic community:

> The apostolic succession has to be understood as a pentecostal event which first established the Church as a community and, within and by this community, the Spirit has appointed, through the apostles, deacons, presbyters, and bishops. It is, therefore, both an act of the community and a transmission of the apostolic ministry, but never an isolated line from Christ through the Twelve to the bishops as a separate divine order outside or above the laity. Apostolicity passes always through the eucharistic community and is recognized in him who presides over a eucharistic gathering. It is the people of God who precede the ministry in eucharistic practice and theological significance.[37]

THE CORPORATE EPISCOPATE

When Orthodoxy insists that the concept of hierarchy does not imply that the bishop has a spiritual superiority over other faithful members of the Church, it does not deny to the bishop a unique status. He succeeds the apostles as the guardian of the true faith.[38] He is the head on earth of the local eucharistic community. In these things the bishops have an essential equality.[39] The bishop's essential function is within the local church. Orthodoxy cannot conceive of a function for the bishop apart from the local church. Each local church is the Catholic Church in its completeness, and each bishop therefore exercises the fulness of episcopacy within it. The bishops together form a collegial body of which each member exercises the totality of episcopal authority within his own sphere. In this collegiate body none has an inherent juridical right over others. Orthodoxy has consistently rejected the idea of 'a bishop of bishops', even though it has admitted, with Cyprian, that the bishop of Rome has a primacy of honour comparable with that of Peter among the apostles. The Orthodox concept of collegiality is well expressed by a Greek, Athanasius, at a meeting held in Constantinople in 1357 at which the papal primacy was discussed. Against a Roman legate who maintained the necessity for a single head of the Church on earth, Athanasius said:

> I have said that the apostles are twelve, I know, but they are not twelve heads of the Church. Just as the faithful, despite their number, form one Church and the unique body of Christ because of identity of worship and religion, as we affirm, in the same way, I urge, you should think of the apostles, although twelve in number, as one sole head of the Church, because of identity of dignity and spiritual power. . . . [After citing John 17.11, 20–22 he proceeds]: you would not say that there are three Gods, for the three are perfectly one. How, then, in the case of those who have the same perfection, will you distinguish the inferior and the superior, or different heads? Should you not rather say that they are one and are the unique head of the Church of Christ? Assuredly, the pope is named first, and sits above the others, but this is only a matter of order,[40] and not because of any special dignity and spiritual power.[41]

The pope, then, is a bishop like any other—the bishop of a particular church. But as Nilus Cabasilas, uncle of the more famous Nicolas Cabasilas,[42] said, 'provided that the pope guards the order of the Church and remains in the truth, he retains the first place, which belongs to him by right'.[43]

Nevertheless, as we have already seen, Orthodoxy has accepted, on the authority of canons of early ecumenical councils, the principle that some sees may be acknowledged, for good historical reasons, as possessing a certain authority over other sees within the same region. Among such reasons were a strong tradition of apostolic foundation, the importance of the see city, the size of the community under the bishop's oversight, and the theological reputation of the see. The sees thus recognized were Rome, Alexandria, Antioch, Jerusalem, and Constantinople, and their bishops were accorded the title of 'patriarch'. From the time of the Council of Chalcedon (451) the five patriarchs were regarded as sharing between them the oversight and a measure of jurisdiction[44] over the whole of the known world (Greek *oikoumene*). This governmental system was known as the pentarchy (Greek *pentarchia*) or 'the rule of the five'. Justinian (Emperor 527–65) spoke of the five patriarchates as the five senses of the Empire. Orthodoxy insists that the pentarchy does not negate the principle of episcopal collegiality. On this Timothy Ware says:[45]

> The system of Patriarchs and Metropolitans is a matter of *ecclesiastical organization*. But if we look at the Church from the viewpoint not of ecclesiastical order but of *divine right*, then we must say that all bishops are essentially equal, however humble or exalted the city over which each presides. All bishops share equally in the apostolic succession, all have the same sacramental powers, all are divinely appointed teachers of the faith. If a dispute about doctrine arises, it is not enough for the Patriarchs to express their opinion: every diocesan bishop has the right to attend a General Council, to speak, and to cast his vote. The system of the Pentarchy does not impair the essential equality of all bishops, nor does it deprive each local community of the importance which Ignatius assigned to it.

AUTOCEPHALY

The patriarchate of Constantinople never claimed jurisdiction over other patriarchates as did the Church of Rome, but the historical circumstances of the submersion of the other eastern patriarchates under Moslem rulers, from the seventh century onwards, inevitably placed it in a position of responsibility for eastern Christendom. As Orthodoxy expanded towards the north through the remarkable missionary activity among the Slavic peoples, the principle of autocephaly[46] was developed, that is, the recognition of the right of a national church to elect its own metropolitan bishop,[47] and eventually to govern itself. This principle is normative in Orthodoxy to this day. It is valued as a true expression of the catholicity and unity of the Church in conformity with the spirit of the general councils. It is maintained that only the true autonomy of the Church within a region can give it the necessary flexibility to provide for the particular, and perhaps unique, needs of the people of that region.

Autocephaly, however, is not separation. The one Catholic Church is thought of as manifesting itself uniquely in each region, and the churches of all regions are bound in unity in the profession of the same faith, and in sacramental communion.

Autocephaly is the working out of a principle enunciated in the canons of early councils by which the Orthodox Church considers itself to be bound, the principle that there may not be more than one ecclesiastical jurisdiction in a single place. Canon 8 of the Council of Nicaea (325) declares 'there may not be two bishops in the city', and Canon 2 of the Council of Constantinople (381) says 'the synod of every province will administer the affairs of that particular province as was decreed in Nicaea'. Adherence to this principle is behind the Orthodox opposition to the papal claim to universal jurisdiction: 'The existence of one "vicar of Christ" for all the churches duplicates (if it does not suppress) the episcopal sacramental ministry of each particular local community.'[48] It places the centre of the ecclesiastical life of the local Christian community outside the community itself in a distant city.

Orthodoxy is uncomfortably aware that circumstances have led to a blurring of its witness to autocephaly and to the underlying principle that it is inadmissible to have different ecclesial communities in one place under different jurisdictions. Movements of population in the twentieth century have brought it about that in many cities of western Europe and North America Orthodox Christians in large numbers are to be found, not under the authority of a single bishop but, although in full communion with each other, under separate metropolitan jurisdictions, Greek, Russian, Serbian, and so on. This is an anomaly which Orthodox theology can only justify by the principle of 'economy'[49] for a limited period while every endeavour is made to restore canonical norms.

Part 4

THE REFORMATION PERIOD

12

Luther; Calvin; Separatism

1 MARTIN LUTHER (1483–1546)

'At the beginning of the sixteenth century everyone that mattered in the Western Church was crying out for reformation.'[1] It was set in motion in 1517, but not in the way, nor with the results, that the majority of those who had longed for it hoped. Western Europe was to be split into two religious camps, Catholic and Protestant, between which there was to be bitter hostility, and often open warfare, and few serious attempts at mutual understanding until late in the twentieth century. Moreover, to the dismay of many reformers, the movement produced splinter groups almost from the beginning, both because of the dissatisfaction of radicals with what they considered its cautious nature, and because of theological differences between the more conservative reformers.

Many factors contribute to explain the rise of the movement, political (rising nationalism in Europe) and social (the grievances of the German peasants) as well as moral and religious. But undoubtedly its immediate cause was the indulgence proclaimed by Pope Leo X to meet his desperate financial needs. The blatant methods of the Dominican friar Tetzel in promoting the indulgence[2] roused the indignation of a young Augustinian (or Austin) friar named Martin Luther. On 31 October 1517 Luther attached to the door of the Castle church in Wittenberg, where he was a university lecturer in Holy Scripture, 'Ninety-five Theses upon Indulgences'. Although outspoken on that subject, the theses were not particularly anti-papal. They assumed that if the Pope knew what was going on, he would disapprove; they called for a public discussion on indulgences, and declared Luther's readiness to defend his theses in such a debate. Little as he can have suspected it, Luther had launched a movement of vast significance for the history of Europe. Copies of the theses were printed, unknown to Luther, and circulated within a few weeks far and wide in Germany. They gained wide support, and gradually he found himself cast in the role of leader in a revolt against papal supremacy over the Church.

THE CHURCH AS THE CONGREGATION OF THE FAITHFUL

The central doctrine of the Luther reformation was that man is justified by faith alone, and not by works. This was a conviction which Luther had reached some years before the affair of the indulgence, as he had struggled with the consciousness that diligence in keeping the rule of the Austin friars and frequent confessions brought him no peace with God, no sense of being redeemed. His rejection of the idea that salvation can be earned by good works prompted his attack on indulgences. He saw them as a particularly odious symptom of the malaise of a Church which, in his view, had come to stand for the doctrine that man might win salvation by reliance on placatory acts performed on his behalf by a clerical hierarchy, in recognition of his pious works or money payments.

The doctrine of justification by faith alone has a direct influence on Luther's ecclesiology. With the acceptance of this doctrine as crucial it is natural to conceive of the Church as essentially the assembly of those who have the faith which justifies, the *congregatio fidelium*. And since those who have justifying faith are redeemed, the Church is defined as 'the congregation of saints'.[3]

THE CHURCH IS WHERE THE WORD OF GOD IS PREACHED AND THE SACRAMENTS ADMINISTERED

Unless the doctrine of justification by faith, however, is understood in a purely subjective way (and Luther did not so understand it), more than this must be said about the Church. Intimately related, in Luther's thought, with the doctrine of justification by faith (which more accurately is to be called the doctrine of justification *by grace* through faith) was the doctrine of the Atonement. This is the doctrine that, by the free gift or grace of God, his Son, Jesus Christ, has redeemed mankind through his life, sacrificial death, and resurrection. The Church of Christ, then, must be where God continues to offer his grace in Christ, and seeks the response which is the faith that justifies. Although Luther differed from Catholic theologians about the nature of grace, the place and importance of preaching, and in sacramental theology, he strongly held that God's grace is received by the preaching of the word of God and the administration of the sacraments. Consequently, while the Church may be described as 'the congregation of saints' one must add 'in which the Gospel is rightly taught and the sacraments are rightly administered'.[4] In *The Papacy at Rome* (1520), Luther writes:[5] 'Baptism, the sacrament, and the gospel are the signs by which the existence of the Church in the world can be noticed externally.'[6]

These signs or marks of the Church are the first three of seven[7] which he lists and treats more fully in a later work:

First, the holy Christian people are recognized by their possession of the holy Word of God. ... Wherever you hear or see this word preached, believed, professed, and lived do not doubt that the true *ecclesia sancta catholica*, 'a Christian holy people', must be there, even though their number is very small. ...

Second, God's people, or the Christian holy people are recognized by the holy sacrament of baptism, wherever it is taught, believed, and administered according to Christ's ordinance. ...

Third, God's people, or Christian holy people, are recognized by the holy sacrament of the altar, wherever it is rightly administered, believed and received according to Christ's institution (*On the Councils and the Church* (1539)).[8]

THE INVISIBLE CHURCH

The true Church, or 'the Christian holy people' as Luther preferred to call it, is hidden or invisible, inasmuch as God alone knows who are the elect. He makes the distinction which we first found in Augustine between the invisible Church of the elect and the empirical 'mixed' Church of saints and sinners:

Christianity is a spiritual assembly of souls in one faith ... no one is regarded as a Christian because of his body. Thus ... the natural, real, true, and essential Christendom exists in the Spirit and not in any external thing. ... This is the way Holy Scripture speaks of the holy Church and of Christendom. ...

We shall call the two churches by two distinct names. The first, which is natural, basic, essential, and true, we shall call 'spiritual internal Christendom'. The second, which is man-made and external, we shall call 'physical, external Christendom' (*On the Papacy at Rome*).[9]

Luther goes further than Augustine when he speaks of the visible Church as man-made. J. S. Whale[10] comments that for Luther

> ecclesiastical institutions have not the divine character claimed for them: all are human, fallible, and alterable; he attaches relatively little importance to ecclesiastical forms as such. He therefore breaks with the specifically medieval conception that Christ's Kingdom is concretely and visibly manifested on earth as an institution hierarchically ordered; and governed, by divine authority, in terms of law. To the Church of history and law he opposes the Church of the Spirit which, ideally considered, has no need of a visible, corporate constitution to make it a reality in the world.

Luther likens the relationship between the 'internal' Christendom and the 'external' to that between soul and body. To the external Christendom belong 'all popes, cardinals, bishops, prelates, monks, nuns, and all those who are regarded as Christians according to externals, no matter whether they are true and real Christians or not'.[11] Some, he concedes, are true Christians, not because of their membership of the external Church ('the body does not keep the soul alive, but the soul does exist in the body as well as without the body'),[12] but because of their faith. Without faith they are 'outside the first community, are dead before God; they are hypocrites and are merely like images of true Christendom.'[13]

Luther's assertion in this context that the soul can exist 'without the body' suggests that he believed that the true Church can and should exist without embodiment in an historical institution and outward forms. In the light of experience, and under the influence of the scholarly and pacific Melanchthon, he came to recognize that this was too idealistic a view. In 1527 in a letter to his friend George Spalatin, the chaplain of the Elector Frederick of Saxony, he admitted that it had been vain to hope that men could be ruled by the gospel alone; men seemed to prefer constraint by law and sword. For, 'round Luther's cry for religious reformation gathered men who wanted other things besides religious reformation'.[14] The excesses of some of these, and the violence of the peasants' risings of 1524–5, led Luther to attach more importance to 'externals' like disciplinary measures and a regular ministry. When in 1539 he wrote the third part of *On the Councils and the Church* he was doing, J. S. Whale remarks,[15] 'very much what Calvin is doing in the second edition of the *Institutio* published that same year—namely coming down to "brass tacks", so to speak;

defining the primary and secondary signs of the Church visible'. In addition to the three signs mentioned above (p. 163), he enumerates the use of the 'keys' (i.e. public and private condemnation of sins); ministers, to whom alone are committed the duties of preaching, baptizing, absolving, and celebrating the eucharist; public prayer, thanksgiving, and praise; and a manner of life which is stamped with the cross of Christ in the face of persecution, temptation, and all adversity.

THE PRIESTHOOD OF ALL BELIEVERS

This is a constant theme with Luther, and 1 Peter 2.9, 'You are ... a royal priesthood' is the text by which he supports it.

> It is pure invention that pope, bishop, priests, and monks are called the spiritual estate while princes, lords, artisans, and farmers are called the temporal estate. This is indeed a piece of deceit and hypocrisy ... all Christians are truly of the spiritual estate, and there is no difference among them except that of office. ...
>
> We are all consecrated priests through baptism, as St Peter says ... 'You are a royal priesthood and a priestly realm'. ...
>
> There is no true, basic difference between laymen and priests, princes and bishops, between religious and secular, except for the sake of office and work, but not for the sake of status. ... All are truly priests, bishops, and popes (*To the Christian Nobility of the German Nation* (1520)).[16]

The same theme is pursued in *The Babylonian Captivity of the Church*, written also in 1520, in a passage in which he says that while all have the same power in respect of Word and sacraments, it is only by the consent of the community that it may be exercised. Luther was never, therefore, quite without a sense of the necessity of a regular ministry, but he repudiated the sharp distinction which the medieval Church had come to make between clergy as a privileged class and a passive, listening, and obedient laity.[17] He maintained that all believers share a common priesthood: they are called, each in his own sphere of life, to preach the gospel, to edify the neighbour in love and to use the 'power of the keys', that is, to rebuke sin, to proclaim forgiveness and salvation, and to reconcile. The essential meaning of apostolic succession is revealed when one Christian proclaims to another the reconciliation in Christ which he himself has heard from others.

It follows that it would be a grave mistake to accuse Luther of encouraging individualism. To him the Christian community was essential. Every individual Christian needs his brother, who is God's representative to him in two ways: it is through a brother that God assures each of his grace (the power of 'the keys' mentioned above); and secondly the brother 'is appointed by God to receive the sacrifices of love and service which God does not need',[18] namely, the good works in which the faith of the justified man is ceaselessly active. The Church as a company of believers exercising a common priesthood is necessary. It is of the Church so understood that Luther, echoing Cyprian, can say: 'Outside the Christian Church there is no truth, no Christ, no blessedness', and even declare that it is necessary to God himself.[19]

THE MINISTRY

Luther's often repeated and enthusiastic language about the priesthood of all believers is not, on the surface, easy to reconcile with any recognition of the necessity of a duly constituted ministry. Yet the mature Luther was clearly not content to sweep aside the ordained ministry with the epithet 'man-made' which he had used of the visible Church in 1520.[20] This can be substantiated by quoting the fifth of the seven signs of the Church in his *On the Councils and the Church* (1539):

> The Church is recognized externally by the fact that it consecrates or calls ministers or has offices that it is to administer. There must be bishops, pastors, or preachers who publicly and privately give, administer, and use the aforementioned four things or holy possessions, viz. Word, baptism, sacrament of the altar, keys, in behalf of and in the name of the Church, or rather *by reason of their institution by Christ* [italics mine], as St Paul states in Ephesians 4, 'He received gifts among men . . .'—his gifts were that some should be apostles, some prophets, some evangelists, some teachers and governors, etc. The people as a whole cannot do these things but must entrust or have them entrusted to one person . . . the others should be content with this arrangement and agree to it.[21]

The ordained ministry as such, then, is not to be described as a man-made contrivance; indeed it is instituted by Christ. What Luther does conceive to be man-made is the distinction of rank and status between ministers. From the interchangeability of the terms 'bishop' and 'presbyter' in the N.T. he argues for the parity of ministers or spiritual rulers. The distinctions between bishops, priests, chaplains, deans, and so on have been introduced 'by men's laws and regulations'. Long usage has led men to think that these distinctions are scriptural and of divine institution.[22] What is of divine institution, scriptural, and to be retained is the careful choice of men from among the faithful to be ministers of Word and sacrament:

> In previous times this matter was handled as follows, and this is the way it should still be done: since in every Christian town they were all equally priests, one of them—the oldest or rather the most learned and most godly—was elected to be their servant, official, caretaker, and guardian in regard to the gospel and the sacraments, just as a mayor is elected from among the common mass of citizens (*Answer to the Hyperchristian, Hyperspiritual, and Hyperlearned Book by Goat Emser* (1521)).[23]

The final words in the above quotation are a reminder that it is the responsibility of the whole body of the faithful to see that the right choice is made of those who are to represent them in the things of God.

THE PLACE OF THE CHRISTIAN PRINCE

In reviewing the development of the idea of the Church in the medieval period, we took note of the complicated questions which arose concerning the relationship of Church and State: the defining of the areas of autonomy of each, and of the rights and duties of each to the other. Such questions certainly belong to ecclesiology in the wide sense of the word, for the various answers which have been given to them have produced different concepts of the nature and the function of the Church. Adequate treatment of this aspect of ecclesiology would require a separate study, which would include an investigation of how the Christian understanding of the Church has been influenced according to whether the temporal ruler or government was hostile, Christian, or indifferent. In the western Europe of Luther's day it could still be taken for granted that emperor, kings, and magistrates were professing Christians. The idea of the Christian prince certainly influenced Luther's ecclesiology. The circumstances of the time ('sixteenth-century Germany was no Garden of Eden,' remarks J. S. Whale)[24] led him to accord to the ruler extensive coercive authority, and disorders within reformed churches[25] led him to demand of the Christian prince protection for the Church, and consequently to allow him a considerable measure of authority in ecclesiastical matters.

In 1523 Luther wrote *Temporal Authority: to what Extent it should be Obeyed*,[26] and dedicated it to the new Elector of Saxony, Duke John. J. S. Whale, who in his book *The Protestant Tradition* provides a thorough discussion of Luther's teaching on Church and State,[27] gives the following useful summary of this work:

A Luther is at pains to establish two scriptural principles:
   (i) The divine sanction of civil government, and its independence of all clerical tutelage and control.
   (ii) The limits of this power, which may be exercised only over the bodies and goods of men, not in the domain of conscience, where man is answerable only to God.

B ... The treatise fights on three fronts; it repudiates three distinct views of the proper relation between State and Church:
   (i) The medieval, Roman view. Luther denies that the State, as the 'secular arm' of the Church, has a duty to undertake religious persecution or coercion.
   (ii) The 'Machiavellian' view. He denies that Christian men may be persecuted as such by the civil power for reasons of State.
   (iii) The 'anarchist' view of Christian idealism and pacifism. He denies the 'anabaptist'[28] thesis that because the Gospel forbids resistance to evil, the Christian state may not use force in the name of law.

C Luther distinguishes between
   (i) Natural society—which, because of sin, cannot subsist without the coercive sanctions of police force and sword.
   (ii) The religious sphere—where the Word is the only agency which may rightly be employed.[29]

Whale adds a comment of his own:

D Luther thus anticipates some of the living issues of our own time. It is doubtful whether he also anticipates those erastian elements in historic Lutheranism which are now criticized and disavowed.[30]

'If all the world were composed of real Christians,' Luther wrote,[31] 'that is, true believers, there would be no need for or benefits from prince, king, lord, sword, or law.' But true Christians were, he admitted, unlikely ever to be numerous enough to make government 'in a Christian and evangelical manner'[32] feasible. And for the protection of the Church itself he called on the Duke of Saxony to conduct visitations of the churches, and began to provide for the government and discipline of the churches by a system of courts, or consistories, whose members were appointed by the prince.

Luther based his doctrine of the place of the Christian prince on that of the priesthood of all believers. All Christians, whatever their calling, were bound to serve the Church, using whatever talents and proper authority they possessed. The Christian who, by a divinely given right, is a ruler, is under obligation to use his authority, which includes the power to coerce, on behalf of the Church when this is necessary. The prince's authority is not, however, absolute. It does not extend to the sphere of conscience. Here Luther claimed the Christian man's right of passive resistance. Nor does that authority include the right to intervene in doctrinal matters. Yet it was admitted that the Christian ruler was obliged to protect the Church against heresy, and the distinction proved hard to draw between what was and what was not interference in purely spiritual matters. The Lutheran churches were to exist under something akin to State absolutism in things spiritual as well as temporal.

J. S. Whale concludes his discussion of Luther's doctrine of the Christian prince with the words:

> It seems that circumstances proved too strong for the author of *The Liberty of the Christian Man*. Not only Melanchthon and later German Lutherans, but the great Reformer himself began to swim with the political current which was everywhere bringing the absolute ruler to port, and to acquiesce in the political opportunism of his princely protectors. The prophet who began by proclaiming the priesthood of all believers at last found himself virtually exalting the temporal prince as *summus episcopus* [i.e. supreme bishop] or as *membrum praecipuum ecclesiae* [i.e. chief member of the Church].[33]

For Lutheranism the authority of pope and bishops had passed to the Christian prince.

2   JOHN CALVIN (1509–64)

The Reformation movement quickly swept from southern Germany to other places. By 1522 Zwingli was leading it in Zürich, by 1523 Martin Bucer in Strasbourg, and by 1530 William Farel in Neuchâtel. Farel, however, went to Geneva in 1535 to organize the reformation there. In 1536 he persuaded John Calvin, who was on a passing visit, to remain and help with the work, which was running into some difficulties. Opposition to some of the disciplinary measures they proposed led to the banishment of both in 1538. Calvin spent three years working with Bucer in Strasbourg. In 1541 he returned to

Geneva where he now met great success. The city rapidly became the favourite place of shelter for Protestant refugees from Catholic countries.[34] Calvin remained in Geneva for the rest of his life. His reputation as a biblical scholar, theologian, and ecclesiastical statesman was acknowledged far beyond the limits of the city of Geneva. He is rightly regarded as the father of those churches of the Reformation which have come to be known as 'The Reformed Churches', and which usually have a presbyterian system of government.

Calvin's *Institutio Christianae Religionis*[35] is one of the great Christian classics. It was first published in 1536, and was greatly expanded in subsequent editions in 1539, 1543, and 1559. It is in four books, the last of which deals with the Church. Much of what he has to say concerns the Church as a visible, organized institution. Keenly aware of the erratic individualism which the Reformation was engendering, and which caused so much concern to Luther, Calvin saw the need for strong churchmanship, and laboured to make Geneva a shining example of it. He is frequently spoken of as the Cyprian of the Reformation, and may with some justice be described as a 'high churchman'.[36]

THE CHURCH VISIBLE AND INVISIBLE

Calvin held a strict doctrine of predestination which would perhaps seem to leave little room for a doctrine of the visible Church. If, by God's eternal decree, some are elected to salvation and others are not, there would seem to be only a peripheral place for the Church as an historical institution: the provision of a ministry and discipline would appear to be unnecessary for the elect, and futile for the reprobate. But Calvin did not see the question in this way. On the contrary, for him the existence of the Church belongs to the mysterious eternal decrees of God. The Church visible is by God's provision the means by which, through the ministry of Word, sacraments, and discipline, he brings the elect to their salvation. Calvin's doctrine of the Church is thus closely linked to his predestinarianism.[37]

Calvin integrates the concepts of the invisible Church and the visible in a way which Luther never succeeded in achieving. There are not two Churches, but

> Holy Scripture speaks of the church in two ways. Sometimes . . . it means that which is actually in God's presence into which no persons are received but those who are children of God by grace of adoption and true

members of Christ by sanctification of the Holy Spirit. . . . [It] includes not only the saints presently living on earth, but all the elect from the beginning of the world. Often however the name 'church' designates the whole multitude of men spread over the earth who profess to worship one God and Christ. By baptism we are initiated into faith in him; by partaking in the Lord's Supper we attest our unity in true doctrine and love; in the Word of the Lord we have agreement, and for the preaching of the Word the ministry instituted by Christ is preserved. In this church are mingled many hypocrites who have nothing of Christ but the name and outward appearance. . . . Just as we must believe, therefore, that the former church, invisible to us, is visible to the eyes of God alone, so we are commanded to revere and keep communion with the latter, which is called 'church' in respect to men (*Institutes* IV, i.7).[38]

Finding that Scripture speaks of the Church as at once visible and invisible, Calvin is content to argue the matter no further, but to devote the rest of the book to the marks of the Church visible, the means of grace which God has given it, and the forms of ministry and discipline which it needs.

TRADITIONAL CONCEPTS: BODY, MOTHER

The traditional images which Calvin most frequently uses are those of the Church as the body of Christ, and as mother. Membership of the body of Christ coincides completely with the invisible Church, but not with the Church visible, among whose membership are some who are not predestined to salvation. Yet because the invisible and visible are one Church and not two, Calvin can use the body image of the Church as institution; for Christ is its Head, and his spirit works within it, distributing varied gifts individually and pre-eminently the gift of love, ordering, unifying, and sanctifying its members.[39]

Calvin fully recognizes the Pauline tension between the 'now' and the 'not yet' of the Church. The Church visible *is* the body of Christ, but it is also in process of *becoming* his body. In a passage where, however, he is using the image of the bride, he says that while it is true that Jesus Christ has sanctified the Church, so that his bride is without wrinkle or blemish,

it is also no less true that the Lord is daily at work in smoothing out the wrinkles and cleansing the spots. From this it follows that the Church's holiness is not yet complete. The Church is holy, then, in the sense that it is daily advancing and is not yet perfect; it makes progress from day to day but has not yet reached its goal of holiness (*Institutes* IV, i.17).[40]

Like Cyprian and Augustine, Calvin boldly uses the mother image of the visible Church, and with them can say that apart from her there is no salvation:

> Because it is now our intention to discuss the visible church, let us learn even from the simple title 'mother' how useful, indeed how necessary, it is that we should know her. For there is no other way to enter into life unless this mother conceive us in her womb, give us birth, nourish us at her breast, and lastly, unless she keep us under her care and guidance until, putting off mortal flesh, we become like the angels ... away from her bosom one cannot hope for any forgiveness of sins or any salvation ... it is always disastrous to leave the Church (*Institutes* IV, i.4).

THE MARKS OF THE VISIBLE CHURCH

But what are the criteria for judging whether a group of people who claim to be Christians have Christ for their Head and are of his body? Calvin, as we have seen, was very conscious that the radicals of the reforming movement were separating themselves into small 'holiness' groups. Were they justified in doing so? Calvin believed that there are certain marks by which one may discern the Church. They are identical with the first three of the external marks which Luther listed:[41]

> Wherever we see the Word of God purely preached and heard, and the sacraments administered according to Christ's institution, there, it is not to be doubted, a Church of God exists (*Institutes* IV, i.9).

Wherever these marks are to be recognized, individuals do wrong to separate themselves. 'Let them ponder how much more important both the ministry of the Word and participation in the sacred mysteries are for the gathering of the church than the possibility that this whole power may be dissipated through the guilt of certain ungodly men.'[42] Calvin argues that differences in 'non-essential matters' do not justify schism: 'We must not thoughtlessly forsake the Church because of any petty dissensions.'[43]

Wendel notices[44] that, although Calvin attaches great importance to disciplinary provision, he did not include this in his marks of the Church. The explanation, he suggests, is that Calvin thought of discipline as belonging not to the definition of the Church, but to its organization as a 'measure of defence and a means of sanctification'. Be that as it may, Calvin certainly recognized the need for ecclesiastical discipline. The streak of puritanism and perfectionism in his own character contributed to the seriousness with which he viewed this matter. At Geneva he provided an elaborate machinery of discipline. The faithful were to be protected from bad example, and sinners prompted to repentance. In serious cases excommunication was to be used, but every effort was to be made to bring the excommunicated person back into fellowship. Calvin is careful to state that excommunication does not imply that the subject is not of the elect, for only God knows about this. The excommunicate are, however, 'assured of their everlasting condemnation unless they repent'. The purpose of excommunication is 'reconciliation and restoration to communion'.[45]

THE MINISTRY

J. S. Whale suggests[46] that Calvin must have been aware that his arguments against the Protestant separatists could equally be used by the Roman Church against Geneva. However, despite certain admissions[47] that some traces of the true Church remained in the Church of Rome of the sixteenth century, he was convinced of the necessity of separation from it. There the Word of God was not purely preached, he believed, nor were the sacraments administered according to the institution of Christ; and the papacy had usurped the headship of Christ.[48] He therefore sees no alternative to an outright rejection of Roman orders.[49]

This does not mean that Calvin rejected the concept of the distinction of ranks within the ministry. Distinctions such as that between patriarch, archbishop, and bishop in the early Church which were 'connected with the maintenance of discipline', are justified.[50] The term 'hierarchy', however, he does reject as 'improper, unscriptural, and likely to encourage ideas of lordship in the government of the Church which are contrary to the will of God'.[51] In his *Commentary on the Book of Numbers* he writes:

> Distinction of a political kind is not to be rejected, for common sense itself dictates it in order to remove confusion. But whatever has this end in view will be so arranged as neither to obscure the glory of Christ nor to minister to ambition or tyranny, nor to hinder all ministers from cultivating a mutual brotherliness among themselves with equal rights and liberties.[52]

His *Letter to the King of Poland*[53] makes clear that he has no fundamental objection to archbishops and bishops provided that they preach the Word of God, rightly administer the sacraments, and make no unjustified claims for status and privilege. The papal Church had failed in these respects. It had destroyed the true relationship between the faithful and Christ, the Head of the Church, and widespread corruption had ensued.

In the third edition of 1543 Calvin introduced into the *Institutes* a detailed account of the ministry by which he believed 'the Lord willed his Church to be governed'.[54] It is not necessary for our purpose to undertake a close examination of the fourfold ministry of pastors, teachers (or doctors), elders, and deacons.[55] It must be said that his attempt to find a scriptural basis for it is not more noticeably successful than that of the papist, episcopalian, or congregationalist endeavouring to provide scriptural justification for the ministry of his own tradition. The evidence is forced, and what does not fit into the preconceived scheme is explained away.

It is more important to notice that for Calvin, unlike the earlier, idealistic Luther, the ministry is no matter of human expediency and contrivance. It is ordained by God. This is implied by the Pauline concept of the body of Christ, not merely because of the obvious analogy between a human body and an institution, each of which possesses members who perform special functions for the benefit of the whole, but rather because Christ as the Head has, through his Spirit, imparted ministry to the Church, his body, as his gift. The Church's ministers 'represent his person'.[56] 'God himself appears in our midst, and, as Author of this order [namely, the ministry], would have men recognize him as present in his institution.'[57] 'No ecclesiology', says Geddes MacGregor, 'has ever more exalted the ministry, under Christ, than does Calvin's.'[58] The words 'under Christ' are important. The headship of Christ over the Church is constitutive of all that Calvin has to say about Church order. Any system which implied the usurpation of Christ's place as Head of the Church, whether by pope or people, was no Church order, but led inevitably to the chaos which Calvin saw both in the Church of Rome and in the anabaptist sects.

Calvin's high doctrine of the ministry is seen also in what he says about the choice and ordination of ministers.[59] Their selection from among those who are of sound doctrine and holy life is the responsibility of ministers who must instruct and examine them, and, if they are approved, present them to the people for their acceptance. At the ordination ministers preside and pray over the candidate. Calvin allows the ceremony of the laying on of hands,[60] although it was not the practice at Geneva in his time. He notes that it is a scriptural custom, observed by the apostles, and commends it accordingly, provided that it is not regarded superstitiously as an act which in itself confers the Holy Spirit. Ordination is accomplished by God through the Holy Spirit; the imposition of hands expresses it symbolically.[61]

Calvin is not unwilling to speak of ordination as a sacrament:

> As far as the true office of presbyter is concerned, which is commended to us by Christ's lips, I willingly accord that place [viz. as a sacrament] to it. ... However, I have not put it as number three among the sacraments because it is not ordinary or common with all believers, but is a special rite for a particular office (*Institutes* IV, xix. 28).[62]

CHURCH AND STATE

It remains to comment briefly on Calvin's teaching on the relationship between the Church's authority and that of rulers. It differs from the position which Luther reluctantly came to adopt, but, as F. Wendel remarks, is close to the latter's personal views. Spiritual and temporal jurisdictions are distinct. Calvin sets out the principle as follows:

> The Church does not have the right of the sword to punish or compel, not the authority to force; not imprisonment, nor the other punishments which the magistrate commonly inflicts. Then, it is not a question of punishing the sinner against his will, but of the sinner professing his repentance in a voluntary chastisement. The two conceptions are very different. The Church does not assume what is proper to the magistrate: nor can the magistrate execute what is carried out by the Church (*Institutes* IV, xi. 3).[63]

Civil government rightly exercises an authority which provides sanctions against crime and unsocial behaviour, and the Christian must acknowledge this. But the Church's concern is with men's consciences, and the purpose of its disciplinary measures is to expel notorious evildoers, to protect the community from bad example, and above all to lead offenders to repentance and restore them to communion.[64]

Many of the things which the Church does in a city or nation ought to cause a ruler to rejoice: the inculcation of honesty and industry, providence and thrift. As G. MacGregor puts it,[65] 'the least to be expected of the ruler and magistrates ... is that they should lend whatever authority and power they possess to the support of the Church through which the land has been so bountifully blessed'.

Calvin did expect it, and considered that the civil and ecclesiastical authorities should complement each other, and work in close collaboration. Calvin's Geneva was not a theocracy which subordinated the temporal to the spiritual power. That this has been so commonly assumed is a measure of the success he achieved (after much initial opposition) in securing the co-operation of the Genevan magistrates and the consistory. For Calvin the Church visible was more than an institution: it was an association, a community. He was not content that it should be a closed community walled off from the life of the population around it; it should embrace the whole people. Twentieth-century man may marvel that this should be so nearly achieved in the Geneva of Calvin's day. He will also probably have little liking for the strictness of the discipline which was exercised. But if the Church is the body of the Christ who came into the world to serve it and redeem it, Calvin's purpose was not at fault despite the faults which hindsight may discern in the relationship which he established between magistrates and Church at Geneva.

3 SEPARATISM

In our study up to this point we have met, broadly speaking, three types of thought about the Church visible. They are sometimes designated Catholic, Protestant, and Separatist; or hierarchical, evangelical, and pentecostal. Such labels, however, can be misleading, for no one of these types altogether excludes what is characteristic of the others. For example, it may not be said that the Catholic or hierarchical type excludes all consciousness of the need for protest and reform. We have come across a number of examples of such consciousness within the hierarchical Church of the Middle Ages. Nor may the great Catholic theologians justly be accused of unawareness of the demands of the gospel of Christ or the significance of the work of the Holy Spirit in the Church. Similar reservations are to be made for the other two types. Bearing this in mind, and also that summaries are certain to be inadequate, the three types are:

CATHOLIC (HIERARCHICAL)

The visible Church consists of all those who have been baptized and who participate in the grace of God given by Word and sacrament through episcopally ordained ministers. Spiritual discipline, worship, and government are ordered by the traditional hierarchy with, in Roman Catholic thought, the pope at its head. Stress is laid on the Church as an institution which is in continuity with the apostles, in that the hierarchy can trace its succession in orders back to the apostles.

PROTESTANT[66] (EVANGELICAL)

This type of Church idea has more in common with the first than is often acknowledged on either side. It sees the visible Church as consisting of the whole company of baptized faithful, nourished in their places of gathering by the preaching of the Word of God and the administration of the sacraments by ministers duly called and ordained. Spiritual discipline, worship, and government are ordered by properly constituted courts, consisting of ministers and laity, either at the local level as in Calvin's Geneva, or in a series of courts from the local to the national levels as in the Church of Scotland and the Lutheran state churches. Continuity with the apostles is conceived as preserved by the purity of the gospel preached rather than by a traceable succession in ministerial ordination.[67]

SEPARATIST (PENTECOSTAL)

We have already met certain of the characteristics of this type of thinking about the Church in the Montanists, the Novatianists, and the Donatists. The visible Church is the spirit-guided company of the holy, separated from the world and gathered together for the worship of God. No rule, discipline, or hierarchy external to the local group is acknowledged. The group itself is regarded as responsible to Christ for its own government. The Separatist church appoints and changes its ministers according to need. It tends to maintain a rigid separation from other Christians who cannot accept the standard of holiness which it sets up.

The Separatist idea was finding expression again in the wake of the Reformation, much to the consternation, as we have seen, of Luther and Calvin. It is true that religious fanatics and political extremists gravitated to the Separatist churches which sprang up in the sixteenth and seventeenth centuries. We are not here concerned with them (other Christian groups have had their share of these). Rather we are concerned with numbers of quiet godly people who almost from the beginning of the Reformation movement began to form themselves into separate local groups. They were motivated by the feeling that the Reformation leaders were not resolute enough and were retaining too much that smacked of the papal Church; by the conviction that religion is essentially a personal matter between God and the soul; that the gathering together of small groups for the breaking of bread and for prayers is the New Testament idea of the Church, and that personal holiness is to be attained by separating oneself from worldly enticements, and indeed from all worldly affairs so far as possible.

Both Luther and Calvin had no little sympathy with some of these convictions, and admiration for the courage of those who held them. But they opposed their separatism. This was destructive of the aim which Luther and Calvin were pursuing, each in his own way. Neither of them was, in intention, setting up a new or separate church. Each hoped for a reformation of the universal Church of Christ, whether city by city or nation by nation, which would be a true and inclusive *volkskirche* (church of the people).

The ecclesiology of the Separatists is well defined by the Englishman, Henry Barrow (executed in 1593):

> The true planted and rightly established Church of Christ is a company of faithful people, separated from the unbelievers and heathen of the land, gathered in the name of Christ, whom they truly worship and readily obey as their only King, Priest, and Prophet, and joined together as members of one body, ordered and governed by such offices and laws as Christ, in his last will and testament, hath thereunto ordained. . . . We hold all believers [to be] ecclesiastical and spiritual. . . . We know not what you mean by your old popish term of 'laymen' (*Discovery of the True Church*).[68]

No difference, then, is drawn between clergy and laity. Pastors are, however, appointed by the congregation. Discipline is the responsibility of 'ruling elders', also appointed by the congregation. The local congregation is thus autonomous, and in the words of a petition to James I of England in 1616 it has 'the right of spiritual administration and government in itself and over itself by the common and free consent of the people, independently and immediately under Christ'.[69]

Another characteristic of the Separatist churches was what is known as 'the voluntary principle'. It developed during the sixteenth century as it became clear that the power of the State was to be used to compel conformity in areas which were Lutheran, Calvinist, or Anglican no less than in countries which adhered to the papacy. Dissent was seen as tantamount to treason, and laws were passed to eradicate it. The voluntary principle was a protest against this Church-State totalitarianism. Its classical definition is given by Robert Browne (1550–1633) in a book with the expressive title, *A Treatise of Reformation without tarying for anie, and of the wickedness of those which will not reforme till the Magistrate command or compell them*[70] (1582):

> The Lord's people is of the willing sorte. It is conscience, not the power of man, that will drive us to seek the Lord's Kingdom. Therefore it belongeth not to the magistrate to compel religion, to plant churches by power, and to force a submission to ecclesiastical government by laws and penalties.

The Separatist groups which explicitly or implicitly adhered to these principles were many and varied.[71] They included the Hutterites of Moravia, the Mennonites of Holland, the English Independents, and many smaller groups. Agreed as they were in their main principles, there were important differences between them. Most, but not all, forbade the taking of civil office and were pacifists. Some practised community of goods. Some were apocalyptists in the sense that, like the second-century Montanists, they believed the Heavenly Jerusalem was soon to appear. Among these were the Melchiorites in Holland, and the violent group at Münster under John of Leyden. Many were pentecostalists in that they claimed for themselves a special guidance of the Holy Spirit. Henry Barrow, questioned in prison about his claim to possess 'a private spirit', answered that he had the spirit of the apostles 'in that measure that God hath imparted unto me, though not in that measure that the Apostles had, by any comparison. Yet the same Spirit. There is but one Spirit.'[72] Although not all these groups claimed special guidance of the Spirit, the name 'Spirituals' was often attached to the whole movement. 'Anabaptists' is another name often fastened on all Separatist groups, although all did not adopt the policy of rebaptizing their converts. Some, like the Quakers, the followers of George Fox (1624–91), dispensed with the sacraments altogether.[73]

J. S. Whale, to whom I have often referred in this chapter, himself a member of the Congregational Union of England and Wales, a union of groups which have their roots deep in the radical movement of the Reformation period, provides an illuminating study of it in Part III of his book *The Protestant Tradition*.[74] He points to its positive contributions to the history of Christianity. While he admits that the truth that religion is an intensely personal matter is complemented by the truth that it is also an intensely social matter, he holds that the radical reformers' insistence on the personal and voluntary principle came at a time when the totalitarian claims of both Catholic and Reformed states called for emphasis of the former truth. The persistence and courage with which the voluntary principle was held contributed much to the eventual achievement of religious toleration in most European countries. The claim to guidance by the Holy Spirit (the spiritual principle), open to question as it is if used to judge all others by the conscience of a small group or single individual, is nevertheless the proclamation, too often neglected in Christian thought and unrecognized in Christian experience, of the guiding work of the Spirit in the Church and its members.

On the other hand the fragmentation of Christian people into small separated sects can lead to disinterest in the unity of the Church; the claim to autonomy and the emphasis on the personal aspect of Christianity can lead to indifference to the note of catholicity; concentration on personal holiness can lead to a contempt for those who do not attain to the standard set by the group, and weakens that sense of missionary responsibility which is essential to apostolicity. These are the dangers of the Separatist ecclesiology. To place a disproportionate emphasis on one of the four credal notes of the Church has always endangered one or more of the others, and our study has revealed instances in which such over-emphasis has led to disaster. It is not being suggested that all churchmen of the Separatist type have succumbed to this danger. Mention of the name of the Baptist William Carey (1761–1834), often described as the father of modern Protestant missions, and of the role that many modern heirs of the sixteenth-century sectarians play in the ecumenical movement, is sufficient to refute any such insinuation.

13

Anglican Doctrine of the Church

The Reformation took a different turn in England, despite the influence of Continental reformers like Martin Bucer and Peter Martyr Vermigli, an Italian who was invited to England by Archbishop Cranmer in the closing years of Henry VIII's reign. Its course ran from its beginnings in the reign of the tyrannical but conservatively Catholic Henry VIII (1509–47), through radical changes in a Protestant direction under the Protector Somerset in the short reign of the boy king Edward VI (1547–53), reaction under Mary (1553–8), so fanatically, if understandably, determined to restore papal authority, and the long reign of Elizabeth I (1558–1603) who, with her ecclesiastical and temporal advisers, attempted to unify the nation on the basis of a moderate reformation of the Church. In this she met with a large measure of success in the face both of numerous supporters of the papacy who received much help and encouragement from Rome, France, and Spain, and of many who looked for a reformation closer to the Swiss pattern.

The Church in England, passing through this experience, and in the seventeenth century through the struggle between episcopalians and Puritans which came to its climax in the reign of Charles I (1625–49), and through a period of radical remodelling on Puritan lines during the Protectorate of Oliver Cromwell (1653–8) emerged after the restoration of the monarchy in 1660 as a reformed Church unlike any other in Europe, with the possible exception of Sweden. The Act of Supremacy bound it to a recognition of the monarch as Supreme Governor of the Church in England.[1] The Act of Uniformity of 1662 (succeeding those of 1549, 1552, and 1559) bound it to a Prayer Book which was an attempt 'to mould the best of the old with the best of the new',[2] and which its admirers claim 'as a ripe fruit of the Christian centuries, bearing within itself the loveliness of a reformed and Catholic devotion'.[3] Subscription to the Thirty-nine Articles of

Religion, which received their final form in 1571, was required of the clergy. While these Articles endorsed the main doctrinal emphases of the Reformation[4] they also maintained that the Nicene, Athanasian, and Apostles' creeds, long accepted by the Church in the West as authoritative, 'ought thoroughly to be received and believed' (Article VIII). The Church retained the threefold ministry of bishop, priest, and deacon in continuity with the medieval Church,[5] and the preface to its Ordinal declared the intention that these orders should be 'continued, and reverently used and esteemed'.

Our concern, however, is with the Anglican doctrine of the Church. English churchmen of the late sixteenth century and the seventeenth wrote a great deal on the subject,[6] and here I shall note the main trends of Anglican ecclesiology and illustrate them from the most prominent of these writers and from Anglican formularies.

THE CHURCH VISIBLE AND INVISIBLE

We have seen that the Reformers developed the idea of the invisible Church against the Roman claim that the visible hierarchical Church centred upon the papacy is the true Church. Anglican writers devoted much space to the meanings and relationships of such terms as 'invisible Church', 'the elect', 'body of Christ', 'mystical body of Christ', and 'visible Church'. H. F. Woodhouse's discussion shows that there is no unanimity among them on these matters, and that even in a single writer different answers seem to be given. He illustrates this from Richard Hooker (*c*. 1554–1600).

Hooker in a number of places clearly identifies the mystical body of Christ with the invisible Church whose members are known to God only.[7] It consists of 'none but only true Israelites, true sons of Abraham, true servants and saints of God'.[8] Hooker also speaks of the visible Church as having Christ for its Head, and as being a body.[9] Thirdly we find him using the phrase 'visible mystical body' in reference to the Church at worship:

> This holy and religious duty of service towards God concerneth us one way in that we are men, and another way in that we are joined as parts to that visible mystical body which is the Church.[10]

Woodhouse briefly discusses[11] whether Hooker is making a triple distinction: visible body, mystical body (invisible), and visible mystical body. He concludes that his distinction is basically between the visible Church and the mystical body. It is not a distinction between false and true, for the visible Church includes faithful and true Christians, although who these are none 'can pronounce, saving only the searcher of all men's hearts, who alone intuitively doth know in this kind who are His'.[12] This may well be the correct elucidation of Hooker's meaning. Woodhouse admits, however, that 'Hooker's qualifications and thought are not fully satisfactory'.[13] This is true, for Hooker gives the term 'mystical body' a meaning which it did not have prior to Wyclif; and since he identifies the mystical body with the invisible Church, his introduction of the phrase 'visible mystical body' can only be confusing.

It is not to be concluded that Hooker had no interest in the visible Church. The very title of *The Laws of Ecclesiastical Polity* proclaims his concern for the Church as an organized society, and of this, its membership, extension, divisions, ministry, sacraments, and life he has many wise things to say.

Richard Field (1561–1616) in his treatise *Of the Church* (1606) provides a clearer discussion in a passage where he seems to follow Calvin's reminder that Scripture speaks of the Church in two ways.[14] He maintains that it is more accurate to speak of different aspects of the one Church than of two churches, one visible and the other invisible:

We say that there is a visible and invisible Church, not meaning to make two distinct Churches, as our adversaries falsely and maliciously charge us, though the form of words may serve to insinuate some such thing, but to distinguish the divers considerations of the same Church; which though it be visible in respect of the profession of supernatural verities revealed in Christ, use of holy Sacraments, order of Ministry, and due obedience yielded thereunto, and they discernible that do communicate therein; yet in respect of those most precious effects, and happy benefits of saving grace, wherein only the elect do communicate, it is invisible; and they that in so happy, gracious, and desirable things have communion among themselves are not discernible from others to whom this fellowship is denied, but are known only unto God. That Nathaniel was an Israelite all men knew; that he was 'a true Israelite, in whom was no guile', only Christ knew (*Of the Church* I, x).[15]

In the discussion which follows the above extract it is clear that Field firmly believes in the necessity of the Church visible and in its divine foundation. It is the locus within which men 'profess the saving truth of God, which all are bound to do that look for salvation'. He defends Luther and other early Reformers against the charge of denying the validity of the idea of the visible Church. They had, however, held (and Field agrees) that there were periods when 'errors and heresies so much prevail ... that the sincerity of religion is upholden and the truth of the profession of Christians defended and maintained but only by some few, and they molested, persecuted, and traduced, as ... enemies to the common peace of the Christian world'. This had been the case in the time of Athanasius, at the height of Arian ascendancy. They had believed also, though Field does not here mention it, that this point had been reached in the later medieval Church. But the great Reformers, and Anglican theologians like Field, did not believe that the Church visible had ceased to exist.[16] It was not the creation of a new Church for which they worked, but for the Church's reformation. Field goes on to say that Robert Bellarmine, the contemporary Roman Catholic apologist,[17] was wasting his time in 'proving that there is, and always hath been a visible Church', for this is not denied by Anglican theologians, although some hold that there have been times in its history when few have been faithful to the truth of God. Field concludes this discussion by declaring that 'touching the visibility and invisibility of the Church' one should say that 'the same Church is at the same time both visible and invisible in divers respects'.

THE VISIBLE CHURCH

A certain preoccupation with the question of the Church invisible, then, does not signify that Anglican theologians lacked interest in the Church visible. They use the Pauline concept of the body, and insist that Christ is its only Head, governing it and imparting to it life and order through the Holy Spirit, in contexts which leave no doubt that they are speaking of the visible Church. They are concerned with questions of the ministry, the preaching of the gospel, the administration of the sacraments, and discipline. Those of the Thirty-nine Articles which deal with the Church speak only of the visible Church. While the doctrine of predestination and election is set out in Article XVII, no attempt is made to link it with ecclesiology by means of a doctrine of the invisible Church.[18]

The articles, or paragraphs of articles, which speak of the Church are set out here, with some comments:

Article XIX, *Of the Church*:

The visible Church of Christ is a congregation of faithful men, in the which the pure Word of God is preached, and the sacraments be duly administered according to Christ's ordinance in all those things that of necessity are requisite to the same.

As the Church of *Jerusalem, Alexandria* and *Antioch* have erred, so also the Church of *Rome* hath erred, not only in their living and manner of Ceremonies, but also in matters of Faith.

It is noteworthy that, although the article is entitled *Of the Church*, its first words are 'The visible Church of Christ. . . .' To be noted also is the closeness of the definition in the first paragraph to that of the Lutheran Augsburg Confession.[19] The four churches mentioned in the second paragraph are the patriarchates of the early Church before the rise of Constantinople in the fourth century. There is no suggestion here that because of their errors they ceased to belong to the Church of Christ.

Article **xx**, *Of the Authority of the Church*, illustrates Anglican insistence on holy Scripture as the criterion in doctrine and forms of worship:

The Church hath power to decree Rites or Ceremonies, and authority in Controversies of Faith: And yet it is not lawful for the Church to ordain anything that is contrary to God's Word written . . . besides the same ought it not to enforce anything to be believed for necessity of Salvation.

Article **xxi**, *Of the Authority of General Councils*, in declaring that 'General Councils may not be gathered together without the commandment and will of Princes' says something that was thoroughly understood and generally accepted in the Reformed churches of sixteenth-century Europe, but is not likely to be considered relevant in the twentieth. The article declares that general councils can err, and that their decisions on matters of faith are not binding unless it is clear that they are 'taken out of holy Scripture'.

Article **xxiii**, *Of Ministering in the Congregation*, rejects the radical claim that any man may preach and administer the sacraments. Only those may do so who are 'lawfully called, and sent . . . by men who have public authority given unto them in the Congregation, to call and send Ministers into the Lord's vineyard'. Standing by itself, this might seem to legislate for the congregational type of church order advocated by the Separatists. But it must be read in conjunction with Article **xxxvi** (below, p. 186).

Article **xxvi**, *Of the Unworthiness of the Ministers, which hinders not the effect of the Sacrament*, is adequately summarized by its title.

It affirms that principle which was established at the Council of Arles in 314,[20] and was also to be affirmed in other Reformed doctrinal statements.[21] That this implies no condonation of wickedness in a minister is shown by the provision in the Article's second paragraph:

> that inquiry be made of evil Ministers, and that they be accused by those who have knowledge of their offences; and finally being found guilty, by just judgement be deposed.

Article xxxiv, *Of the Traditions of the Church*:

> It is not necessary that Traditions and Ceremonies be in all places one, and utterly like. . . . Whosoever through his private judgement, willingly and purposely, doth openly break the traditions and ceremonies of the Church, which be not repugnant to the Word of God, and be ordained and approved by common authority, ought to be rebuked openly. . . .
>
> Every particular or national Church hath authority to ordain, change, and abolish ceremonies or rites of the Church, ordained only by man's authority, so that all things be done to edifying.

The first paragraph is aimed at the English Puritans who held that nothing should be permitted in the worship and life of the Church which was not specifically commended in the Scriptures. The wording 'not repugnant to the Word of God' is, therefore, carefully chosen. The Puritans objected in particular to the use of the ring in marriage and to the sign of the cross in baptism.

The second paragraph anticipates the rejection in Article xxxvii of papal jurisdiction in England.

Article xxxvi, *Of Consecration of Bishops and Ministers*, affirms the adequacy of the Anglican Ordinal, first published in the reign of Edward VI, which provides forms for the consecration of bishops, the ordering of priests, and the making of deacons.[22] The preface of the Ordinal, as previously mentioned, declares the intention of the Church of England to continue the orders of bishop, priest, and deacon and to permit no one who has not had episcopal ordination to exercise ministerial functions in the Church. References to ministers elsewhere in the Thirty-nine Articles (e.g. xxiii) must, therefore, be interpreted in accordance with Article xxxvi.

The ministry of the Church of England is that of bishops, priests, and deacons. Nothing is said in the articles, or in the Ordinal, of a doctrine of apostolic succession, nor is it anywhere implied that churches which do not possess this threefold ministry have forfeited the name of Church.[23]

Article XXXVII, *Of the Civil Magistrates*:

> The King's Majesty hath the chief power in this Realm of England, and other his Dominions, unto whom the Chief Government of all Estates of this Realm, whether they be Ecclesiastical or Civil, in all causes doth appertain, and is not, nor ought to be, subject to any foreign jurisdiction.

Consequently in its third paragraph the Article states: 'The Bishop of Rome hath no jurisdiction in this Realm of England.' The second paragraph defines what is, and what is not, meant by the attribution to the monarch of the title of Supreme Governor in the Acts of Supremacy:

> We give not to our Princes the ministering either of God's Word, or of the Sacraments ... but that only prerogative, which we see to have been given always to godly Princes in holy Scriptures by God himself; that is, that they should rule all estates and degrees committed to their charge by God, whether they be Ecclesiastical or Temporal, and restrain with the civil sword the stubborn and evil-doers.

Dr Erik Routley notes[24] that this Article says nothing about the appointment of bishops by the Crown or parliamentary and royal assent to changes in the Book of Common Prayer: 'That all belongs to the British Constitution. . . . It is not stated in the Articles.' The Erastianism of these practices is greatly lessened by the consultation which now takes place regarding the appointment of bishops, and by powers now given to the Synod of the Church of England in the matter of forms of worship. The national churches and provinces of the Anglican Communion outside the established Church of England have autonomy in these matters.

Dr Routley, a Congregationalist, looks at the Thirty-nine Articles with mingled admiration and exasperation. He finds the articles on the Church to be indefinite and even evasive. Elements from different ecclesiologies are to be found: Catholic, in the implicit acceptance (Article VIII) of the credal descriptions of the Church, and the continuance of the orders of bishop, priest, and deacon (Article XXXVI); Lutheran, in the dependence of Article XIX on the Augsburg Confession; Calvinistic, in the use of the word 'visible' in Article XIX, and in what is said about the authority and obligations of magistrates in Article XXXVII. He finds that 'without the other half of the Calvinist statement (concerning the Church invisible) Article XIX is so vague as to include any doctrine whatever, since all depends on what is a congregation of faithful men and what, in the administration of Word and Sacrament, is deemed right'.[25]

On the other hand he writes:[26] 'It is the distinguishing quality of this document that alone of the sixteenth-century Confessions it seeks to accommodate diverse views rather than to separate its own from those of other bodies.' It may not have been remarkably successful in this, but the attempt had merit. In the ecumenical climate of the twentieth century it is being recognized that points of doctrine which sharply divided Christians 400 years ago are capable of a reconciliation which can enrich and strengthen the Church today, and that Catholic and Protestant have each preserved true insights which the other could not, or would not, recognize in a time of bitter conflict. This may be true of the doctrine of the Church.

THE BOOK OF COMMON PRAYER

Anglican thought and practice has been formed by the Book of Common Prayer at least as much as by the Thirty-nine Articles. In the Anglican Communion of autonomous churches and provinces which developed during the nineteenth and twentieth centuries, the Prayer Book of 1662, although revised by synodical action in many of them, is still regarded as a primary source of Anglican theology.

The book does not include any formal setting-out of a doctrine of the Church. It is to be noted, however, that the recital of one of the ancient creeds which contains the expression of belief in the Church under the marks of unity, holiness, catholicity, and apostolicity is prescribed at the principal acts of corporate worship. The Apostles' Creed is also made one of the bases of catechetical instruction.

Several of the collects prescribed for Sundays and festivals speak explicitly of the Church, and many more do so by implication. Biblical images are used: the household of God (Epiphany v and Trinity xxii), the body (Good Friday), and the temple (St Simon and St Jude). The Church is not a society contrived by men: it is God who built it 'upon the foundation of the Apostles and Prophets, Jesus Christ himself being the head corner-stone' (St Simon and St Jude); it is governed and sanctified by the Spirit of God (Good Friday); its various orders of ministry have been given by God (Ember Days). Several collects make clear that the historical, visible Church is in mind, and that this is 'a mixed society': it needs to pray that God will continually keep it in his true religion (Epiphany v); it acknowledges that the frailty of its members needs God's perpetual mercy (Trinity xv); it needs God's cleansing and defence (Trinity xvi and xxii); it is aware that its ministers may not always be faithful and true (St Matthias); it recognizes the need always to be nourished by the doctrine taught by the apostles and evangelists (collects for St John the Evangelist, St Mark, St Bartholomew, St Simon and St Jude).

There is one collect which introduces the idea of the Church as a society which extends beyond the empirical. The opening words of the collect for All Saints' Day are:

> O Almighty God, who hast knit together thine elect in one communion and fellowship, in the mystical body of thy Son Christ our Lord. . . .

Is this to identify the mystical body of Christ with the invisible Church of the elect as Wyclif had done,[27] and as Hooker seems to do?[28] The sentence is not necessarily to be so interpreted. It certainly implies that the elect are members of Christ's mystical body, but not that all members of the mystical body are elect. Nothing here precludes the interpretation of the term 'mystical body' in its original sense of those who by Christian initiation have become members of Christ. The collect teaches that the saints of the past are still members of the Church, and that the faithful of every generation in following and holding them for an example are in the same fellowship with them:

> . . . Grant us grace so to follow thy blessed saints in all virtuous and godly living, that we may come to those unspeakable joys, which thou hast prepared for them that unfeignedly love thee.

The phrase 'mystical body' occurs also in the prayer of thanksgiving after the communion in the Order for the Administration of the Lord's Supper:

> . . . we most heartily thank thee . . . that we are living members of his mystical body, which is the blessed company of all faithful people; and are also heirs through hope of thy everlasting kingdom. . . .

Here the mystical body clearly includes the visible, worshipping community in which there are many who still need to pray:

> . . . although we are unworthy, yet we beseech thee to accept this our bounden duty and service, not weighing our merits, but pardoning our offences; through Jesus Christ our Lord.

JOHN PEARSON ON THE CHURCH

One of the most influential Anglican theological works in the seventeenth century was *An Exposition of the Creed* by John Pearson (1612–86), Bishop of Chester. This commentary on the Apostles' Creed was published in 1659, had four further editions during Pearson's lifetime, and has been frequently reprinted. The section on the Church[29] deserves special notice here for its evidence of biblical and patristic scholarship, and because of its long continuing influence on Anglican theology.

He begins by stating that the Church is a society of 'the sons of men'. The Scriptures do not mention angels as members of the Church, nor can angels be said to be 'built upon the foundation of the apostles and prophets' (Eph. 2.20). He also excludes from his notion of the Church the people of Israel as such. He holds that all those who 'from the beginning pleased God' are saved through Christ; but because the catholicity of the Church 'must be understood in opposition to the legal singularity of the Jewish nation', the notion of the Church must be restricted to Christianity. Jesus spoke in the future tense to Peter: 'I will build my Church.' The Church, then, came into being at Pentecost by the gift of the Holy Spirit. Its first members were the apostles and other disciples of Jesus, about 120 in all, to whom were added those who were baptized in response to Peter's preaching, and who 'devoted themselves to the apostles' teaching and fellowship, to the breaking of bread and the prayers' (Acts 2.42).

THE UNITY OF THE CHURCH

This church in Jerusalem was one. Yet its members soon became members of several churches. How then can we speak of one Church? There follows an acute discussion of the N.T. use of the word *ekklesia* sometimes in the singular and sometimes in the plural. He finds that although there were several congregations or churches at Corinth (he cites 1 Cor. 14.34), Paul addresses his letter to 'the Church of God which is at Corinth'. A group of churches is properly spoken of as one Church because they are under one ruler or bishop. Similarly all churches in all cities and nations may be said to be one Church because all are under one supreme Governor, Jesus Christ, the bishop of our souls.

The unity of the churches in the one Church is sixfold. It is a unity of *origination* because Christ is their one foundation; of *faith* because they hold the doctrines taught by the apostles who received them from Christ; of the *sacraments* because they all acknowledge and receive baptism and the Lord's Supper; of *hope* because all are called, and this calling is in the hope of righteousness and eternal life, which are God's promises to those he calls; of *charity* because all 'endeavour to keep the unity of the spirit in the bond of peace' and heed Christ's words, 'by this shall all men know that ye are my disciples, if ye have love one to another'; and of *government and discipline* because they are united in having the same pastoral guides, appointed of God under the direction of the Spirit, to lead them in the same way of eternal salvation. 'As therefore there is no Church where there is no order, no ministry, so where the same order and ministry is there is the same Church.' By these six marks of unity 'millions of persons and multitudes of congregations are united into one body, and become one Church'.

THE CHURCH'S INDEFECTIBILITY

Pearson now asks whether this Church, which has had a continuous existence from the apostles to the present, will continue to the end of the world. In itself 'the Church is not of such a nature as would necessarily, once begun, preserve itself for ever'. Thousands have fallen away from it, and particular churches have disappeared. If this is possible of particular churches it is possible also of the universal Church. Nevertheless, the answer to the question is affirmative because, and only because, of the promises of God in Christ: 'The gates of hell shall not prevail against it'; 'lo, I am with you alway, even to the end of the world'.

THE CHURCH'S HOLINESS

The Church may properly be described as holy in several respects. Its members are called to holiness; the offices appointed and the powers exercised in the Church are holy 'by their institution and operation'; its members profess the holy name of Christ and are committed to holiness of life; God's purpose was to communicate sanctity through the Church so that men might become a 'holy and a precious people'.

But the unblemished holiness of which Paul speaks in Ephesians 5.21 ff clearly does not belong to the Church taken in the wide sense of all those who have been called and baptized. We have, then, to ask where, 'within the great complex body of the universal Church', may be found the Church to which this perfect holiness belongs. Pearson's answer is that it is beyond death. The Church of those who continue in this life is a mixed society of good and bad, as is taught in the parable of the wheat and tares and in similar parables.

> I conclude, therefore, as the ancient Catholics did against the Donatists, that within the Church, in the public profession and external communion thereof, are contained persons truly good and sanctified, and hereafter saved, and together with them other persons void of all saving grace, and hereafter to be damned; and that Church containing these of both kinds may well be called *holy*, as St Matthew called Jerusalem *the holy city* ... when we know there was in that city a general corruption in manners and worship.

The hypocrites and profane who have communicated with the rest of the Church while they lived are

> by death separated from the external communion of the Church, and having no true internal communion with the members and the head thereof, are totally and finally cut off from the Church of Christ.

Pearson, then, does not accept a distinction between the Church visible and invisible in any such way as to suggest that Christ founded two churches:

> Not that there are two Churches of Christ, one, in which good and bad are mingled together, another, in which there are good alone ... but one and the same Church, in relation to different times, admitteth or not admitteth the permixtion of the wicked, or the imperfection of the holy. . . . The same Church is really holy in this world in relation to all godly persons contained in it, by a real infused sanctity; the same is farther yet at the same time perfectly holy in reference to the saints departed and admitted to the presence of God; and the same Church shall hereafter be more completely holy in the world to come, when all the members actually belonging to it shall be at once perfected in holiness and completed in happiness.

THE CHURCH'S CATHOLICITY

Pearson notes that the word 'catholic' is not scriptural, but came into early use among patristic writers. He discusses its various secular and ecclesiastical usages: a title for the emperor's chief revenue officer; to describe those epistles which are addressed to the Church in general; a title for Christian patriarchs. Most frequently, however, it was used for the Church as a whole. Its signification when so used is fourfold. First, it refers to the diffusiveness or extent of the Church as it fulfils its commission to 'teach all nations'. Second, it refers to the whole-ness of the Church's doctrine: it teaches all things 'necessary for a Christian to know'. Third, it refers to the universal obedience which the Church requires from all persons of all conditions to all the precepts of the gospel. Finally, the Church is catholic because God has provided in it all the necessary graces whereby men may become perfect in Jesus Christ.[30]

NO SALVATION OUTSIDE THE CHURCH

Pearson holds as strongly as did Cyprian and Augustine that

> Christ hath appointed [the Church] as the only way unto eternal life. We read at the first, that 'the Lord added to them daily such as should be saved'; and what was then daily done hath been done since continually. Christ never appointed two ways to Heaven, nor did He build a Church to save some, and make another institution for other men's salvation.

Although the ark of Noah contained both good and bad, one had to be in it to be saved from the flood. Pearson presents the doctrine of *extra ecclesiam nulla salus* in all its starkness, showing no awareness of any problem for theodicy in supposing that millions who have had no opportunity of becoming members of the Church are damned. 'None shall ever escape the eternal wrath of God, which belong not to the Church of God.' He therefore stresses the great danger of in-curring excommunication and of falling into heresy or schism. Nor must there be any complacent reliance on merely formal church membership. The means of grace must not be neglected: 'It is necessary that the persons abiding in the communion of (the Church) should be really and effectually sanctified.'

THE CONTINUITY OF THE CHURCH

Pearson concludes this section of his book by maintaining that there are no new Churches:

> (Since) the Church which is truly Catholic containeth within it all which are truly Churches, whosoever is not of the Catholic Church cannot be of the true Church. That Church alone which first began at Jerusalem on earth will bring us to the Jerusalem in Heaven; and that alone began there which always embraceth the 'faith once delivered to the saints'. What-soever Church pretendeth to a new beginning pretendeth at the same time

to a new Churchdom, and whatsoever is so new is none, so necessary it is to believe 'the Holy Catholic Church'.

Implicit here is the Anglican rejection of the suggestion that it is a new Church, founded in the sixteenth century.

14

Catholic Reformation and Protestant Confessions

The Church of Rome's response to the reforming movement was a vigorous introduction of reforms which many of its adherents recognized to be necessary. Much was achieved in the areas of discipline, education, and pastoral care as a result both of a renewed devotion on the part of the clergy and the rise of new Orders founded by saintly men and guided by wise superiors. The most important of these were the Society of Jesus (Jesuits), founded by Ignatius Loyola and sanctioned in 1540, and the Congregation of the Oratory, founded by Philip Neri and sanctioned in 1575. This response is known as the Counter-Reformation,[1] and under this heading Church-history textbooks usually discuss the Council of Trent.

THE COUNCIL OF TRENT

The Emperor Charles V had long demanded a council which he hoped would address itself to the reform of the Church. Popes, while not refusing the demand outright, spoke much of the difficulties in the way, but at length a Council was summoned by Pope Paul III. It held twenty-five sessions between 1545 and 1563, at Trent (1547–9), at Bologna (1551–2), and again at Trent (1562–3) under Pius IV. An early decision that voting should be by individual bishops and not by nations ensured that the results of the Council would be conservative, since Italian pro-papal bishops far outnumbered those of any other nation. The Council examined many of the major theological issues raised by the Reformers. Much time was spent on the authority of the Scriptures, justification, predestination, and the theology of the sacraments, and the Reformers' views on these subjects were firmly rejected. In the areas of discipline and practice, however, the Council tacitly admitted the validity of many of the Reformers' protests. The

Council's 'Decrees of Reformation' called for significant reforms, among them a greater control over monasteries by diocesan bishops, stricter regulations for the issuing of indulgences, and provisions for raising the standards of holiness, learning, and competence of the clergy.

Our concern, however, is whether the Council contributes to the discussion of the nature of the Church. Since Article VII of the Augsburg Confession[2] had offered a definition of the Church, the Council might have been expected to formulate canons on this subject. Yet nowhere do we find any formal treatment of the doctrine of the Church. Yves Congar[3] opens a brief discussion of the Council with the words: 'Strange fact: this Council which had to give an answer to the Reformation did not deal with the ecclesiological problem.' Nor did it deal with the currently controversial topic of the papacy.[4]

Nevertheless, throughout the documents of the Council the papal and hierarchical conception of the Church is assumed. In the 'Bull of Indiction' which prefaces the decrees, Pope Paul III speaks of himself as one who has 'been called to guide and govern the bark of Peter'[5] in the troubles of the time and as exercising on earth the authority of the apostles Peter and Paul.[6] He does not fail to remind the archbishops, bishops, abbots, and all others who have the privilege of sitting in a general council, of the oath which they have taken 'to us and to this Holy See'.[7] At the close of the Council the decrees and canons were submitted for the confirmation of 'the most blessed Roman Pontiff'.[8] The hierarchical nature of the Church is asserted to be of divine ordinance in a canon which anathematizes whoever says 'that in the Catholic Church there is not a hierarchy instituted by divine ordination, consisting of bishops, priests, and ministers (deacons)'.[9]

THE CATECHISM OF THE COUNCIL OF TRENT

At the conclusion of the Council certain matters in connection with the implementation of its decrees were entrusted to the pope. Among these was the compilation of a catechism. Charles Borromeo was largely responsible for its drafting, and after revision by a committee it was published in 1566 by Pope Pius V. It is not strictly a catechism, but a theological exposition of the Apostles' Creed, the seven sacraments, the ten commandments, and prayer, intended for the edification of the clergy and for their use in preaching and teaching.

Part I, Chapter X deals with the credal article 'I believe the holy

Catholic Church' in twenty 'questions', and concludes with five questions on 'the Communion of Saints'. The questions treat in turn of the meaning of the word *ecclesia* (ii); other scriptural names and descriptions of the Church (iv); the distinction between the Church militant and the Church triumphant (v); the nature of the Church militant (vi–vii); what persons are excluded from it (viii); the use of the word 'church' for parts of the Church (ix); the Church's unity and the Roman pontiff as its visible head (x–xii); the Church as holy (xiii), catholic (xiv), and apostolic (xv); the inerrancy of the Church (xvi); the prefiguration of the Church in the O.T. (ark of Noah, city of Jerusalem) (xvii); why 'to believe the Church' is an article of faith (xviii–xix); the reason for the credal wording 'I believe the holy Catholic Church' (instead of 'I believe in . . .') (xx); the link between the articles on the Communion of Saints and the Church (xxi); communion in the fruit of the sacraments (xxii); co-operation in the body of the Church (xxiii); the use of graces for the common good (xxv).

The ecclesiology presented in this section of the catechism is traditional, and St Augustine is cited far more frequently than any other of the early Fathers. Here I shall mention points of particular interest.

1 The word ecclesia is defined in a way which most Reformers would have endorsed. It is noted that the N.T. ordinarily uses the word

> to designate the Christian commonwealth only, and the congregation of the faithful; that is, of those who were called by faith unto the light of truth and the knowledge of God. . . . 'The Church', says St Augustine, 'consists of the faithful, dispersed throughout the world' (part I, ch. x, q. ii).[10]

The Church differs from other societies of men in origin and end:

> [It rests] on the wisdom and counsel of God; for he called us by the inward inspiration of the Holy Ghost, who opens the hearts of men, and outwardly, through the labour and ministry of his pastors and preachers. . . . The Christian people are justly called a Church . . . because, despising earthly and mortal things, they pursue only things heavenly and eternal (q. iii).

That the Church is the body of Christ is noted in q. iv, but the concept of the Church as the mystical body is not developed. The nearest approach to such a development is in q. xxii where the communion of saints is interpreted as 'a communion of sacraments'. The sacraments 'unite us to God and render us partakers of him whose grace we receive'; and 'the word "communion" belongs in a more special manner to the Eucharist, which accomplishes this communion itself'. But in q. xxiii the body image, following 1 Cor. 12.14 ff, is used quite pragmatically to illustrate the contributions which each member of the Church makes to the health and welfare of the whole.

2   The Church triumphant and the Church militant. No reference is made to the doctrine of the invisible Church. The distinction which the catechism dwells on is that between the Church triumphant and the Church militant:[11.]

> The Church triumphant is the most glorious and happy assemblage of blessed spirits, and of those who have triumphed over the world, the flesh, and the devil, and who, now free and secure from the troubles of this life, enjoy everlasting bliss. But the Church militant is the society of all the faithful who still dwell on earth, and is called militant, because it wages eternal war with those most implacable enemies, the world, the flesh, and the devil (q. v).

They are not, however, two churches, but constituent parts of the one Church. The Church militant consists of both good and bad. The good 'are linked together not only by profession of the same faith, and the communion of the same sacraments, but also by the spirit of grace, and the bond of charity' (q. vi). None can know with certainty who belongs to this class. There then follows the sentence:

> Of this part of the Church, therefore, we are not to suppose Christ our Saviour to speak when he refers us to the Church, and commands us to obey her (Matt. 18.17); for, unknown as is that portion of the Church, how can anyone be certain to whose decision he should recur, whose authority obey? (q. vi).

Where, then, can authority within the Church be identified? The answer is not provided until q. ix in which we are told that Matthew 18.17 refers to the Church in the sense of 'the prelates and pastors', that is, 'the authorities of the Church'. Q. xi moreover makes plain that ultimate authority in the Church militant is exercised by the Roman pontiff.

The bad members of the Church are likened to the chaff which is mingled with the grain on the threshing-floor, and to 'dead members' which 'sometimes remain attached to a (living) body' (q. vii). Being still in the Church they may yet be 'assisted in recovering lost grace and life' by the faithful, and they 'enjoy those fruits which are ... denied to such as are utterly cut off from the Church' (q. xxiv). What these fruits are is not explained.

Three groups are excluded from the Church: unbelievers, who have never belonged to it; heretics and schismatics, who have quitted it, though these are still under the Church's power (*potestas*) and 'may be cited before her tribunal, punished and condemned by anathema'; and the excommunicated, who are excluded 'until they repent'.

> With regard to the rest, although shameful and wicked persons, there is no doubt that they still continue in the Church; and of this the faithful are frequently to be informed, in order that they may convince themselves, that, even were the lives of her ministers debased perchance by crime, they are still included within her pale, nor do they on that account lose any part of their power (*potestas*).[12]

3   The unity of the Church and the papacy. Papal primacy is discussed under the heading of the Church's unity.

> This Church has ... one ruler and one governor, the invisible one, Christ, whom the eternal Father 'hath made head over all the Church, which is his body' (Eph. 1.22); but the visible one is he, who, the legitimate successor of Peter, the Prince of the Apostles, occupies the See of Rome (q. x).

In q. xi the visible headship of the pope is supported by quotations from Jerome, Irenaeus, Cyprian, Optatus, Basil, and Ambrose.[13] No historical or theological arguments are adduced to support the claim of the bishop of Rome to be the legitimate successor of Peter, or to have universal jurisdiction over the Church. There is simply the assertion that

> as a visible Church requires a visible head, our Saviour appointed Peter head and pastor of all the faithful, when, in the most ample terms, he committed to his care the feeding of his sheep, so as that he wished his successor to have the very same power of ruling and governing the whole Church (q. xi).

There is no allusion to the temporal claims of the papacy.

4   Holiness. The Church is holy, even though it contains sinners, because, like the things called holy in the Scriptures (vessels, vestments, altars, the firstborn), it is dedicated to God. Similarly St

Paul calls the Corinthian Christians, grievous sinners though some of them were, 'sanctified and holy'. The Church is also holy because it is united to Christ, 'the fountain of all holiness'. Moreover,

> the Church alone has the legitimate worship of sacrifice, and the salutary use of the sacraments, by which, as by the efficacious instruments of divine grace, God effects true holiness, so that whosoever are really holy cannot be outside the Church (q. xiii).

5 Catholicity. The Church is catholic or universal because it is limited neither by territorial frontier, race, class, or sex, nor by time. All the faithful who have lived from the time of Adam and who shall live as long as the world exists are included.

> She is also called universal because, like those who entered the ark, lest they should perish in the flood, all who desire to attain eternal salvation must cling to and embrace her (q. xiv).

This last somewhat forced simile does not seem to illustrate very aptly the Church's catholicity.

6 Apostolicity. The true Church is to be recognized by its derivation from the apostles. Its doctrines are those which the apostles handed down. Moreover,

> the Holy Ghost, who presides over the Church, governs her by no other than apostolic ministers; and this Spirit was first imparted to the apostles, and has, by the supreme goodness of God, always remained in the Church (q. xv).

The apostolic succession is seen here as a tradition of doctrine, and a succession in ministry by the reception of the Holy Spirit.[14]

7 The Church's inerrancy.

> As this one Church, seeing it is governed by the Holy Ghost, cannot err in delivering the discipline of faith and morals, so all other societies which arrogate to themselves the name of Church, because guided by the spirit of the devil, are necessarily sunk in the most pernicious errors both of doctrine and morals (q. xvi).

8 The Church as an article of faith. Since the existence of the Church is a fact not doubted by any, why does the creed speak of the Church as an object of faith? The answer is that

> it is by the light of faith only, and not by any process of reasoning, that

the mind can comprehend those mysteries, which . . . are contained in the holy Church of God . . . the origin, privileges, and dignity of the Church (q. xviii).

The Church was not created by man, but by God. Its powers come not from man, but by a divine gift. Therefore

by faith alone can we understand that with the Church are deposited the keys of the kingdom of heaven; that to her has been confided the power of remitting sins; of excommunicating; and of consecrating the real body of Christ; and that her children have not here a permanent dwelling, but look for one to come (q. xix).

9 The meaning of 'I believe the Church'. The catechism notices that whereas the clauses of the creed which speak of the three divine Persons are introduced by *Credo in* (I believe in), this clause begins simply with *Credo* (I believe the Church). The reason is

that by this difference . . . we may distinguish God, the author of all things, from the things he has created, and acknowledge ourselves indebted to the divine goodness for all those exalted benefits, which have been conferred on the Church (q. xx).

10 The communion of saints. This clause is said to provide an interpretation of the preceding article on the Church and to declare also 'what ought to be the use of the mysteries which are contained in the Creed':

For all our researches and knowledge ought to be directed to one end, viz., to our admission into this so august and so blessed a society of the saints, and our most steady perseverance therein (q. xxi).

The communion of saints consists in communion in the fruits of the sacraments and communion in charity. The sacraments are divine gifts in the benefits of which all share.[15]

Fruit of all the sacraments appertains to all the faithful (q. xxii).

But there is also another communion in the Church which demands our attention; for every pious and holy action undertaken by one appertains to all, and becomes profitable to all, through charity, which 'seeketh not her own' (q. xxiii).

That the communion of saints is essentially a communion in charity is shown by Christ who 'taught us to say *our*, not *my*, bread, and other similar petitions, not looking to ourselves alone, but also to the general interests and salvation of all'. Paul's treatment of the aid which the members of the human body render to each other for the advantage of the whole body[16] teaches the same lesson. Nevertheless, the hierarchical structure of the Church is emphasized:

> To each member of this Church is also assigned his own peculiar office; for as some are appointed apostles, some teachers, but all for the public benefit, so to some it belongs to govern and to teach, to others, to be subject and to obey (ibid.).

Particular gifts which the faithful may possess are given to them 'for the public benefit, for the building up of the Church . . . the gift of healing . . . for the sake of him who is sick'. All must be ready to relieve the misery of the needy. He who is well supplied with this world's goods 'and seeth his brother in want, and will not assist him, is at once convicted of not having "the love of God within him" ' (q. xxv).

During succeeding centuries the Roman Catholic Church has authorized innumerable catechisms in all languages. On all of them the Catechism of the Council of Trent was a major influence until the appearance of the Dutch Catechism, authorized by the bishops of the Netherlands in 1966.[17]

ROBERT BELLARMINE (1542–1621)

In the post-Reformation period the Roman Catholic Church paid much attention to the defence of its position, and many of its theologians concentrated on apologetics or controversial theology. Peter Canisius (1521–97) and Thomas Stapleton (1535–98) were notable amongst these, but the most influential was Robert Bellarmine, an Italian Jesuit. He became engaged in controversy at Louvain where he was professor of theology, 1569–76. In 1576 he was appointed to the *Collegium Romanum* in Rome to teach a course in controversial theology which had just been introduced. Bellarmine possessed ideal qualities as a controversialist. He was reasonable, temperate, and fair. He was ready to recognize the strengths of the Reformed theology as well as to probe its weaknesses. In 1599 he was made a cardinal, and devoted his last years to writing on the spiritual life.

His best known work is *Disputations against the Heretics of the present time on the Controversies regarding the Christian Faith*,[18] usually referred to as the *Controversies*. It was based on his lectures at the *Collegium Romanum*, and was published during 1586–93.

THE VISIBILITY OF THE CHURCH

Bellarmine's ecclesiology is marked by an insistence on the visibility of the Church. He minimizes the idea of the Church as existing from Abel or Adam, thus differing from Turrecremata[19] and others before him. Though it may be said that the Church in some sense had a beginning in Adam, its true existence is derived from Christ who founded a society and placed his vicar at its head. The Church is

> the congregation of men bound by the profession of the same Christian faith and by communion in the same sacraments under the rule of lawful pastors, and especially of the only vicar of Christ on earth, the Roman pontiff (*Controversies* IV, iii.2).

He emphasizes the visibility of the Church in startling fashion when he writes:

> For one to be said to be part of the Church in some degree, I do not consider any interior virtue is required, but only an exterior profession of faith and participation in the sacraments, things which our sense perception can confirm. For the Church is a congregation of men which is as visible and palpable as are the assembly of the people of Rome, or the Kingdom of Gaul, or the republic of Venice (ibid. IV, iii.10).

Bellarmine is not here asserting that no more is required of Church members than a formal profession of faith and attendance at worship which may or may not be willing and sincere. He is speaking of the Church as it appears to those outside. A little later he speaks of the inward graces which are characteristic of the soul of the Church. He is, in fact, making the distinction which some schoolmen of the thirteenth century had made between membership *numero* and membership *merito*.[20] It may be, as Congar says,[21] that the distinction intended is between two ways in which men belong to the Church which is at once a spiritual and a visible body. But Congar admits that 'the way in which Bellarmine expressed himself long encouraged the idea of a distinction *within the Church itself* between a body made of what is visible therein, and a soul made of the interior elements of grace'.

THE PAPACY

Bellarmine strongly supported the papal supremacy. The pope

represents Christ as head of the body. He inherits the universal authority given by Christ to Peter. This authority is transmissible, whereas that given to the other apostles was delegated and not transmissible (III, v. 23). Hence, the authority which bishops possess in their dioceses is received from the pope (III, iv. 24).

The *Controversies* narrowly escaped being placed on the Index of prohibited books by Pope Sixtus V on the ground that it attributed to the pope only indirect temporal power:

> The pontiff, as pontiff, does not directly and immediately possess any temporal power, but only spiritual; nevertheless in a spiritual way he does indirectly possess a power, and that the highest, in temporal matters (III, v. 4).

This was considered to put an unjustifiable restriction on the papal powers, even though Bellarmine himself could derive from his doctrine the papal right to forbid the implementation of any laws which denied the Church's rights and to depose heretical monarchs. Sixtus V died before his proposed action against Bellarmine could be effected, and his successor dropped the matter.

REFORMED CONFESSIONS

The development of the doctrine of the Church in the Reformed Churches during the immediate post-Reformation period can best be illustrated from some of the Confessions and other documents of those Churches from the mid-sixteenth to the mid-seventeenth centuries.[22]

THE FRENCH CONFESSION OF FAITH (1559)

was issued by the first National Synod of the Reformed Church of France. It is largely the work of Calvin. Articles xxv to xxxii deal with the Church and its ministers.

> The true Church ... is the company of the faithful who agree to follow (God's) Word, and the pure religion which it teaches. ... Among the faithful there may be hypocrites and reprobates, but their wickedness cannot destroy the title of the Church (xxvii).[23]

The Church, properly speaking, only exists where the Word of God is received, and submitted to, and the sacraments are administered according to Christ's institution. Papal assemblies are condemned 'as the pure Word of God is banished from them, their sacraments are corrupted . . . and all superstitions and idolatries are in them'. Those who take part in them are separated from the body of Christ. Yet 'some trace of the Church is left in the papacy' and the efficacy of baptism in the papal church is admitted: 'Those baptized in it do not need a second baptism' (XXVIII).

Pastors, overseers, and deacons are needed for teaching, for the correction of errors, and for the care of the poor (XXIX). God is not 'bound to such aid and subordinate means' but it has pleased him to provide the Church with this order. 'Visionaries' who would like to destroy the ministry are denounced (XXV). All pastors have the same authority and power under the 'one only sovereign and universal bishop, Jesus Christ' (XXX). Thus the principle of parity of ministers is asserted.

'No person should undertake to govern the Church upon his own authority.' This should be by election. When the times demand, God may 'raise men in an extraordinary manner to restore the Church', but this rule must always be binding: 'that all pastors, overseers, and deacons should have evidence of being called to their office' (XXXI).

THE SCOTTISH CONFESSION OF FAITH (1560)

This was chiefly the work of John Knox, and was ratified by the Scottish Parliament in 1567. Chapters V and XVI–XVIII deal with the Church.

Chapter V on 'The Continuance, Increase, and Preservation of the Kirk' presents a brief summary of O.T. history in order to show that 'God preserved, instructed, multiplied, honoured, adorned, and called from death to life His Kirk in all ages since Adam until the coming of Christ Jesus in the flesh'.[24]

There has always been one Kirk, and always will be to the end of the world. It is catholic 'because it contains the chosen of all ages, of all realms, nations, and tongues'. It is the communion of saints, who have 'one God, one Lord Jesus, one faith and one baptism'. Outside it 'there is neither life nor eternal felicity'. It is invisible, known only to God, and includes the elect who are departed (the Kirk triumphant), and the elect who yet live or shall live (XVI).

The true Kirk is characterized by the notes of the true preaching of the Word of God, the right administration of the sacraments, and 'ecclesiastical discipline uprightly ministered'. It is contrasted with 'the horrible harlot, the false Kirk'. 'Neither antiquity, usurped title, lineal succession, appointed place, nor the numbers of men approving an error' are notes by which the spotless bride of Christ may be known. By the Word of God is meant the Scriptures of both Testaments, whose interpreter is the Holy Spirit (XVIII). These Scriptures are received from God, and it is blasphemous to say that they are received through the Kirk. The true Kirk is obedient to them and does not claim to control them.

THE BELGIC CONFESSION OF FAITH (1561)

This was drawn up by Guido de Brès. It is an expansion of the French Confession. It received the approval of Geneva, was endorsed by several synods in the Low Countries and declared authoritative by the Synod of Dort (1619), since when it has been the doctrinal standard of the Reformed Churches in Holland and Belgium and of the Dutch Reformed Church in America. Articles XXVII–XXXII deal with the Church.

This Confession, like the Scottish, adds Church discipline to the pure teaching of the gospel and the administration of the sacraments among the marks of the Church. Those who are members of the Church

> may be known by the marks of Christians, namely, by faith; and when they have received Jesus Christ the only Saviour, they avoid sin, follow after righteousness, love the true God and their neighbour. . . . But this is not to be understood as if there did not remain in them great infirmities; but they fight against them through the Spirit . . . continually, taking their refuge in the blood, death, passion, and obedience of our Lord Jesus Christ (XXIX).[25]

The 'false Church', by which is meant the Church of Rome, 'ascribes more power and authority to herself and her ordinances than to the Word of God . . . [and] relieth more upon men than upon Christ' (ibid.). Neither the Belgic nor the French Confession mentions the doctrine of the invisible Church,[26] though both teach the doctrine of predestination.

> There must be ministers or pastors to preach the Word of God, and to administer the Sacraments; also elders and deacons, who together with the pastors, form the Council of the Church (XXX).

These should be chosen by election. Parity of ministers of the Word is asserted (XXXI).

THE SECOND HELVETIC CONFESSION (1566)

The First Helvetic Confession, drawn up at Basel in 1536, was an attempt to provide a document which could unify Lutherans and the Swiss Reformed Churches. It failed in this purpose, but did unite the German-speaking Swiss Reformed Churches. The much longer Second Helvetic Confession (1566), was based upon it and was composed by Johann Heinrich Bullinger who had contributed to the former document. It was adopted by all the Swiss Reformed Churches except Basel, and remained authoritative until the mid-nineteenth century. Chapter xvii treats 'Of the Catholic and Holy Church of God and of the One Only Head of the Church', and xviii 'Of the Ministers of the Church, their Institution and Duties'.

> Because God from the beginning would have men to be saved ... (1 Tim. 2.4), it is altogether necessary that there always should have been, and should be now, and to the end of the world, a Church (xvii).[27]

The Church is 'an assembly of the faithful called or gathered out of the world'; a communion of all saints, who by faith share in the benefits offered through Christ. It is called catholic because it is not limited to times and places: 'Therefore we condemn the Donatists who confined the Church to I know not what corners of Africa. Nor do we approve of the Roman clergy who have recently passed off only the Roman Church as catholic.' The Church militant on earth and the Church triumphant are parts of the same Church, each in fellowship with the other. The former has always had many particular churches because of the diversity of its members. The Church militant has been set up differently at different times, for example by the patriarchs, by Moses, and by Christ through the gospel. The claim is made 'that now the ceremonies being abolished, the light shines unto us more clearly, and blessings are given to us more abundantly, and a fuller liberty'.

The Church cannot err, provided it rests on Christ 'and upon the foundation of the prophets and apostles'. Christ is the sole Head. It needs no vicar of Christ. Christ does not need a substitute as though he were absent. To the charge that the Reformation brought confusion, dissension, and schism, the answer is given that the Roman Church had experienced much contention and division. Such things were not unknown in the early Church. Yet God uses dissensions to illuminate the truth and to test and strengthen those who are in the right.

Earlier Confessions are followed very closely in treating of the notes of the Church, and the marks of membership.

The principle that 'outside the Church of God there is no salvation' is asserted, but the interesting discussion which follows under this heading indicates unwillingness to apply it in a rigoristic manner. It is implied that it would be better to say 'outside Christ there is no salvation':

> For as there was no salvation outside Noah's ark when the world perished in the flood, so we believe that there is no certain salvation outside Christ, who offers himself to be enjoyed by the elect in the Church; and hence we teach that those who wish to live ought not to be separated from the true Church of Christ.

It is noted that 'God had some friends outside the commonwealth of Israel'. Biblical instances are cited. Not all those who do not participate in the sacraments, whose faith sometimes fails, or who are subject to imperfections and errors, are outside the Church. This is why the Church 'may be termed invisible ... because, being hidden from our eyes and known only to God, it often secretly escapes human judgement':

> Hence we must be very careful not to judge before the time, nor undertake to exclude, reject, or cut off those whom the Lord does not want to have excluded or rejected, and those whom we cannot eliminate without loss to the Church. On the other hand, we must be vigilant lest, while the pious snore the wicked gain ground and do harm to the Church.

The Confession also recognizes that not all who are in the number of the Church are living and true members. There are some who outwardly hear the Word, receive the sacraments, seem to pray and to exercise charity: 'They are not of the Church, just as traitors in a state are numbered among its citizens before they are discovered.'

The unity of the Church is said to consist not in outward rites and ceremonies but in the truth of the Catholic faith which is given by holy Scripture and summarized in the Apostles' Creed. Within this Catholic faith both a diversity of rites and a freedom is possible which does not dissolve the Church's unity.

Chapter XVIII deals at considerable length with the ministry. 'The office of ministers is a most ancient arrangement of God himself' for the establishing, governing, and preservation of the Church. Ministers in the N.T. were called apostles, prophets, evangelists, bishops (overseers), elders, pastors, and teachers. In the course of time many other names for ministers were introduced:

> Some were appointed patriarchs, others archbishops, others suffragans; also metropolitans, archdeacons, deacons, subdeacons, acolytes, exorcists, cantors, porters, and I know not what others, as cardinals, provosts, and priors; greater and lesser fathers, greater and lesser orders. But we are not troubled about all these. . . . For us the apostolic doctrine concerning ministers is sufficient.

The Confession speaks of bishops, defined as 'the overseers and watchmen of the Church who administer the food and needs of the life of the Church', elders, pastors, and teachers as being sufficient for the times.

Ministers must be called and elected by the Church or by those delegated by the Church. They must be ordained by the elders with the laying on of hands. Those who set themselves up as ministers are condemned.

Emphasis is placed on the ministers of the Church as servants. They are not priests. Christ is 'the only priest for ever, and lest we derogate anything from him, we do not impart the name of priest to any minister'. The N.T. indeed speaks of all believers as priests, but this is because they are able to offer spiritual sacrifices to God through Christ, and not in respect of any office. Ministers are servants of Christ and stewards of the mysteries of God, called to preach the gospel and administer the sacraments:

> The apostle wants us to think of ministers as ministers. Now the apostle calls them *hupēretas* (1 Cor. 4.1), rowers, who have their eyes fixed on the coxswain, and so men who do not live for themselves, or according to their own will, but for others—namely, their masters, upon whose command they altogether depend.

Ministers are equal in power and authority. Yet the scriptural practice is admitted by which

> some one of the ministers called the assembly together, proposed matters to be laid before it, gathered the opinions of the others, in short, to the best of man's ability took precaution lest any confusion should arise.

So St Peter acted, according to the Acts of the Apostles, but 'was not on that account preferred to the others, nor endowed with greater authority than the rest'. Jerome is quoted[28] as a witness that the distinction between bishops and elders is not scriptural. The drift of the passage, however, is that, while some may rightly be chosen in the Church for a role of leadership, this is to be interpreted in terms of service.

The ancient principle that the efficacy of the Word and sacraments is not dependent on the worthiness of ministers[29] is affirmed. Yet there must be proper discipline among ministers, and the synods of the Church must have authority to depose.

THE WESTMINSTER CONFESSION (1647)

During the Civil War in England the 'Long Parliament' set up the Westminster Assembly to make recommendations for the reform of the Church of England. Although it included some Episcopalians and Independents the majority of its members were Calvinists who favoured a presbyterian form of government. The Assembly drew up a Confession of Faith, which was accepted by the General Assembly of the Church of Scotland in 1647, and approved by Parliament in 1648. It has become the standard of Presbyterian doctrine in the English-speaking world. Chapters xxv, xxvi, xxx, and xxxi deal with the Church.

The doctrine of the invisible Church in distinction from the visible Church is set out very clearly in Chapter xxv.

1 The catholic or universal Church, which is invisible, consists of the whole number of the elect, that have been, are, or shall be gathered into one, under Christ the head thereof; and is the spouse, the body, the fulness of him that filleth all in all.

2 The visible Church, which is also catholic or universal under the gospel (not confined to one nation as before under the law) consists of all those, throughout the world, that profess the true religion, and of their children; and is the kingdom of the Lord Jesus Christ, the house and family of God, out of which there is no ordinary possibility of salvation.

3 Unto this catholic visible Church Christ hath given the ministry, oracles, and ordinances of God, for the gathering and perfecting of the saints, in this life, to the end of the world: and doth by his own presence and spirit, according to his promise, make them effectual thereunto.

4 This catholic Church hath been sometimes more, sometimes less visible. And particular churches, which are members thereof, are more or less pure, according as the doctrine of the gospel is taught and embraced, ordinances administered, and public worship performed more or less purely in them.

5 The purest churches under heaven are subject both to mixture and error; and some have so degenerated as to become no churches of Christ, but synagogues of Satan. Nevertheless, there shall be always a Church on earth to worship God according to his will.

There is no other head of the Church but the Lord Jesus Christ.... (xxv).[30]

The communion of saints is the unity which men have with Christ by his spirit and by faith, and with one another by love. It involves community in service, edification, and works of charity. It is specifically stated that it does not imply community of goods (xxvi).

The Church's officers have 'the keys of the kingdom of heaven ... by virtue whereof they have power respectively to retain and remit sins'. They may admonish, censure, and excommunicate; and they may absolve the penitent and readmit to communion (xxx).

Synods are needed for the government of the Church. They may properly be called by civil rulers, but if these are enemies of the Church, the ministers may meet 'of themselves, by virtue of their office or ... upon delegation from their churches'. The decisions of synods must be in accordance with the Word of God. Synods may err, and their decisions 'are not to be made the rule of faith or practice, but to be used as a help in both'. They may not 'intermeddle with civil affairs', except by way of 'humble petition', or of advice if requested by the magistrate (xxxi).

The office of the civil magistrate is dealt with earlier in Chapter XXIII. His duty is to preserve peace and minister to the public good. He may not assume the administration of the Word and sacraments or exercise ecclesiastical discipline, but he has the responsibility of preserving order in the Church, suppressing blasphemies, and preventing corruptions.[31]

THE SAVOY DECLARATION (1658)

This Declaration was drawn up at a meeting of representatives of churches of the congregational type of government, held at the Chapel of the Savoy Palace in London. It was based on the Westminster Confession, but makes alterations in the chapters which concern the government of the Church, and civil magistrates.

The main points of difference are these:

(1) While 'the magistrate is bound to encourage, promote, and protect

the professors and profession of the gospel', and to prevent the publication of blasphemies and errors, he has no right to intervene in matters of doctrinal and liturgical dispute.

> In such differences about the doctrines of the gospel, or ways of the worship of God, as may befall men exercising a good conscience, manifesting it in their conversation, and holding the foundation, not disturbing others in their ways of worship that differ from them, there is no warrant for the magistrate under the gospel to abridge them of their liberty.[32]

Savoy is thus more explicit than Westminster in limiting the magistrate's powers.

(2) There is a greater emphasis on the invisible Church. Savoy omits Westminster's assertion that 'there is no ordinary possibility of salvation' outside the visible Church. Against Westminster xxv, 3, Savoy XXVI declares of the visible Catholic Church of Christ that 'as such it is not intrusted with the administration of any ordinances, or hath any officers to rule or govern in or over the whole body'.

(3) There is also emphasis on the autonomy of the local congregation in line with the Independent position. This appears in the 'Platform of Polity' which follows the Declaration of Faith and sets out the Church polity of Independency. The emphasis is on the local gathered Church, which possesses from Christ all the necessary power and authority to conduct worship and exercise discipline, and to choose and set apart by the laying on of hands pastors (or teachers, or elders) and deacons to minister in the congregation.

> Besides these particular Churches, there is not instituted by Christ any Church more extensive or Catholic intrusted with power for the administration of his Ordinances or the execution of any authority in his Name (Platform vi).

Chapter XXVI of the Platform, however, appears to jeopardize the principle of the completely autonomous local congregation in providing for a synod comprised of representatives of other congregations to meet when there are 'cases of difficulties or differences, either in point of doctrine or in administrations'. But it is declared that such a synod has no 'church power properly so called', cannot impose its decisions, and can only give advice.

THE CAMBRIDGE PLATFORM (1648)

This document, 'The Platform of Church Discipline',[33] was drawn up at a synod held at Cambridge, Massachusetts, with the purpose of setting forth the principles of the churches founded in New England by the Pilgrim Fathers. These were English Independents who had sailed for America after a period of exile in Holland. The document, largely the work of Richard Mather, consists of seventeen chapters and deals throughout with the doctrine of the Church, its order and discipline.

The Catholic Church is declared to be the whole company of the elect (II, 1), triumphant in heaven and militant on earth (II, 2).

> This Militant Church is to be considered as Invisible and Visible. Invisible, in respect of their relation wherein they stand to Christ, as a body unto the head, being united unto him, by the Spirit of God, and faith in their hearts: Visible, in respect of the profession of their faith, in their persons, and in particular Churches: and so there may be acknowledged a universal visible Church (II, 3).

The next paragraph (II, 4) asserts that the members of the militant visible Church are to be considered as those who 'walk according to the church-order of the Gospel' (and II, 5 explains that this order is congregational). 'Besides the spiritual union and communion common to all believers, they enjoy moreover a union and communion ecclesiastical-political: so we deny a universal visible church.' These last words apparently contradict the last sentence of II, 3 above. Williston Walker interprets this as meaning that although those who profess the faith, wherever they may be, may be regarded as a universal visible Church, this is not in any corporate sense: 'There is no *corporate* union and communion of all the professed followers of Christ, only an association of local churches.'[34] The text of the Platform at this point, however, is far from clear. What is clear is that the document envisages the Church as being essentially the gathering together of believers in particular places.

> A Congregational-church is by the institution of Christ a part of the Militant-visible-church, consisting of a company of saints by calling, united into one body, by a holy covenant, for the public worship of God, and the mutual edification one of another, in the Fellowship of the Lord Jesus (II, 6).

Particular churches are to be constituted by a covenant or voluntary agreement to meet regularly for worship and instruction, and to accept church discipline. Such a covenant rather than 'faith in the heart', a formal profession of faith, the fact of residing close at hand, or even baptism, provides the true 'form' of a church, though the importance of none of these things is denied. Emphasis is thus placed on a voluntary act of joining a particular congregation (IV).

Membership of a congregation should not be 'of greater number than may ordinarily meet together conveniently in one place: nor ordinarily fewer than may conveniently carry on Church-work' (III, 4). When a congregation grows too large, another church should be founded from it (XV, 4).

Authority resides in the congregation itself which receives it immediately from Christ and may exercise it immediately; and in the eldership which has the power of office. The ministers, however, possess their power through the congregation, and cannot, therefore, be said to exercise their power 'immediately' (V, 2). As the congregation has power to call, test, and ordain its officers, so it has power to depose them if they prove unworthy (VIII, 7).

The officers of the church are elders of whom 'some attend chiefly to the ministry of the word, as the Pastors and Teachers; others attend especially unto Rule, who are therefore called Ruling Elders' (VI, 4); and deacons whose office is 'limited unto the care of the temporal good things of the church' (VIII, 4). These church officers are to be freely elected by the congregation (VIII) and ordained by the laying on of hands by elders. If the congregation has no elder to perform this function, members of the congregation, duly chosen, may do so, or elders invited from another church (IX).

Chapter X sums up the concept of authority as the Platform perceives it:

> This Government of the church is a mixed Government. ... In respect of Christ, the Head and King of the church, and the Sovereign power residing in him, and exercised by him, it is a Monarchy. In respect of the body, or Brotherhood of the church, and power from Christ granted unto them, it resembles a Democracy. In respect of the Presbytery (i.e. the Elders) and power committed to them, it is an Aristocracy (X, 3).

On the relation between the authority of the congregation and that of the elders it has this to say:

> This power of Government in the Elders doth not any wise prejudice the power of privilege in the brotherhood; as neither the power of privilege in the brethren doth prejudice the power of government in the Elders; but they may sweetly agree together, as we may see in the example of the Apostles, furnished with the greatest church power, who took in the concurrence and consent of the brethren in church administration (X, 10).

Chapter xv deals with 'the communion of churches one with another'. 'Although churches be distinct, and therefore have not dominion one over another' yet they are encouraged to care for each other's welfare, to consult and to admonish each other. The practice of worshipping occasionally at another church, especially to partake at the Lord's table, is commended. The calling of synods is provided for (xvi) when necessary 'to determine controversies of faith and cases of conscience'. Magistrates also may call synods 'to counsel and assist them in matters of religion', but it is made clear that 'the constituting of a synod is a church act' which is not dependent on the will of the magistrate.

It is lawful and necessary for Christians to form churches without the consent of magistrates, as happened in the early days of the Church (xvii, 1). Church government and civil government are not opposed. Each has its distinct jurisdiction, but each can help the other (xvii, 2). But it is unlawful for either to 'meddle' in the work proper to the other (xvii, 5). Magistrates have no power, therefore, to compel subjects to become church members or to reinstate members who have been excommunicated (xvii, 4), but they are called on to 'take care of matters of religion', to see that God's commandments are kept (xvii, 6), to restrain idolatry, blasphemy, and heresy (xvii, 8) and:

> If any church, one or more, shall grow schismatical, rending itself from the communion of other churches, or shall walk incorrigibly or obstinately in any corrupt way of their own, contrary to the rule of the Word; in such case, the Magistrate is to put forth his coercive power, as the matter shall require (xvii, 9).

The Cambridge Platform, says Dr Erik Routley,[35] 'expounds the Congregational doctrine of the Church more completely than any other English-speaking document'. It was intended, he points out, 'to lay down a polity for no dissenting minority, but for a Church whose universal hold over a whole country (as they then saw it) was more confidently to be hoped for than any Church which could have been founded at Savoy'. It envisaged also a situation in which the community and the congregation were almost identical, in which church members alone had voting rights and magistrates, therefore, would always be supporters, if not members, of the church.

The Cambridge Platform quickly won assent from a great number of congregations in New England, some of them of Anglican and Presbyterian ancestry. In 1651 the General Court at Boston legalized it as the polity of the church in Massachusetts, and so it remained until 1780. But long before this, the experiment had broken down. Men of strong independent views could not accept even the qualified powers given to the magistrates, and left Massachusetts to form or to join communities elsewhere. In Massachusetts itself difficulties quickly appeared. Not everybody shared the enthusiasm of the colony's founders. There were those in the community who, while well qualified for leadership, were not qualified for church membership. Others, being unwilling to accept the responsibilities of civic office, refrained from making the covenant. Church membership was dwindling. Assemblies held in 1657 and 1662 agreed upon a solution known as 'The Half-way Covenant'. This permitted those who were baptized, but had not made the covenant, to vote in civic elections and to accept office, but excluded them from the Lord's Supper and from any part in the deliberations of the congregation. That such a compromise departed from the principles of the Cambridge Platform is evident.[36]

The subject matter of this chapter bears witness to a certain tendency during the sixteenth and seventeenth centuries to define theological, and therefore ecclesiological, positions very closely. On the part of the Catholic Church there was determination to 'hold the fort', while the great concern of theologians of Protestant bodies was to define their doctrine of the Church not only against Rome, but against one another. The old orthodoxy and ecclesiology was challenged, but only to be replaced by various new orthodoxies and new ecclesiologies, strongly held, and often rigidly enforced in the differing Protestant churches. What we may call a hardening process was going on. But already in the seventeenth century new interests, scientific, cultural, and philosophical, had begun to engage men's minds. The changing image of the Church in relation to modern modes of thought will be the subject of our second volume.

Notes

CHAPTER 1

[1] Some have argued that it was written later, from Ephesus, on Paul's third missionary journey, but the earlier date of A.D. 50, from Athens, gains the widest acceptance.

[2] Each appears well over a hundred times. Hebrew has several other words with similar meanings, but these occur rarely. Both words are translated in the English versions by 'assembly', 'congregation', and less frequently by 'company' and 'council'.

[3] Êdhah appears with great frequency in Exodus, Leviticus, Numbers, and Joshua. Occurrences in later books are rare.

[4] In these three instances qāhāl is the word used. The meanings of qāhāl and êdhah are clearly set out by George Johnston, The Doctrine of the Church in the New Testament (Cambridge 1943), p. 36, n. 2 and p. 37, n. 2.

[5] See H. B. Swete, Introduction to the Old Testament in Greek (Cambridge 1902), p. 317; K. L. Schmidt, article 'Ekklesia', in G. Kittel, Theological Dictionary of the New Testament, vol iii (Grand Rapids, Michigan 1965), pp. 528–9.

[6] Swete, op. cit., p. 315.

[7] Schmidt, op. cit., p. 528. George Johnston in his article 'The Doctrine of the Church in the New Testament' in Peake's Commentary on the Bible, ed. M. Black and H. H. Rowley (London 1962) makes the new suggestion that the Hebrew yahadh (community or union) may lie behind the N.T. use of ekklesia in view of its frequent use in the Qumrân literature. In the 'Manual of Discipline', e.g., it is used 'for the Qumrân brotherhood or that community to which the Qumrân "camp" belonged. It is not distinct from Israel, but embodies the true Israel' (p. 719).

[8] Schmidt, op. cit., pp. 516–17.

[9] There are eight occurrences of sunagoge in Josephus, six of which refer to the synagogue building.

[10] Schmidt, op. cit., p. 517, suggests this as a reason why LXX translators preferred ekklesia as a translation for qāhāl.

[11] G. Johnston, op. cit., pp. 43–4.

[12] Cf. also Romans 16.5 and 1 Corinthians 16.19.

[13] See Schmidt, op. cit., p. 505.

[14] The singular ekklesia is a better manuscript reading than the plural which is reproduced in the Authorized (King James) Version.

[15] This is clear in the case of Luke, because of his frequent use of ekklesia in the Acts of the Apostles.

[16] Schmidt, op. cit., pp. 525–6. Schmidt argues (pp. 519–25) that Matthew 16.18 is an authentic saying of Jesus. He does not discuss the papal interpretation of the verse.

[17] See G. Johnston, op. cit., p. 49.

[18] Ibid., p. 58.

[19] See Schmidt, op. cit., p. 531, n. 92 for other suggestions which have been made.

CHAPTER 2

[1] The most complete discussion in English of the N.T. images of the Church is Paul S. Minear, *Images of the Church in the New Testament* (Philadelphia 1950). See also A. Richardson, *Introduction to the Theology of the New Testament* (London 1958), pp. 242–90.

[2] G. Johnston, op. cit., p. 43, n. 2.

[3] Cf. Paul's argument in the Epistle to the Romans, especially ch. 9.

[4] T. W. Manson, *The Teaching of Jesus* (Cambridge 1931). See ch. 9, the argument of which he sums up on pp. 234–6. Another influential book, published in the same year, E. C. Hoskyns and F. N. Davey, *The Riddle of the New Testament* (London 1931), likewise insists that the significance of the life and death of Jesus and the question of the origin of the Church are to be elucidated as do the Synoptic Gospels and the other N.T. books, i.e. in the context of the O.T. Scriptures. See especially ch. 4.

[5] Hoskyns and Davey, op. cit., pp. 82–4.

[6] G. Henton Davies, article 'Remnant', in A. Richardson, ed., *A Theological Word Book of the Bible* (London 1950), p. 191.

[7] Ibid.

[8] Note the references to numbers in Acts 1.15; 2.41, 47; 4.4; 6.1, 7.

[9] This German word, meaning 'salvation history', is used here in the sense of an interpretation of certain historical events as being specially significant of the working-out of a divine purpose for man's salvation.

[10] E. Best, *One Body in Christ* (London 1955), has a full exegetical discussion of these phrases.

[11] Ibid., p. 184.

[12] Note the 'all' of 1 Corinthians 15.22 (and cf. v. 28), and the 'for all men' of Romans 5.18.

[13] J. A. T. Robinson, *The Body* (London 1952), p. 9. The whole Introduction to this book (pp. 7–10) is illuminating on Paul's solidarity doctrine.

[14] E. Best, op. cit., pp. 98–101.

[15] Ibid., p. 184.

[16] Ephesians 1.3–10.

[17] Cf. G. Johnston, op. cit., p. 92: 'Whether or not the apostle Paul wrote (Ephesians), it offers nothing which is untrue to his thought.'

[18] For commentary on the passage see, e.g., E. Best, op. cit., pp. 139 ff; J. A. T. Robinson, op. cit., pp. 65 ff. Note the translations suggested in text and notes of the New English Bible.

[19] A. E. J. Rawlinson, 'Corpus Christi', in G. Bell and A. Deissmann, eds., *Mysterium Christi* (London 1930), pp. 223 ff.

[20] Note that the context of Paul's main discussion of the eucharist (1 Cor. 11.17–34) is a strong protest against the divisions, even schisms, of the Corinthian Christians which were manifest even in their gatherings for the Lord's Supper.

[21] G. Johnston, op. cit., pp. 98–9.

[22] The theme of Christ as the bridegroom of the Church is also found in John 3.27–30 and in several passages in Revelation, most clearly in 19.6–9; 21.2; 22.17.

[23] Consult 'holiness of the C.' in Index of Subjects, p. 248.

[24] R. J. McKelvey, *The New Temple* (Oxford 1969), provides a thorough examination of the many passages in which the temple theme is to be detected. See also E. Best, op. cit., ch. ix, 'The Building in Christ'.

[25] 1 Corinthians 14.12; 2 Corinthians 10.8; 12.19; 13.10.

[26] Most recently, R. J. McKelvey, op. cit., pp. 114, 195–204.

[27] E.g. J. Jeremias, article '*Akrogoniaios*', in G. Kittel, *Theological Dictionary of the New Testament*, vol. 1 (1964), pp. 792–3; E. Best, op. cit., pp. 165–6.

[28] Op. cit., pp. 182–3.
[29] G. Johnston, op. cit., p. 99.
[30] Ibid., p. 74. Cf. Galatians 5.22–3; 2 Corinthians 6.16.
[31] Matthew 18.21 ff; John 13.34; 1 Corinthians 1.10; Galatians 6.1 ff, 10; Philippians 2.1 ff; Hebrews 13.1 ff; 1 Peter 3.8 ff; 1 John 2.7 ff are a few of many instances.
[32] Similarly the phrase 'love of God', also in 2 Corinthians 13.14, includes the idea both of God's love for us, and our love for God.
[33] Cf. John 14.16–17, 26; 15.26; 16.7, 13.
[34] G. Aulén, *The Faith of the Christian Church* (London 1954), pp. 329, 333.
[35] G. Johnston, op. cit., p. 100.
[36] Ibid., p. 101, n. 2.
[37] J. A. T. Robinson, op. cit., p. 79.

CHAPTER 3

[1] See below, pp. 69–71.
[2] *Smyrnaeans* VIII, 2. English translation (E.T.) of the 'Apostolic Fathers' is from Kirsopp Lake, *The Apostolic Fathers* (London 1959).
[3] *The Martyrdom of Polycarp* VIII.
[4] E. T. of J. N. D. Kelly, *Early Christian Doctrines* (London 1958), p. 192.
[5] There is no reason to doubt the early tradition which attaches the name of Clement to this Letter.
[6] If this be doubted, compare Acts 20.17 (*presbuteroi*) with 20.28 (*episkopoi*); and in 1 Timothy note that in 3.5 it is the bishop (*episkopos*) who is said to have the care of God's Church, while in 5.17 it is the elders (*presbuteroi*) who rule. Chapter 3, which describes the qualifications and responsibilities of ministers, mentions bishops and deacons, but not presbyters. Clearly *episkopos* and *presbuteros* are alternative words for the same ministerial office.
[7] 'Monarchical' in this connection has no overtone of despotism. It simply describes the bishop as the one who has the authority to rule in a given Christian community.
[8] The address of the letter is: 'The Church of God which sojourns in Rome to the Church of God which sojourns in Corinth'.
[9] H. Bettenson, *The Early Christian Fathers* (Oxford 1956), p. 47, is surely right in denying that Clement intends an equation between High Priest, priests, and Levites and bishop, priests, and deacons.
[10] Note the words 'with the consent of the whole Church' in 1 Clement XLIV, quoted above, p. 32. Cyprian of Carthage (see below, p. 71) constantly makes the same point. On the significance and history of the distinction between 'layman' and 'cleric', see Hans Küng, *The Church* (New York 1967), pp. 363–87.
[11] The council certainly consisted of the presbyters. Ignatius does not make clear whether or not deacons and any non-officeholders were included.
[12] Instances of this are very numerous, e.g. *Eph.* II, V, XX; *Magn.* IV, VI, XIII; *Trall.* II; *Phil.* VII; *Smyrn.* VIII; *Polycarp* VI.
[13] Kirsopp Lake's translation is the ambiguous 'to refresh the bishop'. The Greek verb used literally means 'to lift up the soul'.
[14] E.g. Justin Martyr, *Apology* LXVII; Hippolytus, *The Apostolic Tradition* I, 9.
[15] The Greek texts have *eis topon*, 'in the place', but Syriac and Armenian versions suggest that the original Greek may have been *eis tupon*, 'as a type'. Cf. the excerpt from *Trall.* III which follows on p. 37.
[16] Evidence is lacking that in Ignatius' day the office of bishop as he understood it existed outside Syria and Asia Minor.

[17] B. H. Streeter, *The Primitive Church* (London 1929). For a different estimate of Ignatius' motives, character, and temperament see Virginia Corwin, *St Ignatius and Christianity in Antioch* (New Haven, Connecticut 1960).

[18] 'Monepiscopacy', 'monepiscopate', 'monarchical episcopate' are all terms used of the form of Church government in which a single bishop exercises oversight (*episkope*) and is the centre of authority in a local Christian community.

[19] Discovered in the eighteenth century by Ludovico Muratori. It is a Latin translation of an eighth-century manuscript of a list of early Christian writings. Its Greek original is thought to date from the later second century.

[20] Examples, each however with its own emphasis, are Montanism, Novatianism, Donatism, and a number of medieval and post-Reformation sects.

[21] See p. 30 above.

[22] '[God] chose us in him [Jesus Christ] before the foundation of the world, that we should be holy and blameless before him.'

[23] See pp. 60 and 63 below.

[24] *Kathedra*, usually translated 'throne', does not necessarily mean an elaborate piece of furniture like the bishop's throne in medieval and modern cathedral churches. It does, however, denote a seat of authority. The teacher in ancient Greek schools lectured sitting on a *kathedra*. Its adoption in Christian usage was probably in order to emphasize the bishop's teaching authority. The throne, therefore, is a symbol of the bishop's responsibility to teach the pure doctrine of Christ rather than of exaltation over other members of the Church. Those churches where the bishop's *kathedra* was placed were later known as cathedral churches. Note that the English term 'episcopal see (seat)' refers primarily to the bishop's throne.

[25] Justin came to Rome from Ephesus where, if Ignatius' teaching was still heeded, the *episkopos* or his delegate was the celebrant of the eucharist.

[26] See below, pp. 44–6.

[27] See below, p. 56.

[28] But Harnack dates it in the third century.

[29] *Adversus Haereses* was written in Greek, but apart from fragments it has come down to us in a Latin translation.

[30] Irenaeus' work is one of our chief sources of information about the details of Gnostic systems.

[31] The Gnostic presupposition that the Supreme Being can have no contact with the physical world precludes, however, any doctrine of incarnation.

[32] The E.T. of passages from Irenaeus is from A. Roberts and J. Donaldson eds., The Ante-Nicene Christian Library (ANCL), vol. i (Edinburgh 1864 ff); published also in New York under the title *The Ante-Nicene Fathers*.

[33] Tertullian, *De Praescriptione Haereticorum* 13.

[34] Origen, *De Principiis*, Preface.

[35] The significance of this passage as an early acknowledgement of the primacy of the bishop of Rome does not concern us here. For a brief discussion, see J. N. D. Kelly, op. cit., pp. 192–3.

[36] See above, pp. 31–3.

[37] See below, p. 88.

[38] Jerome, *On the Epistle to Titus* I, 6–7. The passage is quoted below on p. 93.

CHAPTER 4

[1] *Apologeticus* XXXIX.

[2] *Contra Marcionem* IV, xi; *De Pudicitia* I.

[3] *Ad Martyres* I.

[4] The E.T. of passages from Tertullian is from The Ante-Nicene Christian Library, vols. iii and iv.

[5] *De Praescriptione* xx.

[6] Ibid. xxxvi.

[7] Tertullian also gives a shorter version which he attributes to the Church of Rome in *De Virginibus Velandis* i.

[8] See p. 44 above.

[9] *Early Christian Doctrines*, p. 41.

[10] Marcion, who taught in Rome *c*. 140–50, e.g. rejected the whole of the O.T., and retained only a reduced version of Luke's Gospel and ten epistles of Paul in his canon of Scripture.

[11] Note, e.g., the many scriptural references in *De Carne Christi* where Tertullian is defending the Church's belief in both the divinity and the humanity of Christ.

[12] Kelly, op. cit., p. 41.

[13] Tertullian, *De Fuga* ix.

[14] *De Anima* ix.

[15] *Adversus Praxean* xxx.

[16] *De Pudicitia* xxi. This short work begins with a trenchant condemnation of a bishop who had recently admitted to communion some who had committed adultery. It is usually assumed that the bishop was Zephyrinus of Rome (d. 217) or his successor Callistus. But it may have been an African bishop.

[17] I.e. 'gathers together'.

[18] R. C. Moberly, *Ministerial Priesthood* (New York 1916), pp. 48 ff.

[19] *Adversus Marcionem* iv, v.

[20] *De Exhortatione Castitatis* vii. The ambiguity in Tertullian's later (Montanist) attitude to the episcopal system is discussed by R. F. Evans in a chapter on Tertullian in his *One and Holy* (London 1972), pp. 27–35. He tends to agree with Moberly: 'The motto "No bishop, no Church" is at the farthest point removed from Tertullian's late thought' (p. 33).

[21] The E.T. is that of Gregory Dix in *The Apostolic Tradition of St Hippolytus* (London 1937). Words in brackets are either introduced by Dix to assist the sense in English, or are judged by him not to have belonged to the original Greek (which is not extant), although having support in the versions.

[22] I hold that it is most probable that in the early decades in many places the council of presbyters ordained one of their number to the office of bishop. No principle of apostolic succession is thereby contradicted, provided that apostles or apostolic men appointed these collegial bodies of presbyters and authorized them so to act. See C. Gore, *The Church and the Ministry* (London 1893), pp. 73–6. But evidence is lacking about any such explicit commission from the apostles to the presbyteral colleges.

[23] See p. 34 above, and p. 75, n. 9.

[24] *Summus sacerdos* and *sacerdos* are the Latin for the Greek *archiereus* and *hiereus*, High Priest and priest. In the N.T. these terms are never used of a Christian minister. Christ is the High Priest; the Church is a priestly community, a kingdom of priests (Rev. 1.6).

[25] Note the words 'propitiate Thy countenance' in the passage quoted above, p. 57.

[26] See, e.g., Romans 3.25; 1 John 2.2; 4.10, and the whole argument of Hebrews, 7–10.

[27] E.g. *summus sacerdos* (High Priest), *sacerdos* (priest), *sacerdotalis* (priestly), *sacerdotium* (priesthood).

[28] From Justin Martyr we learn that the deacon also had liturgical functions which included the distribution of the eucharist to those present, and those absent through age or infirmity. In his function of distributing the Church's alms to the needy, the deacon was closely attached to the bishop.

[29] *Protreptikos* (An Exhortation to the Greeks); *Paidagogos* (The Tutor); and *Stromateis* (Miscellanies).

[30] *Paidagogos* I, vi. The E.T. of passages from Clement is from ANCL, vol. ii.

[31] The Greek phrase is *he kuriōs ekklesia*, which can be translated 'that which is properly the Church'.

[32] E.T. of Origen is my own except where otherwise stated.

[33] See p. 44 above.

[34] *Homilies on Leviticus* VI, 3.

[35] *Commentary on Matthew* XII, 14.

[36] *Contra Celsum* III, 51. Cf. also *Hom. on Numbers* XX, 4.

[37] *Hom. on Leviticus* IX, 1.

[38] Ibid. IX, 9.

[39] Cf. also *Hom. on Ezekiel* I, 11.

[40] *Hom. on Joshua* XXI, 1.

[41] *Hom. on Ezekiel* VI, 5; *Hom. on Numbers* III, 1; *Comm. on John* VII, 17.

[42] *On Prayer* XX, 1; commenting on Ephesians 5·27.

[43] The theme is constant in Origen's mystical treatment of the Song of Solomon in his *Commentary on the Song of Songs*; e.g. in I, 1.

[44] *Hom. on Exodus* IX, 3.

[45] E.T. of R. P. Lawson in *Origen: The Song of Songs, Commentary and Homilies*, vol. 26 in the 'Ancient Christian Writers' series (London; and Westminster, Maryland 1957).

[46] Origen places Adam among the prophets in view of Genesis 2.24, taken as a prophecy concerning the Church.

[47] See below, pp. 88–9.

[48] *Hom. on Joshua* III, 5.

[49] *Hom. on Jeremiah* XX, 3. It is a passage in which he interprets the scarlet cord in Rahab's window (Josh. 2) allegorically as the redemptive blood of Christ, and her house as the place of salvation.

[50] *Hom. on Psalm 36* II, 1.

[51] *De Principiis* I, vi. 1–2.

CHAPTER 5

[1] See R. F. Evans, op. cit., p. 64.

[2] See above, pp. 55–6.

[3] Cyprian, *Epistles* L, 3 (LIII). The numbering of Cyprian's *Epistles* followed here is that in ANCL, vol. v. Many edns use the numbering of the Oxford edn of 1682: I place this in square brackets when it differs from ANCL.

[4] The full title is *De Catholicae Ecclesiae Unitate*, 'On the Unity of the Catholic Church'. E.T. of passages from Cyprian is that of Ernest Wallace in ANCL, vol. v.

[5] *Epistles* LXXV, 3 (LXIX).

[6] This passage strongly implies that Peter and the other apostles were the first bishops. 'Cyprian took a crucial step in the history of thought about the episcopate: the Apostles themselves were the first bishops of the Church' (R. F. Evans, op. cit., p. 49). Cf. also *Epp.* LXIV, 3 [III]; LXVIII, 4 [LXCI]; and LXXIV, 16 (LXXV).

[7] Cyprian frequently speaks of bishops as *sacerdotes*, a word which he also uses to denote the presbyters. The context usually makes clear what the word signifies.

[8] *Ep.* LXXII, 21 [LXXIII].

[9] *Ep.* LXXIII, 8 (LXXIV).

[10] *Ep.* LXXI [LXXII].

[11] Some later sects of the 'Holiness' type have not observed it. And it is to be noted

that both Novationists and the Donatists of the fourth century rebaptized their 'converts'.

[12] 'On the Unity of the Catholic Church', *c.* 251, referred to hereafter as *De Unitate.*
[13] *De Unitate* 3.
[14] Another version of this section of *De Unitate* is extant, usually known as the Papal or Primacy Text. See below, p. 70.
[15] Ibid. 5.
[16] E.g. in *Ep.* LI, 21 [LV]; LXVIII, 8 [LXVI], quoted above, p. 000.
[17] Kelly, op. cit., p. 205.
[18] R. H. Bettenson, op. cit., p. 363.
[19] *Ep.* LIV, 5 [LIX].
[20] *Ep.* LXVIII, 1 [LXVI].
[21] *Ep.* LXVII, 3.
[22] See above, p. 57.
[23] The English word 'priest' (French *prêtre*, German *priester*) derives from the Greek *presbyteros*, and in itself has no sacerdotal connotation. As the presbyter came rapidly to be regarded as having the right to celebrate the eucharist in virtue of his ordination, and not solely by delegation from the bishop, we find the word *sacerdos* increasingly used of the presbyter.
[24] *De Unitate* 5.
[25] Ibid. 6.
[26] Ibid.
[27] E.g. by those who urge that divided Christendom should be seen as a state of schism *within* the Church, and that the notion that among the historic churches there is any one which is the true Church in relation to which all others are in schism should be abandoned. See the last paragraphs of Oliver C. Quick, *Doctrines of the Creed* (London 1963).
[28] See below, pp. 87.

CHAPTER 6

[1] Diocletian (Emperor, 284–305) created the administrative structure of the empire which Constantine inherited. The empire was divided into twelve dioceses (Greek *dioikesis*) or 'exarchies' (Greek *exarchia*). Each diocese consisted of a number of provinces or eparchies (Greek *eparchia*). The smallest, Britain, had four and the largest, the East (*Oriens*) had sixteen.
[2] Although ecclesiastical districts coincided closely with civil boundaries, there was no such close correspondence in nomenclature. This is a somewhat confusing matter since terms were often used interchangeably. Generally speaking, in the East *dioikesis* described the area of jurisdiction of a metropolitan bishop, and 'eparchy' or *paroikia* that of other bishops. In the West the area of a bishop was denoted either by *dioecesis* or by *parochia* (Latinizations of *dioikesis* and *paroikia*). Much later *paroikia* and *parochia* came to be used of a smaller unit, the 'parish' of today.
[3] Pontus and Asia comprised the northern and western parts of Asia Minor.
[4] There are twenty-three Lectures. The last five were delivered on the days immediately following the Easter baptism.
[5] E.T. of Cyril of Jerusalem from The Nicene and Post-Nicene Fathers (NPNF), 2nd ser., vol. 7, ed. P. Schaff and H. Wace (New York; London 1894).
[6] See above, pp. 13–17.
[7] *Cat.* XIX, 1.
[8] Ibid. XX, 3.
[9] From the Greek *chrisma*, consecrated oil. *Christos* (Christ) literally means 'the anointed one'.

[10] Ibid. XXI, 1.

[11] Ibid. XXI, 2.

[12] Ibid. XXI, 5.

[13] Ibid. XXII, 1.

[14] Athanasius, *De Incarnatione* 54.

[15] Gregory of Nyssa, *Oratio Catechetica* 25 ('The Great Catechism').

[16] *In illud 'Tunc Ipse'*, a short treatise which expounds 1 Corinthians 15.28. Greek text in *PG*, vol. 44, column 1317.

[17] The Greek *musterion*, mystery, is also the Greek word for 'sacrament'. The reference here is doubtless both to the mystery of the incarnation and to the eucharist.

[18] Hilary, *De Trinitate* VIII, 7. E.T. of passages from Hilary are from NPNF, 2nd ser., vol. ix.

[19] The 'gradation and sequence' is 'you' (Christians), I (Christ), and the Father. Hilary's point seems to be that a 'unity of will' or mutual agreement is an arrangement between equals. The unity of the Church is not of that kind; it is given to the Church by God through Christ in virtue of Christ's participation in the nature of God and the Christian's participation in the nature of Christ who took flesh. Hence it is a union of natures, or a 'natural unity'. But Hilary would not deny that it may also be said to be supernatural, since it comes by the grace of God.

[20] Ibid. VIII, 7.

[21] From the Latin *trado*, to hand over. The English 'traitor' is derived from *traditor*.

[22] J. N. D. Kelly, op. cit., p. 411.

[23] See above, p. 68.

[24] E.g. Thomas Aquinas, *De Articulis Fidei et Sacramentis Ecclesiae* 2.

[25] The passages in which Optatus refers to Peter, and Peter's chair (*De Schism. Donat.* I, 10; II, 2; VII, 3) have sometimes been supposed to support the idea of papal supremacy. Optatus' argument, following Cyprian, is that Christ provided for the unity of the Church by giving first to Peter authority which was later to be communicated to all the apostles. The see of Rome, whose first bishop was Peter, is then to be regarded as the centre of unity, and it is a schismatic act to set up a chair (or see) in opposition to it. The passages support the idea of the primacy of the see of Rome, but certainly not the later claims for papal supremacy. J. N. D. Kelly (op. cit., p. 419) says 'we should note that he laid almost equal stress on the desirability of communion with the Oriental Churches' (*De Schism. Donat.* II, 6; VI, 3). The text of Optatus' work may be found in *Corpus Scriptorum Ecclesiasticorum Latinorum*, vol. xxvi (Prague; Vienna; Leipzig 1893).

CHAPTER 7

[1] Hippo Regius was about 100 miles west of Carthage on the coast of modern Algeria.

[2] *Sermon* 341.

[3] E.g., ibid. 341.10.

[4] *Homilies on 1 John* VI, 10.

[5] *Sermon* 341.9.

[6] See Yves Congar, *L'Eglise de Saint Augustin à l'époque moderne* (Paris 1970), p. 12; S. J. Grabowski *The Church: an Introduction to the Theology of St Augustine* (London; St Louis, Missouri 1957), pp. 18–19; J. N. D. Kelly, op. cit., p. 413.

[7] Early liturgists insist that at the conclusion of the eucharistic prayer the 'amen' should be unanimously and audibly said. See Justin Martyr, *Apology* 65, 67.

[8] E.T. of passages from St Augustine is from The Nicene and Post-Nicene Fathers (NPNF), 1st ser., ed. P. Schaff (New York 1886–9) where available. Elsewhere it is the author's translation.

[9] *Sermon* 267.4.

[10] See *On the Trinity* VI, 7; XV, 29, 38.

[11] The reference to the Spirit's gift of languages (Acts 2.4 ff) is directed against the Donatists, whose sect was confined to North Africa and therefore to its languages.

[12] *On Baptism* IV, 17 (25).

[13] Cyprian, *De Unitate Ecclesiae* 7. Cyprian's language, however, is not consistent. In the same passage he speaks of the Church being rent and divided.

[14] E.g. in *Letters* XLIII, 21.

[15] Acceptance of the notion that there may be schisms *within* the Church has been urged as a promising approach to modern problems of Church unity, e.g. by O. C. Quick, *Doctrines of the Creed*, op. cit., pp. 338–9; S. L. Greenslade, *Schism in the Early Church* (London 1953), pp. 212 ff; B. C. Butler in *The Idea of the Church* (London 1962) reacts against the suggestion.

[16] *On Baptism* VI, 1. The distinction is usually spoken of as that between validity and efficacy.

[17] See above p. 82.

[18] See above, pp. 59–60 and 62–3.

[19] *On Baptism* V, 27 (38).

[20] Ibid.

[21] Op. cit., p. 417.

[22] *Letters* XLIX, 3.

[23] *Expositions on the Psalms* LVI, 13; *Contra Faustum* XXVIII, 2; *Letters* XCIII, 7.23.

[24] *Expositions on the Psalms* LVI, 1.

[25] See Yves Congar, op. cit., p. 12.

[26] See H. R. T. Brandreth, *Episcopi Vagantes* (London 1947).

[27] *Against Petilian* III, 10.

[28] *On Baptism* I, 10 (13) to 17 (26).

[29] Ibid. I, 15 (23).

[30] Ibid. I, 10 (14).

[31] Ibid. I, 17 (26).

[32] See, e.g., 'Dogmatic Constitution on the Church', 64, in *The Documents of Vatican II*, ed. W. M. Abbott (New York 1966), pp. 92–3.

[33] As is recognized in 'The Decree on the Ministry and Life of Priests', ibid., p. 546.

[34] E.g. *Sermons* 191, 2–3; 192, 2; *On Virginity* VI, 6.

[35] *De Civ. Dei* XIV, 28.

[36] Augustine makes the identification also in *De Civ. Dei* XIII, 16.

[37] S. J. Grabowski, op. cit., pp. 532–7, gives a full account of these.

[38] *De Civ. Dei* XI, 9.

[39] *Encheiridion* LXVI.

[40] Ibid.

[41] R. W. Battenhouse in *A Companion to the Study of St Augustine*, ed. Battenhouse (New York; Oxford 1955), p. 54.

[42] Cf. *Epistle* CXLVI, 1 (Letter to Evangelus): 'What, apart from ordaining, does a bishop do which a presbyter does not do?'

[43] Acts 20.17, 28; Philippians 1.2.

[44] The evidence is set out by W. Telfer, 'Episcopal Succession in Egypt', in *The Journal of Ecclesiastical History*, vol. 3, no. 1, April 1952.

CHAPTER 8

[1] See above, pp. 45, 70–1, 75, 83, 94

[2] Op. cit., pp. 419–20.

[3] The exegesis on which this statement is based is tenuous.
[4] Migne, *Patrologia Latina* (hereafter cited as *PL*), vol. 54, 671.
[5] *PL* 59, 42.
[6] R. C. Petry, *A History of the Christian Church* (Englewood Cliffs, New Jersey 1962), p. 181.
[7] R. W. Southern, *Western Society and the Church in the Middle Ages* (Harmondsworth 1970), p. 94.
[8] Yves Congar, op. cit., pp. 47–8.
[9] See above, p. 98.
[10] Einhard, *Vita Karoli Magni* 24. E.T. in A. J. Grant, *Early Lives of Charlemagne* (London 1905).
[11] R. W. Southern, op. cit., p. 92.
[12] Ibid., p. 93.
[13] See above, p. 41.
[14] Petry, op. cit., pp. 221–30 provides material for such a debate.
[15] *PL* 117, 564.
[16] See above, pp. 69–70.
[17] See Congar, op. cit., pp. 58–60, 65–6.
[18] Ibid., p. 65.
[19] The works of Hincmar are contained in *PL* 125 and 126.
[20] Congar, op. cit., p. 57.
[21] Florus, *Capitula*, *PL* 119, 421c.
[22] John VIII, *Epistles* 5. Its authorship is doubtful, though of this period.
[23] See below, pp. 144–5.
[24] Southern, op. cit., p. 100.
[25] Congar, op. cit., p. 97.
[26] O. J. Thatcher and E. H. McNeal, *A Source Book for Medieval History* (New York 1905) gives the full text in E.T., pp. 136–8.
[27] Ibid., p. 156.
[28] Liemar of Bremen, in a letter written in 1075.
[29] Thatcher and McNeal, op. cit., pp. 153–5.
[30] E.g. Ivo of Chartres (d. 1116).
[31] See above, p. 98.
[32] Congar, op. cit., pp. 116–18.
[33] Canticle XXIX, 7 (*PL* 183, 932).
[34] *De Consideratione* IV, 3, 6 (*PL* 182, 776). Bernard addressed the five books of *De Consideratione*, 'On Meditation' and the ascetic life, to Pope Eugenius III.
[35] Ibid. I, 1–2 (*PL* 182, 727–31).
[36] See above, p. 98.
[37] *De Consideratione* III, 4, 14 (*PL* 182, 766–7).
[38] Canticle LXXXIII, 4 (*PL* 182, 1183).
[39] Corrupt attempts of Roman noble families to influence papal elections had long been scandalous. These had been made more difficult, by a papal decree in 1159 giving the cardinals the exclusive right to elect, and by the Third Lateran Council, (1179), which decided that all cardinals had an equal vote, and that a two-thirds majority was necessary.
[40] For the full text of Canon 1 see Petry, op. cit., pp. 322–3.
[41] Canon 21; ibid., p. 323.
[42] Ibid.
[43] Petry, op. cit., pp. 319–21 gives the text of Innocent's letter to John to which John's submission is attached. (E.T. of C. R. Cheney and W. H. Semple, *Selected Letters of Pope Innocent III concerning England* (Edinburgh 1953).
[44] *PL* 214, 292.

[45] The full text is given in Thatcher and McNeal, op. cit., pp. 314–17.

[46] Boniface's exegesis of Psalm 22.20 is not altogether clear. He seems to identify the 'darling' of the psalm both with the body of Christ and with the bride of Christ of John 3.29, and so with the Church (cf. Eph. 5.22 ff). As there is one Bridegroom, so there is but one Church.

[47] The exegesis of the 'two swords' text had occupied theologians and canonists for a long time. The question at issue was whether the two swords (spiritual and temporal power) were given into the hands of distinct and autonomous authorities (pope and emperor), or into the hands of the pope alone. There is no doubt about Boniface's answer.

[48] Again, Boniface's argument is not crystal-clear, since Peter presumably was wielding only one sword in Gethsemane.

[49] The reference is to a writer of about 500 who used the pseudonym of Dionysius the Areopagite (Acts 17.34). Among his works were treatises on the celestial hierarchy and the ecclesiastical hierarchy.

[50] E.g. it is not clear whether Boniface saw himself as the vicar of Peter or the vicar of Christ.

CHAPTER 9

[1] Congar, op. cit., p. 217.

[2] Hans Küng, *Structures of the Church* (Notre Dame 1968), p. 260.

[3] *De Sacramentis* I, 12. i (*PL* 176, 347–9).

[4] Ibid. (*PL* 176, 415 D).

[5] Ibid. (*PL* 176, 417 A).

[6] Congar, op. cit., p. 164.

[7] Ibid.

[8] See above, p. 93.

[9] *Glossa in* IV *Sent.* d. 24, n. 3.

[10] 'Faith' here means assent. The 'faith which has been formed' (*fides formata*) is much closer to Paul's 'faith working through love' (Gal. 5.6), and to what Luther meant by faith.

[11] *Summa* II. II. *in qu.* 2.

[12] *Opera* II, p. 709 (*S. Bonaventurae Opera Omnia*, 10 vols., Quaracchi, 1882–1907).

[13] Ibid. IV, p. 203.

[14] Congar, op. cit., p. 222.

[15] *Opera* VIII, p. 375.

[16] *Opera* V, p. 198b.

[17] Ibid. VIII, p. 235a.

[18] The works (*opera*) of Albertus were edited by A. Borgnet in 38 vols. (Paris 1890–99).

[19] *Opera* XXXVIII, pp. 64–5.

[20] Congar, op. cit., p. 231.

[21] *Opera* XXIX, p. 440.

[22] Ibid. XXXVIII, pp. 104–6.

[23] Ibid. XXIII, p. 685.

[24] *Summa Theologica* IIIa, 8, 1.

[25] Ibid. IIIa 8, 3. E.T. from *The Summa Theologica of St Thomas Aquinas,* tr. Fathers of the English Dominicans (London 1920 ff).

[26] See above, p. 115.

[27] *Summa Theologica* Ia, 92, 3; cf. also IIIa, 64, 2 *ad* 3.

[28] But in *Summa* IIIa, 8, 1 *ad* 3 Thomas likens the Holy Spirit to the heart which quickens the body.

[29] E.T. of passages from the *Exposition* is from T. Gilby, *St Thomas Aquinas: Theological Texts* (Oxford 1955), pp. 340–43.

[30] Ibid.

[31] *Summa* IIa–IIae, 183, 3 *ad* 3; cf. *Compendium Theologiae* I, 147.

[32] Congar, op. cit., pp. 234–5.

[33] 'Habitual grace' is 'the gift of God inhering in the soul, by which men are enabled to perform righteous acts. It is held to be normally conveyed in the Sacraments' (F. L. Cross, ed., *Oxford Dictionary of the Christian Church* (Oxford 1957), p. 577).

[34] *Summa* IIIa, 8, 3 *ad* 2.

[35] Hans Küng, *Structures of the Church*, pp. 13, 260. In addition to the passage under discussion Küng lists seven other occurrences. See also Congar, op. cit., p. 233.

[36] See below, p. 136.

[37] See below, pp. 136–7.

[38] This image, frequent in medieval ecclesiology, is used by Boniface VIII in *Unam Sanctam*; see above, p. 110.

[39] E.g. in Jerome; see above, p. 94.

[40] No patristic or scholastic writer has provided a systematic treatment of the Trinitarian nature of the Church as at once the People of God, the Body of Christ, and the Fellowship of the Spirit (the three basic N.T. themes of the Church).

[41] We have here the well-known threefold division of the Church as militant, expectant, and triumphant. Augustine had spoken of the Church on earth as *perigrans*, 'on a journey' (e.g. *Encheiridion* LVI). The expression 'Church militant' appeared about the middle of the twelfth century, perhaps with reference to the crusades against the Turks and the struggle against heresy. Departed souls who are being purged of their sins and awaiting the resurrection of the body are the Church expectant.

[42] This notion is derived from Augustine, *De Civ. Dei* XV, 1; *On the Psalms* LXIV, 2. It is taken up by Gregory the Great. 'From righteous Abel to the last elect' is a frequent description of the membership of the true Church; see list of occurrences in Y. Congar, *L'Ecclésiologie du haut Moyen-Age* (Paris 1968), p. 68, n. 43.

[43] IV *Quodlibets* VIII, 13. E.T., Gilby, op. cit., p. 398.

[44] See below. pp. 136–8.

[45] E.T., Gilby, op. cit., pp. 399–400.

[46] Ibid., p. 399.

CHAPTER 10

[1] Some representative documents both from Albigensian and Catharist sources are gathered together in Petry, op. cit., pp. 342–50.

[2] This catechism was long accepted as an early Waldensian document. Recent examination, however, has shown its dependence on the writings of Martin Bucer, the sixteenth-century reformer. See G. MacGregor, *Corpus Christi* (Philadelphia 1958), pp. 37–8. But there is no doubt that the Waldensians anticipated Reformation teaching in some important respects.

[3] Tr. R. C. Petry, op. cit., p. 353 from A. Monastier, *Histoire de l'Eglise vaudoise* (Paris 1847), II, pp. 301 ff.

[4] Petry, op. cit., p. 334 gives some excerpts, quoted from F. S. Stevenson, *Robert Grosseteste, Bishop of Lincoln* (London 1899), pp. 286–8.

[5] *De potestate regia et papali,* ed. J. LeClercq (Paris 1942).

[6] Many of his works suffered destruction on account of his condemnation. Extant ser-

mons, treatises, and fragments have been edited by G. Thery and R. Klibansky, *Opera Latina* (Leipzig 1934 ff).

[7] Text ed. C. W. Previté-Orton (Cambridge 1928). Petry, op. cit., pp. 510–13 provides some extracts in E.T. including the 'Conclusions' in the E.T. of Thatcher and McNeal.

[8] Erastianism is so called after Thomas Erastus (1524–83). It signifies the complete submission of the Church to State control. Erastus himself did not, however, teach so sweeping a doctrine. He opposed excommunication by Church authorities without permission of the lay ruler.

[9] See Thatcher and McNeal, op. cit., pp. 317–24, or Petry, op. cit., pp. 511–13.

[10] Marsilius distinguishes between the inseparable (essential) and separable (inessential) functions of the clergy. The inseparable functions are the power to administer the sacraments. The separable functions are the control of one priest over others (e.g. as archbishop or bishop), and the administration of the sacraments in a particular place or to a particular group.

[11] *Conclusions* 17 and 18.

[12] *Dialogus* I, 1, 4. (Edn of text in M. Goldast, *Monarchia S. Romani Imperii*, vol. 2 (Hanover 1612).

[13] *Opera Politica*, vol. iii, p. 191, ed. J. G. Sikes *et al* (Manchester 1940).

[14] Congar, *L'Eglise*, pp. 294–5.

[15] *De Imperatorum et Pontificum Potestate*, ed. C. K. Brampton (Oxford 1927).

[16] Quoted in Petry, op. cit., p. 515 from the E.T. of Ewart Lewis, *Medieval Political Ideas* (New York 1954), vol. ii, p. 608.

[17] I.e. a priest who is not a member of a religious Order.

[18] Among these are *De Dominio Divino* ('On Divine Lordship'), *De Civili Dominio* ('On Civil Lordship'), *De Ecclesia* ('On the Church'), *De Eucharistia* ('On the Eucharist'), *De Ecclesia et Membris eius* ('On the Church and its Members'), *De Officio Regis* ('On the Office of the King'), *De Potestate Papae* ('On the Authority of the Pope'). His *Trialogus* (1382) restates his main theses in sharper fashion. Most of these have been published by the Wyclif Society: *Wyclif's Latin Works* (London 1884 ff).

[19] *Trialogus* IV, 22. The *Trialogus* is ed. G. V. Kechner (Oxford 1869).

[20] See above, pp. 120, 228, n. 41.

[21] G. Macgregor, op. cit., pp. 34–7.

[22] *Tractatus de Ecclesia*, ed. J. Loserth, Wyclif Society (London 1886): pp. 17, 22, 57, 132–3.

[23] Ibid., pp. 298–328.

[24] *Tractatus de Officio Regis*, ed. A. W. Pollard and C. Sayle, Wyclif Society (London 1887): pp. 13, 137.

[25] Matthew Spinka, *John Hus' Concept of the Church* (Princeton 1966).

[26] See below, pp. 136–8.

[27] See G. Macgregor, op. cit., pp. 25–8.

[28] Ibid., pp. 23–4.

[29] See Petry, op. cit., pp. 526–7. He quotes the whole document from Francis Oakley, 'The *Propositiones Utiles* of Pierre d'Ailly: an Epitome of Conciliar Theory', in *Church History* XXIX, 4 (December 1960), pp. 399–402.

[30] Cf. William of Ockham, above, p. 131.

[31] This Council first met at Ferrara, was transferred to Florence in 1439 and to Rome in 1442.

[32] See below, pp. 146–7.

[33] Küng, *Structures of the Church*, p. 242.

[34] Thatcher and McNeal, op. cit., pp. 328–9.

[35] G. Macgregor, op. cit., p. 40.

[36] *Summa de Ecclesia* I, 21.

[37] Ibid., especially I, 67–8.
[38] Ibid. I, 22.
[39] Ibid. I, 6.
[40] Ibid. II, 32–4.
[41] Turrecremata's understanding of astronomy may, of course, be ignored.
[42] Ibid. II, 54. For Latin text see Congar, *L'Eglise*, p. 342, n. 7.
[43] Küng, *Structures of the Church*, pp. 271–5.
[44] *Summa de Ecclesia* II, 93, 102; IV, 18.
[45] It is noticeable that Turrecremata interprets the 'rock' of Matthew 16.18 not as the person of Peter, but as faith in Christ.
[46] See Küng, *Structures*, pp. 256–7.
[47] *Summa de Ecclesia* III, 16.
[48] Ibid. III, 64.

CHAPTER 11

[1] For brief accounts of the history see Timothy Ware, *The Orthodox Church* (Harmondsworth 1963), chs. 1–3; R. W. Southern, op. cit., ch. 3.
[2] See above, pp. 75–6.
[3] Quoted from Southern, op. cit., p. 71.
[4] See above, p. 104.
[5] Hans Küng, *The Church*, p. 446.
[6] Southern, op. cit., p. 74.
[7] Ibid., p. 75.
[8] Ibid., p. 82. A twentieth-century example is A. Harnack's treatment of eastern Christianity in his popular *What is Christianity?*
[9] John Meyendorff, *Orthodoxy and Catholicity* (New York 1966), p. 88.
[10] Yves Congar, *L'Ecclésiologie du Haut Moyen-Age*, pp. 324–5.
[11] John of Damascus, *c.* 675–*c.* 749, one of the most influential of Greek theologians. His *De Fide Orthodoxa* is a systematic treatment of the main articles of Christian faith.
[12] Greek, *mustagogia*, literally, 'introduction to the mysteries'.
[13] T. Ware, op. cit., p. 247.
[14] *PG*, vol. 91, 658–718.
[15] Congar, op. cit., p. 327.
[16] *PG* 98, 383f.
[17] Greek, 'all-sovereign'. Whether or not in the central dome, an ikon of Christ the *Pantokrator* is prominent in every Orthodox church.
[18] See above, p. 78. For a brief discussion of the modern Orthodox understanding of the deification of man, see T. Ware, op. cit., pp. 240–42.
[19] 'On our Strict Doctrines of Truth', *PG* 89, 1340.
[20] Alexis Khomiakov, *The Church is One*, section 9, quoted in T. Ware, op. cit., p. 247.
[21] For St Paul, see above, pp. 17–18; Cyril of Jerusalem, p. 78; Cyril of Alexandria, p. 79; Augustine, p. 85.
[22] In a preparatory document for the seminar on Orthodox Theology and Worship held at the Ecumenical Institute, Bossey, Switzerland in April 1971.
[23] Literally, 'calling upon'.
[24] It is expressed in the title *Pantokrator*. See above, p. 150.
[25] See T. Ware, op. cit., p. 49; J. Meyendorff, *The Orthodox Church* (London 1962), pp. 20 ff.
[26] The Greek *leitourgia* means 'service'. Orthodox theology does not (and no theology

should) make a sharp distinction between the service of God in worship and the service of God in work.

[27] See above, pp. 86–90.

[28] A common western misconception is that the Church of the East has been inactive in mission. The Slavonic missions from the ninth century on, and Orthodox activity in eastern Asia in the eighteenth century alone are sufficient to disprove this charge.

[29] Ignatius, *Smyrn.* viii; see above, pp. 35–6.

[30] E.g. above, pp. 16–17, 20, 88.

[31] T. Ware, op. cit., p. 248, briefly discusses this tension.

[32] Quoted by T. Ware, ibid.

[33] J. Meyendorff, 'What Holds the Church Together?' in *Ecumenical Review*, vol. xii (1960), p. 298.

[34] Orthodoxy is quite clear that bishops are not to be equated with apostles. See J. Meyendorff, *Orthodoxy and Catholicity*, p. 12 where he quotes from Nilus Cabasilas' (d. 1363) *On the Primacy of the Pope*: 'The apostles did not ordain other apostles, but pastors and teachers.'

[35] J. Meyendorff, ibid., p. 5.

[36] The western practice of 'private masses' with a single layman present as server is foreign to Orthodoxy.

[37] N. A. Nissiotis in the document mentioned in n. 22 above.

[38] Orthodox theologians often appeal to the authority of Irenaeus on this point.

[39] On this point Orthodox theologians appeal to the authority of Cyprian. See J. Meyendorff, *Orthodoxy and Catholicity,* pp. 158–9.

[40] The Greek word is *taxis*, 'order' in the sense of 'placing'.

[41] E.T. of quotation by Y. Congar, *L'Eglise*, p. 265, from J. Darrouzès, 'Conférence sur la Primauté du Pape à Constantinople en 1357' in *Revue des Etudes Byzantines*, 19 (1961).

[42] Nicolas Cabasilas, *c.* 1320–*c.* 1370, author of *The Life of Christ* and *Interpretation of the Divine Liturgy*.

[43] Nilus Cabasilas, *On the Primacy of the Pope, PG* 149, 728–9.

[44] This jurisdiction included the right to hear appeals, to judge disputed cases in the eparchies of the patriarchate, to confirm elections to metropolitical sees. Larger claims by the patriarch of Rome were resisted in the East.

[45] T. Ware, op. cit., p. 35.

[46] From the Greek *autos* (self), and *kephale* (head).

[47] The title of patriarch has been accorded to the metropolitan bishops of some autocephalous churches, e.g. Russia, Serbia, Rumania, Bulgaria.

[48] J. Meyendorff, *Orthodoxy and Catholicity*, p. 115.

[49] J. Meyendorff, ibid., p. 117, defines 'economy' as 'a conscious relaxation by the ecclesiastical authorities of the letter of the canons in cases when a strict legalistic observance would do more harm than good to the entire body of the Church'.

CHAPTER 12

[1] Owen Chadwick, *The Reformation* (Harmondsworth 1964), vol. 3 in 'The Pelican History of the Church', p. 11.

[2] There is no reason to doubt that Tetzel used words like 'the moment the money tinkles in the box a soul flies out of purgatory'.

[3] So in the Augsburg Confession, Article vii, which was largely drawn up by Luther's friend and colleague, Melanchthon.

[4] Ibid. 7.

[5] E.T. of quotations from Luther is from *Luther's Works*, 55 vols. (St Louis, Missouri;

Philadelphia 1955 ff). General eds. Jaroslav Pelikan and H. T. Lehmann. This is designated *LW*.

[6] *LW*, vol. 39, p. 75.

[7] For the other four marks see below, p. 165.

[8] *LW* 41, pp. 148–52.

[9] *LW* 39, pp. 69–70.

[10] *The Protestant Tradition* (Cambridge 1955), p. 110.

[11] *The Papacy at Rome*; *LW* 39, p. 70.

[12] Ibid.

[13] Ibid.

[14] Owen Chadwick, op. cit., p. 61.

[15] Whale, op. cit., pp. 112–13.

[16] *LW* 44, pp. 127–9.

[17] See R. W. Southern, op. cit., pp. 37–8 for a brief comment on the medieval demotion of the laity. See also Hans Küng, *The Church*, pp. 363–87, for a modern Roman Catholic discussion of the N.T. usage of the words 'priest' and *clerus* (Greek *kleros*) in relation to 'people' (*laos*). Of Luther, Küng says (ibid., p. 280): 'He helped to revive original N.T. perspectives (the primacy of grace, the priesthood of all believers, ecclesiastical office as ministry, the importance of the Word, the opposition between the law and the Gospel, the ethos of everyday life and work, etc.) and ... made an important contribution to the reform of the Church—indirectly to the reform of the Catholic Church too.'

[18] J. S. Whale, op. cit., p. 98.

[19] Ibid., p. 111.

[20] See above, p. 164.

[21] *LW* 41, p. 154.

[22] *Answer to the Hyperchristian, Hyperspiritual, and Hyperlearned Book by Goat Emser*, *LW* 39, p. 155.

[23] Ibid.

[24] Whale, op. cit., p. 301.

[25] An early example is the radical activity, including incitement to riot of Carlstadt and others in Wittenberg as early as 1522. A later example is the attempt of John of Leyden to make Münster the New Jerusalem in 1534–5, entailing the banishment or slaughter of opponents, and the institution of communism not only in goods, but in wives.

[26] *LW* 45, pp. 81–129.

[27] Ch. 18, 'The Crown Rights of the Redeemer', pp. 288–305.

[28] 'Anabaptist' (Greek, *anabaptistes*, rebaptizer) describes those groups of reformers who rejected infant baptism and baptized their 'converts' again. They condemned the use of force, courts of law, and taking oaths. The word later became a label for all radical reformers, many of whom were only too ready to use force themselves.

[29] Whale, op. cit., p. 290.

[30] Ibid., p. 291.

[31] *Temporal Authority*; *LW* 45, p. 89.

[32] Ibid., p. 91.

[33] Whale, op. cit., pp. 303–4.

[34] John Knox, who was one of them, said of Calvin's Geneva that it was 'the most perfect school of Christ that ever was'.

[35] Literally, 'Instruction in the Christian Religion'. The plural *Institutiones* was sometimes used in edns after Calvin's death. It is usually known in English as *The Institutes*.

[36] A North American professor, teaching a course on the doctrine of the Church, was accustomed to read to his students a paragraph or two from the beginning of

Institutes IV, and to ask them to name the writer. Thomas Aquinas was the most frequent response.

[37] For a discussion of this, and a criticism of Calvin on this point, see G. MacGregor op. cit., pp. 48–50. Calvin did not arrive at his mature doctrine of the Church quickly. F. Wendel, *Calvin* (E.T., London 1965), p. 294, says that in 1536 Calvin had hardly considered the Church except under its invisible aspect. J. S. Whale, op. cit., pp. 146–62 traces the development of Calvin's ecclesiology in the succeeding editions of the *Institutes*.

[38] E.T. of passages from the *Institutes* is from the translation of F. L. Battles in the edn of J. T. McNeill in vols. xx and xxi of the 'Library of Christian Classics' (London; Philadelphia 1961) entitled *Calvin: Institutes of the Christian Religion*.

[39] *Institutes* IV, i. 2–3.

[40] See also ibid. IV, i. 13.

[41] See above, p. 163.

[42] *Institutes* IV, i. 16.

[43] Ibid. IV, i. 12.

[44] Wendel, op. cit., pp. 300–301.

[45] *Institutes* IV, xii. 10.

[46] Whale, op. cit., p. 155.

[47] E.g. *Institutes* IV, ii. 11–12.

[48] *Institutes* IV, vi. 9.

[49] For a discussion of this, see Benjamin C. Milner, *Calvin's Doctrine of the Church* (Leiden 1970), pp. 150–57.

[50] *Institutes* IV, iv. 4.

[51] Ibid.

[52] *Commentary on Numbers* III, 5: *Ioannis Calvini Opera quae supersunt omnia*, ed. G. Baum *et al.*, in 'Corpus Reformatorum', (Brunswick 1863–1900; reprinted, New York and London 1964), vol. 52 (vol. 24 of Calvin's works), pp. 444–5.

[53] 'Corpus Reformatorum', vol. 43 (vol. 15 of Calvin's works), pp. 329–36. Students of Calvin differ on the question whether he was prepared to accept episcopacy in the sense of a distinct order of ministry. See the brief discussion in B. C. Milner, op. cit., pp. 147–8 and footnotes. Milner's view is that Calvin admitted distinction of ministry for practical purposes ('distinction of a political kind'), but that he strongly held that 'the office of bishop . . . cannot be different from that of the pastor'.

[54] *Institutes* IV, iii. 1.

[55] It is described also in the *Draft Ecclesiastical Ordinances* of 1541, drawn up by Calvin and his colleagues. See J. K. S. Reid, ed., *Calvin, Theological Treatises* in 'The Library of Christian Classics', vol xxii (1954), pp. 58 ff.

[56] *Institutes* IV, iii. 1.

[57] Ibid. IV, i. 5.

[58] G. MacGregor, op. cit., p. 57.

[59] *Institutes* IV, iii. 10–16.

[60] Ibid. IV, iii. 16; IV, xix. 31.

[61] *Comm. Acts* 6.6; *Comm. 1 Tim.* 4.14; *Comm. 2 Tim.* 1.6. The relevant passages are quoted in B. C. Milner, op. cit., p. 143.

[62] Cf. *Institutes* IV, xix. 31, 'I concede that it [the laying on of hands] is a sacrament in true and lawful ordinations.'

[63] Cf. also III, xix. 15; IV, xx. 1–2.

[64] Ibid. IV, xii. 5.

[65] MacGregor, op. cit., p. 107.

[66] The word 'Protestant' has a positive as well as the negative connotation which it is usually given. The Latin *protestor* means literally 'bear witness for'. The Reformers, while protesting against what they held to be abuses in the medieval Church, were at

the same time bearing witness for principles which they believed to have been submerged. 'Protestant' came into use as a term to describe a reformer after the Diet of Speyer (1529), at which a reforming minority made a formal *Protestatio* in defence of the rights of minority groups.

[67] The Lutheran Church of Sweden, however, retained the office of bishop in succession from the pre-Reformation bishops, and values this aspect of continuity with the apostolic Church. There are also Presbyterians who claim 'a succession of presbyters both by office and by ordination in direct descent from the days of the apostles': see R. Newton Flew, ed., *The Nature of the Church* (London 1952), p. 114.

[68] Quoted from J. S. Whale, op. cit., pp. 186–7. Barrow's works are contained in Leland H. Carson, ed., *The Writings of Henry Barrow, 1587–90* (Elizabethan Nonconformist Texts, vol. iii, London 1962).

[69] Quoted from J. S. Whale, op. cit., p. 193. It was drawn up by John Robinson, author of *Justification of Separation from the Church of England* (1610), who was to sail in the *Mayflower* as one of the Pilgrim Fathers in 1620.

[70] Browne's book is regarded as a foundation document of modern Congregationalists: see R. N. Flew, op. cit., p. 169. Browne, however, recanted in 1585 and conformed to the Church of England.

[71] See Owen Chadwick, op. cit., ch. 6, for a brief account of the Separatists of the sixteenth century and the early seventeenth.

[72] Quoted from J. S. Whale, op. cit., pp. 215–16.

[73] See chs. 14 and 15 of Robert Barclay, *Apology for the True Christian Religion, as the same is set forth and preached by the People called in Scorn 'Quakers'* (London 1701).

[74] See also J. S. Whale, *Christian Doctrine* (London 1957), pp. 130 ff.

CHAPTER 13

[1] Henry VIII had insisted on the words 'Supreme Head'.

[2] Owen Chadwick, op. cit., p. 119.

[3] Ibid., p. 215.

[4] E.g. the prevenience of grace (x), justification by faith alone (xi), predestination (xvii), the sufficiency of holy Scripture for salvation (vi).

[5] This claim has been disputed by Roman Catholic theologians. The adverse judgement on the validity of Anglican Orders by Pope Leo XI in the Bull *Apostolicae Curae* (1896) is still the Church of Rome's last official word on the subject.

[6] See H. F. Woodhouse, *The Doctrine of the Church in Anglican Theology, 1547–1603* (London 1954), published for the Church Historical Society, for an account of those of the sixteenth century; and P. E. More and F. L. Cross, eds., *Anglicanism* (London 1957), for biographies and extracts from the works of those of the seventeenth century on ecclesiology, as well as other major theological topics.

[7] *The Laws of Ecclesiastical Polity* III, i. 3, 8; v, lvi. 7, 11; *Sermon* II (*Of Justification, Works, and how the Foundation of Faith is overthrown*) 23, where the 'body mystical' is said to be a 'building undiscernible by mortal eyes'.

[8] *LEP* III, i. 8.

[9] Ibid. VIII, iv. 5, 7.

[10] Ibid. v, xxiv. 1.

[11] Woodhouse, op. cit., pp. 50–51.

[12] *LEP* III, i. 2.

[13] Op. cit., p. 51.

[14] See above, p. 170. Richard Hooker makes the same point, though with less clarity, in *LEP* III, i. 3: 'And as those everlasting promises [viz., in the Scriptures] of love,

mercy, and blessedness belong to the mystical Church; even so on the other side when we read [i.e. in the Scriptures] of any duty which the Church of God is bound unto, the Church whom this doth concern is a sensibly known company.'

[15] P. E. More and F. L. Cross, op. cit., p. 41. Hooker also uses the illustration of Jesus' knowledge of Nathaniel in *LEP* III, i. 2.

[16] For the views of sixteenth-century Anglican writers on whether the Church of Rome had ceased to be part of the Church of Christ, see ch. 10 in Woodhouse, op. cit. For the views of selected seventeenth-century Anglican writers, see More and Cross, op. cit., pp. 53–72. The views expressed have a wide range. John Bradford condemns Rome as a 'strumpet-church' and the spouse of the Antichrist. From men like Hooker, John Cosin, and Isaac Barrow we have reasoned and scholarly examinations of Roman claims in the light of Scripture and the writings of the Fathers.

[17] Bellarmine's *De Ecclesia Militante* (a section of his *Controversies*) was published in 1586. See below, pp. 202–4.

[18] The words 'we must receive God's promises in such wise, as they be generally set forth to us in holy Scripture' in the final paragraph of Article XVII may readily be interpreted as implying that the elect will be found within the visible Church.

[19] See above, pp. 163 and 231, nn. 3, 4.

[20] See above, p. 82.

[21] E.g., the Second Helvetic Confession (1566), Article XVIII; The Westminster Confession (1647), Article XXVII.

[22] The Ordinal, or 'The Form and Manner of Making, Ordaining, and Consecrating of Bishops, Priests, and Deacons' is printed with the Book of Common Prayer, although, like the Thirty-nine Articles, it is a separate document.

[23] Anglicans have differed on these matters. For the views of Richard Hooker and seventeenth-century Anglican theologians, see More and Cross, op. cit., pp. 345–403.

[24] Erik Routley, *Creeds and Confessions* (London 1962), p. 112.

[25] Ibid., p. 111.

[26] Ibid., p. 108.

[27] See above, p. 133.

[28] See above, pp. 182–3.

[29] The text of this may be read in More and Cross, op. cit., pp. 23–9, from which quotations here are taken. More and Cross use the 1864 Oxford edn of Edward Burton which was first published in 1833.

[30] Cf. Cyril of Jerusalem on catholicity; above, pp. 76–7.

CHAPTER 14

[1] Roman Catholics prefer to use the terms 'Catholic Reformation' or 'Catholic Renewal' which lay less stress on these reforms as a mere response to the Protestant Reformation; see Y. Congar, *L'Eglise,* pp. 380–81.

[2] See above, pp. 163 and 231, nn. 3, 4.

[3] Y. Congar, op. cit., p. 364.

[4] See H. Küng, *The Church,* p. 11.

[5] *The Canons and Decrees of the Council of Trent,* translated by T. A. Buckley (London 1851), p. 2.

[6] Ibid., p. 9.

[7] Ibid., p. 10.

[8] Ibid., p. 255.

[9] Hans Küng, op. cit., pp. 418–19 discusses this sentence, and remarks: 'The Tridentine proposition, if strictly interpreted, does not agree with historical realities.' There is no dominical ordinance concerning distinctions in office between bishops, priests, and

deacons. The distinctions emerged later than the N.T. period. He notes that Vatican II is more in accordance with recent exegetical and historical research in saying: 'The divinely established ecclesiastical ministry is exercised on different levels by those who from antiquity (*ab antiquo*, not *ab initio*) have been called bishops, priests, and deacons' (*Constitution on the Church* III, 28).

[10] The E.T. used is that of T. A. Buckley, *The Catechism of the Council of Trent* (London 1852). The translation has been checked with the Latin in *Catechismus ex Decreto Concilii Tridentini* (Leipzig 1872).

[11] It is to be noted that there is no mention here of the Church expectant (in purgatory). However, the doctrine of purgatory is alluded to in Part II, ch. IV, q. lxxvi (Buckley, op. cit., p. 255), and in Part IV, ch. V, q. iv (ibid., p. 489).

[12] Cf. Article XXVI of the Thirty-nine Articles (see above, pp. 185–6).

[13] The passage from Ambrose (*Commentary on Luke*, Book IX, 9) is curiously omitted from some Latin editions, including the Leipzig edition mentioned in n. 10 above. It is not a particularly strong witness to the papal claims.

[14] The catechism treats of the sacrament of order in Part II, ch. VII (Buckley, op. cit., pp. 312–32).

[15] See above, pp. 197–8.

[16] See above, pp. 14–15.

[17] *A New Catechism: Catholic Faith for Adults* (New York 1967).

[18] *Disputationes de Controversiis Christianae Fidei adversus huius temporis Haereticos* (Ingolstadt 1586–93), in 3 vols. Modern edns in *Opera Omnia* (Naples 1856–62, 8 vols.; and Paris 1870–74, 12 vols.).

[19] See above, p. 140.

[20] See above, pp. 115–17.

[21] Congar, *L'Eglise*, p. 373.

[22] Texts are to be found in A. C. Cochrane, *Reformed Confessions of the 16th Century* (E.T., Philadelphia 1966); P. Schaff, *The Creeds of Christendom*, vol. 3, 'The Evangelical Protestant Creeds' (New York 1877); Williston Walker, *The Creeds and Platforms of Congregationalism* (New York 1893).

[23] E.T. from Cochrane, op. cit.

[24] E.T. from Cochrane, op. cit.

[25] E.T. from Cochrane, op. cit.

[26] See E. Routley, *Creeds and Confessions* (London 1962), p. 90.

[27] This and the following quotation from chs. xvii and xviii are from the E.T. of Cochrane, op. cit.

[28] See above, p. 93.

[29] See above, p. 82.

[30] Quotations are taken from Schaff, op. cit.

[31] This chapter was altered in the later American revision to bring it into line with the principle of the separation of Church and State and of the neutrality of the State in ecclesiastical matters.

[32] Quotations from Schaff, op. cit.

[33] The full text is given in Williston Walker, op. cit., from which quotations here are taken, the spelling, however, being modernized, and the punctuation sometimes altered.

[34] Williston Walker, op. cit., p. 205, n. 3; see also p. 204, n. 2.

[35] Routley, op. cit., p. 130.

[36] See G. R. Cragg, *The Church and the Age of Reason, 1648–1759* (Harmondsworth 1970), pp. 176–7. For an account of the 'Half-way Covenant' decisions of 1657 and 1662, and of the connected controversies, see Williston Walker, op. cit., pp. 238–339.

Bibliography

The dates given are those of the editions used in this volume, and do not necessarily indicate the dates of the original publications.

A. TEXTS OF COLLECTED OR SINGLE WORKS; TRANSLATIONS; SELECTIONS

Migne, J. P., ed., *Patrologia Graeca*. Paris 1857–66.

Migne, J. P., ed., *Patrologia Latina*. Paris 1844–55.

Roberts, A. and Donaldson, J., eds., The Ante-Nicene Christian Library, 9 vols. Edinburgh 1864 ff. Published also in New York under the title *The Ante-Nicene Fathers*.

Schaff, P., ed., The Nicene and Post-Nicene Fathers, 1st ser., 14 vols. New York 1886–9.

Schaff, P. and Wace, A., eds., The Nicene and Post-Nicene Fathers, 2nd ser., 28 vols. New York; London 1890–1900.

Lake, Kirsopp, ed., *The Apostolic Fathers*, 2 vols. Heinemann, The Loeb Classical Library 1959.

Bettenson, R. H., ed., *The Early Christian Fathers*. Oxford University Press 1956.

Bettenson, R. H., ed., *The Later Christian Fathers*. Oxford University Press 1970.

Dix, Gregory, ed., *The Apostolic Tradition of St Hippolytus*. SPCK 1937.

Lawson, R. P., ed., *Origen; The Song of Songs, Commentary and Homilies*, vol. 26 of 'Ancient Christian Writers'. Longmans Green; Westminster, Maryland, Newman Press, 1957.

Goldast, M., ed., *Monarchia Sancti Romani Imperii*, 3 vols. Hanover 1612.

S. Bonaventurae Opera Omnia, ed. Franciscan Brethren of Quaracchi, 10 vols. 1882–1907.

Albertus Magnus, *Opera*, ed. A. Borgnet, 38 vols. Paris 1890–99.

The Summa Theologica of St Thomas Aquinas, tr. Fathers of the English Dominican Province. Burns, Oates & Washbourne. 1914 ff.

Gilby, T., *St Thomas Aquinas: Theological Texts*. Oxford University Press 1955.

John of Paris, *De potestate regia et papali*, ed. J. LeClercq, in *Jean de Paris et l'ecclésiologie du xiiie siècle*. Paris 1942.

Meister Johann Eckhart, *Opera Latina*, ed. G. Thery and R. Klibansky. Leipzig 1934 ff.

Marsilius of Padua, *Defensor Fidei*, ed. C. W. Previté-Orton. Cambridge University Press 1928.

William of Ockham, *Opera Politica*, ed. J. G. Sikes *et al.* University of Manchester Publications 1940.

William of Ockham, *De Imperatorum et Pontificum Potestate*, ed. C. K. Brampton. Oxford University Press 1927.

John Wyclif, *Trialogus*, ed. G. V. Kechner. 1869.

Wyclif's Latin Works, published by the Wyclif Society. 1884 ff.

Johannes de Turrecremata (Torquemada), *Summa de Ecclesia*. Venice 1560.

Corpus Reformatorum. Brunswick 1863–1900; reprinted, New York and London, Johnson Reprint Corporation, 1969.

Luther's Works, 55 vols., ed. J. Pelikan and H. T. Lehmann. St Louis, Missouri, Concordia Publishing House; Philadelphia, Fortress Press, 1955 ff.

Calvin: Institutes of the Christian Religion, tr. F. L. Battles, ed. J. T. McNeill, vols. xx and xxi of 'The Library of Christian Classics'. SCM Press; Philadelphia, Westminster Press, 1961.

Calvin: Theological Treatises, ed. J. K. S. Reid, vol. xxii of 'The Library of Christian Classics'. SCM Press; Philadelphia, Westminster Press, 1954.

Anglicanism, ed. P. E. More and F. L. Cross. SPCK 1957.

The Works of that Learned and Judicious Divine, Mr Richard Hooker, ed. J. Keble 1836; rev. R. W. Church and F. Paget 1888.

Richard Hooker, *The Laws of Ecclesiastical Polity*. J. M. Dent, Everyman's Library 1907.

Richard Field, *Of the Church*, ed. Ecclesiastical History Society. 1847.

The Writings of Henry Barrow, 1587–90, ed. Leland H. Carson, Elizabethan Nonconformist Texts, vol. iii. Allen & Unwin 1962.

John Pearson, *An Exposition of the Creed*, ed. E. Burton. 1864.

Robert Barclay, *Apology for the True Christian Religion, as the same is set forth and presented by the People called in Scorn 'Quakers'*. 1701.

The Canons and Decrees of the Council of Trent, tr. T. A. Buckley. 1851.

The Catechism of the Council of Trent, tr. T. A. Buckley. 1852.

Robert Bellarmine, *Disputationes de Controversiis Christianae Fidei adversus huius temporis Haereticos*, 3 vols. Ingolstadt 1586–9. Modern edns in *Opera Omnia*, Naples 1856–62, 8 vols. and Paris 1870–74, 12 vols.

Reformed Confessions of the 16th Century, ed. A. C. Cochrane. Philadelphia, Westminster Press, 1966.

The Evangelical Protestant Creeds, ed. P. Schaff, vol. 3 of 'The Creeds of Christendom'. New York 1877.

The Creeds and Platforms of Congregationalism, ed. Williston Walker. New York 1893.

B. GENERAL WORKS

Aulén, Gustaf, *The Faith of the Christian Church*. SPCK 1954.

Battenhouse, R. W., *A Companion to the Study of St Augustine*. New York, Oxford University Press, 1955.

Best, Ernest, *One Body in Christ*. SPCK 1955.

Brandreth, H. R. T., *Episcopi Vagantes*. SPCK 1947.

Butler, B. C., *The Idea of the Church*. Darton, Longman & Todd 1962.

Chadwick, Owen, *The Reformation*, 'Pelican History of the Church', vol. 3. Penguin Books 1964.

Congar, Yves, *L'Ecclésiologie du haut Moyen-Age*. Paris, Les Editions du Cerf. 1968.

Congar, Yves, *L'Eglise de Saint Augustin à l'époque moderne*. Paris, Les Editions du Cerf, 1970.

Corwin, Virginia, *St Ignatius and Christianity in Antioch*. New Haven, Connecticut, Yale University Press, 1960.

Cragg, G. R., *The Church and the Age of Reason, 1648–1759*, 'Pelican History of the Church', vol. 4. Penguin Books 1970.

Cross, F. L., ed., *The Oxford Dictionary of the Christian Church*. Oxford University Press 1957.

Davies, G. Henton, 'Remnant', in A. Richardson, ed., *A Theological Word Book of the Bible*. SCM Press 1950.

Evans, R. F., *One and Holy*. SPCK 1972.

Flew, R. Newton, ed., *The Nature of the Church*. SCM Press 1952.

Gore, Charles, *The Church and the Ministry*. Longmans Green 1893.

Grabowski, S. J., *The Church: An Introduction to the Theology of St Augustine*. London; St Louis, Missouri, Herder, 1957.

Greenslade, S. L., *Schism in the Early Church*. SCM Press 1953.

Hoskyns, E. C. and Davey, F. N., *The Riddle of the New Testament*. Faber 1931.

Jeremias, J., 'Akrogoniaios', in G. Kittel, ed., *Theological Dictionary of the New Testament* (see below).

Johnston, George, *The Doctrine of the Church in the New Testament*. Cambridge University Press 1943.

Johnston, George, 'The Doctrine of the Church in the New Testament', in M. Black and H. H. Rowley, eds., *Peake's Commentary on the Bible*. Nelson 1962.

Kelly, J. N. D., *Early Christian Doctrines*. Black 1958.

Kittel, G., ed., *Theological Dictionary of the New Testament*, 9 vols. Grand Rapids, Michigan, Eerdmans, 1964 ff.

Küng, Hans, *The Church*. New York, Sheed & Ward, 1967.

Küng, Hans, *Structures of the Church*. Nelson 1964; Notre Dame, University of Notre Dame Press, 1968.

MacGregor, Geddes, *Corpus Christi*. Philadelphia, Westminster Press, 1958.

McKelvey, R. T., *The New Temple*. Oxford University Press 1969.

Manson, T. W., *The Teaching of Jesus*. Cambridge University Press 1931.

Meyendorff, John, *Orthodoxy and Catholicity*. New York, Sheed & Ward, 1966.

Meyendorff, John, *The Orthodox Church*. Darton, Longman & Todd 1962.

Meyendorff, John, 'What Holds the Church Together?', in *Ecumenical Review*, vol. xii. 1960.

Milner, B. C., *Calvin's Doctrine of the Church*. Leiden, E. J. Brill, 1970.

Minear, P. S., *Images of the Church in the New Testament*. Philadelphia, Westminster Press, 1950.

Moberly, R. C., *Ministerial Priesthood*. New York, Longmans Green, 1916.

Nissiotis, N. A., unpublished paper on 'Orthodox Theology and Worship'. 1971.

Petry, R. C., *A History of the Christian Church,* vol. 1. Englewood Cliffs, New Jersey, Prentice-Hall, 1962.

Quick, O. C., *Doctrines of the Creed*. Collins 1963.

Rawlinson, A. E. J., 'Corpus Christi', in G. K. A. Bell and A. Deissmann, eds., *Mysterium Christi*. Longmans Green 1930.

Richardson, Alan, *Introduction to the Theology of the New Testament*. SCM Press 1958.

Richardson, Alan, ed., *A Theological Word Book of the Bible*. SCM Press 1950.

Robinson, J. A. T., *The Body*. SCM Press 1952.

Routley, Erik, *Creeds and Confessions*. Duckworth 1962.

Schmidt, K. L., 'Ekklesia', in G. Kittel, ed., *Theological Dictionary of the New Testament*, vol. iii (see above).

Southern, R. W., *Western Society and the Church in the Middle Ages*, 'Pelican History of the Church', vol. 2. Penguin Books 1970.

Spinka, Matthew, *John Hus' Concept of the Church*. Princeton University Press 1966.

Streeter, B. H., *The Primitive Church*. Macmillan 1929.

Swete, H. B., *Introduction to the Old Testament in Greek*. Cambridge University Press 1902.

Telfer, W., 'Episcopal Succession in Egypt', in *The Journal of Ecclesiastical History*, vol. 3, no. 1, April 1952.

Thatcher, O. J. and McNeal, E. H., *A Source Book for Medieval History*. New York, Scribner's, 1905.

Ware, Timothy, *The Orthodox Church*. Penguin Books 1963.

Wendel, F., *Calvin*. Collins, Fontana Library 1965.

Whale, J. S., *Christian Doctrine*. Collins, Fontana Library 1957.

Whale, J. S., *The Protestant Tradition*. Cambridge University Press 1955.

Woodhouse, H. F., *The Doctrine of the Church in Anglican Theology, 1547–1603*. SPCK 1954.

Index

NAMES

SUBJECTS

C. indicates Church